Working
for
Yourself

How to Be
Successfully
Self-Employed
Working
for
Yourself

by
Geof Hewitt

Photographs by T.L. Gettings

 **Rodale Press** Emmaus, PA

Printed in the United States
of America on recycled paper

2   4   6   8   10   9   7   5   3   1

Library of Congress Cataloging in Publication Data

Hewitt, Geof.
   Working for yourself.

   Bibliography: p.
   Includes index.
   1. Self-employed.   2. New business enterprises.
I. Title.   II. Title: How to be successfully self-
employed.
HD8036.H48   658.1′141   77-22783
ISBN 0-87857-162-0

"Concerning Necessity," by Hayden Carruth, is reprinted
complete from *From Snow and Rock, From Chaos*.
Copyright © 1973 by Hayden Carruth. Reprinted by permission of New Directions.

Contents

Preface

To research this book, I traveled across the country with Janet and our son Ben, who at four years of age, enjoyed the trip immensely. We started by driving to Maine, where we were amazed by the large number of self-employed people we met. I attributed this to the Yankee tradition of independence, evident throughout New England, but more extreme the farther east you go. But as we progressed in our travels, visiting "independent" people in Virginia, Iowa, New Mexico, and California, I realized that New England may have the *tradition*, but the phenomenon of self-employment is *everywhere*. Opening our eyes, asking around, we discovered a powerful web of people who, mostly in the last five or six years, have recognized that happiness and security are often illusions when you work for someone else at the same job day after day.

As we traveled, I read *Working*, by Studs Terkel. I contrasted the realities of the 40-hour week his book so thoroughly describes with the seemingly more-flexible lives of the people we were visiting. Within weeks of starting our travels, I realized how wasteful my practice was of writing in advance to make appointments. I learned, instead, that driving through town and phoning from the gas station at lunchtime ("We're just passing through and I wondered if we could stop by sometime this afternoon to see you in action . . . ?") was the best way to get a candid view of these small businesses. "Come anytime!" "My time is my own!" were typical replies. And yet, we learned, such time is dearly bought.

I first employed this drop-in technique on John Cole, editor of *Maine Times*, a forthright little newspaper published in Topsham, Maine, that pays close and sympathetic attention to the activities of people who have abandoned—or never entered—"the great American work force." While we talked, Cole introduced me to the term "Post-Industrial Activity," which informed the researching of and thus, I hope, describes, the principal thrust of this book.

Driving from Topsham, we visited first Joan and Rob Lee Johnston, whose seed business had been featured in a recent *Maine Times* issue, then farther east to Harborside, where Eliot and Sue Coleman are working to expand the one-acre, intensive organic garden they've hacked out of a heavily wooded piece of land sold them by their nearest neighbors, Helen and Scott Nearing. How wonderful to discover that we could help the Colemans, who were building a root cellar, in exchange for a fresh vegetarian meal and overnight camping privileges. The next morning we saw an old, old man down on the beach, raking up seaweed with the assistance of three or four people who all seemed to be in their mid-20s.

The seaweed, we learned, was for the potato patch at Nearings'. The man, 93 years old, was Scott himself; the young people were his friends from months of helping with what the Nearings call "the Good Life," a highly regimented program that includes four hours of morning labors devoted to the chores of survival. We were immediately welcomed into the fellowship of work. We learned from one of his helpers that Scott Nearing's last regular job ended in 1917 when he was fired from his teaching job for protesting the war. Nearing has been self-employed ever since. After a morning of raking and trucking and spreading the seaweed we were invited into the Nearings' home for a hearty, vegetarian soup in wooden bowls, with wedges of fresh cabbage and whole wheat loaves spread on the kitchen table. Helen Nearing sat on a flat-top wood stove (possible only during the summer!) and explained that Maine Yankee Power Company holds an option on seaside land bordering their property and the Colemans'. It strikes me as especially cruel that the nuclear power sites are chosen largely for their remoteness in conjunction with access to a body of cold water, which is warmed considerably and thermally polluted, at the least, in the deal.

I had asked Eliot Coleman about local sentiment toward the possibility of a nuclear power plant right there in tiny Harborside. "They think it'll create jobs," he said. "So I'm afraid a lot of people are in favor of it. Some nice-looking man in a suit says, 'Nuclear power won't hurt you,' and they stop worrying about the dangers, because jobs will be created. The trouble with some folks is they want the job to come to them. Not enough people look around to see what needs to be done. Instead, they've come to rely on having a job created for them."

Acknowledgments

During the 18 months I worked on this book, more than 200 people shared their ideas and experiences, their homes, and the names of their friends who might offer something to the effort. And my family—in-laws and out-laws alike—provided generous encouragement and numerous clippings that have become a tangible part of this book. Rather than try to list names, and thus make omissions, I simply wish to acknowledge this generosity.

I also wish to acknowledge gratefully the *Cornell Alumni News*, which originally published, in slightly different form, the material on Charlie Lee.

And to Janet and Ben, who have shared the burdens as well as the pleasures, my loving thanks.

1. A CLEAR DREAM

"A Clear Dream"

This book is not concerned with ways to become a grim success in Business, but with ways to apply certain basic business principles to activities you feel can be rewarding to everyone. If you like what you're doing, you're more likely to attract customers.

Knowing yourself and what you really enjoy doing is the most important single factor in determining the difference between happy enterprise and bankruptcy. Rob Lee Johnston, the seedsman from Maine, calls it "a clear dream," the first necessity for setting up a small business.

With this in mind, I set out to explore the ways of getting by (if not rich) in a world where more and more emphasis on quality and personal service is working to break the terrible hold of corporate merchandising that has so many people scowling.

"*If you enjoy doing it*, you'll be able to master the business and formal steps necessary to keep your head above water," is a rule of thumb commonly expressed by successfully self-employed people. Confidence in the product or service is integral with self-confidence. They grow together, and (as they say) are "good for business."

If the interviews here are mostly positive, that reflects a number of clear dreams made into reality. Yet, occasionally, the self-employed person has become "independent" because the larger system, with its well-established practices and ready-made "jobs," does not meet the individual's needs. In the case of a musician, this translates into cynical terms; the cynicism is not hers, but the system she rejects, a system that wires teenagers to electrically charged meters that measure "basal skin response" (BSR) as the subjects listen to pop tunes being considered for major promotional efforts.

Ideally your favorite activities have led you to wondering: Could I make a living at it? Answering such a question requires a painstaking overall personal and financial self-assessment. First, what are the activities I enjoy most? Do I enjoy being with people? Do I want to be primarily outdoors? In all seasons? What commercial possibilities exist in the ideal combinations?

It is a mistake to start your plans for business independence by tallying imaginary profits. Financial considerations, unless you have unlimited wealth, must include the worst contingencies. A compelling reason for selecting a business that you already enjoy on a "hobby" basis is that presumably, you have much of the necessary equipment and the know-how to reduce expensive purchases and costly fumbling. Such experience will help convince your local banker of your potential in a chosen field and improve your chances of receiving a loan.

Insurance is a costly item, but it is a deductible business expense, and you should carry a realistic insurance policy to cover your business in case of fire, theft, and for all potential liabilities. If a customer slips on your shiny floors and suffers whiplash, you can be wiped out overnight, so find a reliable insurance agent and ask him what you need. Compare his advice, and his policy, with that of another insurance agent, and with people who are already established in a business similar to yours.

Be prepared, in making a financial assessment, to calculate all the "hidden costs." These include taxes (federal income, state income, real estate, property, school, road, sales, capital gains, and who knows what else), necessary licenses and permits, alterations of existing structures, tools, maintenance, construction of new structures and how these will affect taxes, electricity, gas, oil, mailing, travel, telephone, and extra help. In estimating these expenses, figure *high*: Remember, between the time you make original calculations and the time you pay the actual bills, inflation will have been at work too! What professional expenses will you incur? Will you need a lawyer to check your plans and to help with deeds, taxes, and contracts? A good accountant may be necessary. When in doubt, figure that you will need such professional services, and then phone around to learn who can help you most favorably. Don't go asking professional friends for free advice too often; if you like their ideas and they have professional training, they're in the best position to work for you. Try to select lawyers and accountants and insurance agents from among personal friends, who already have an interest in your well-being. To retain such friendships, be sure your "understandings" are written out on paper. Contracts may be anathema to some amateur small-business people, but professionals hold a healthy respect for the value of a simple written agreement.

Acquiring a Business

If a good business is for sale that actually corresponds with your chosen field, you might consider buying all, or part of it. In cases where the entire business is for sale, and not just a portion of its inventory or goodwill, you will rightfully want to assess its proven earnings record. Larry Farchi, who bought Feil's Motel, calculated the value of the motel at four-and-a-half times its gross annual income, and was willing to pay that amount. Similarly, as the business has appreciated since he acquired it, he carries insurance calculated on the same basis.

The best way to determine the veracity of a seller's income-claim is to review the IRS forms that report the business' annual or quarterly income. An owner of a business is not likely to exaggerate income when he reports it for tax purposes!

One other aspect of acquiring a business I observed in common among The Quincy Hotel's new owners, and the new owners of Appleyard Corporation, is a genuine interest in maintaining a personal friendship with the previous owners. This may be a difficult matter, following the rigors of legal negotiations, but if at all possible, warm relations and the friendly advice of the previous owners should be sought.

Among early items on the agenda for the first meeting of the new Appleyard Corporation was a gift for the previous directors.

Location

"We made a terrible mistake by locating in an area which has become a 'suburb'," Dorothea Noback, a Hartland, Wisconsin, herb grower, told me. "As such my business is threatened, and I am forced to fight for a 'Compatible Use' permit. Just a bit of testimony to the idiocy of do-gooder conformists. Try to be certain when you start in business that you will not encounter future zoning problems!"

Location is very important to you. Analyze your choice of business very carefully in terms of its location. Realize that even if you do not want to be located as near to potential customers as possible, you want to be near a good supplier of your professional needs. Ordering materials by mail can delay and sometimes spoil the work. An option, if you are located in a remote place, is the occasional "supply run" where you travel once or twice a year to acquire all necessary items.

Even after careful evaluation of your location, the circumstances of your growing business may someday force a move. Eric and Francine Chittenden spent two hard years establishing their cider press in a dairy barn they converted for cider pressing in Bakersfield, Vermont, before deciding that local zoning regulations, and the hilly terrain around their barn were prohibitive to the scale of effort and income they had in mind. Now they are moving to a more-favorably located farm, 35 miles downstate.

I met an antique dealer in Wayland, Missouri, in his father's shop. "I'd take you across the street and show you my stuff," he said, "but I can't. They passed a law last month that to have a shop open to the public you've got to have a toilet. And that place hasn't got any plumbing." I suppose anyone who wants to buy an old antique shop quick and cheap could get one in Wayland. But check the local environmental codes to be sure the installation of plumbing is feasible. How he could have forseen the change in law I don't profess to know. I guess luck plays its part, too.

    Check out: The Water.
                  The Law.
                  The Neighbors.
                  The Schools.

Look at water supply in the driest possible season. If possible, test rate of flow to insure the supply replenishes itself fast enough to meet your needs. For "Law," read environmental codes as well as zoning regulations, and any possible future encumbrances on your freedoms. The neighbors, needless to say, are potentially your closest friends—so it's always a good idea to know whether they are sympathetic to your plans, and, even if the law allows your sort of business, you should be sure it will not infringe on their sensibilities. If you're a potter, you want to locate where the kiln's fumes won't offend others. And check local ordinances to be sure you're in compliance. Musicians should know that electric music carries literally for miles in the country. So if you're electric, play very good, or very softly, and at reasonable hours.

Remember that people who live in the country are there usually because they like their own, personal space. That space is precious and sometimes threatened by well-meaning people who move out of the rat race.

Schools are best visited during normal school hours. Introduce yourself at the main office and ask permission to attend a few random classes. As you walk the halls, listen to the children. Are they happy? Are they complaining? Is the school bright or dingy? Do you hear any teachers shouting? Were there students participating at the reception desk—or do they only go to the office when they're incorrigible or sick? Are you welcome at the school? Do students need a bathroom pass? Are there live animals and plants in the elementary classrooms? Does the school have good windows and an active outdoor program?

If you are moving to the country will your children have companions near enough to visit without using a car? How long will they actually be in the school bus each day? How many hours of study hall do the students have? If you can, talk with the students themselves, who know how to exaggerate what the administrators will try to minimize. Do you like these people who will be your children's closest friends?

Self-Sufficiency and Living Off the Land

If you think about "living off the land," remember that land itself requires rent or a large initial payment and taxes ever after.

The tools of farming and transportation are costly. Medical and dental expenses are another almost unavoidable financial link to a world that sometimes seems terribly unbalanced by monetary realities.

The key to self-sufficiency, as opposed to "living off the land," is providing as much of your own materials and labor as you can for all your endeavors, while specializing in one aspect of your life that is useful to others. Maintaining your own tools is an almost indispensable requirement for anyone seeking self-sufficiency. In farming, for instance, being able to repair the tractor on the spot, when it is needed, often means the difference between a full barn or fields of spoiled hay. Anyone interested in "homesteading" simply has to be interested in both thinking about and *doing* myriad chores of carpentry and mauling, building pens and driving fence posts. A good friend of mine who loves to drive a tractor around and around, day after day, bought a farm, which he quickly sold, because he learned that the only way to drive a tractor full time is to hire out at the minimum wage. "In planning my homestead I just didn't count on so many hassles," he told me. "Even when I got to drive my tractor, I couldn't stop thinking about the other things I had to do."

Promotion

If your product or service costs too much, it simply won't sell, regardless of quality. Once high quality and reasonable prices have attracted a group of steady customers, word of mouth will swell your business and once you have all the customers you need, you can consider raising your prices.

If possible, your name and address should be embossed on anything you make; if yours is a service, be sure to leave your card with all satisfied customers. Consider printing your card on adhesive paper, which you apply to a flat surface nearest the place where your work is performed. An appliance repairman, for instance, might glue his card to the appliance itself, with bright, bold letters, in case the appliance is normally in a dark place. "Chief LeMay, Furnace Repairs, 933-1000," is all it has to say. Just wait for the first cold night that furnace quits!

Word of mouth really makes a difference. Your best advertisement is your work itself. A shed full of overpriced wooden toys is worth a lot less to you than those same toys placed strategically among energetic children with lots of friends. Consider selling your product, at a small percentage above cost, to a few institutions. If you're a potter, go to restaurant managers and offer a complete set of your dishware, at cost. "My only request is that you permit me to mention your establishment in my promotional messages," you might say. The restaurant person is likely to jump at this idea, because your advertisements will help promote his restaurant. Perhaps he'll agree to share the cost of such advertising, or reciprocate by mentioning your business in *his* advertising.

In addition, the restauranteur may agree to display your card on his bulletin or near the cash register. And he will undoubtedly wind up buying replacement dinnerware from you! But keep the initial asking price as low as you can; if you absorb a loss, deduct it from your income tax. "He's new and he needs the business" will grow to "he deserves the business," to, finally, "he's good if you can get him."

Paid Advertising

Although word of mouth is the best form of promotion, printed advertisements can also be effective, and radio and TV spots are also of use in promoting your business. Most seasoned salespeople agree that a single message spread by a combination of the media is by far the best form of paid advertising. Your message on a poster in the bus and in the morning paper, broadcast on radio and perhaps on TV, repeated daily for a number of days, tells the world who and where you are and what you have to offer. The same message, simply repeated on a variety of media, will achieve better results than a variety of messages. Such advertising is probably best used to announce a special sale, or event. For a craftsperson, this might mean an "open house" where he can be seen at work.

Coding

If you code your promotional message, your customers will automatically let you know, in responding, where they learned of you. Such coding is easiest in mail-order operations where the customer actually addresses an envelope or mails a coupon to you. Assume you've placed three ads, each to run the same week, in the local newspaper, the radio, and on television. The newspaper ad would say: "Write to Dept. 1," the radio ad would list "Dept. 2," and TV responders would be directed to "Dept. 3." If you received 50 orders addressed to Dept. 1, and the message cost you $100, you could see that each response to your newspaper advertising had cost you $2. Coding demonstrates which of the media, in your case, has worked best to promote your product or service.

It is also important to place appropriate ads with the appropriate media. Promotions for wind generators, for instance, are probably more successful in newspapers than on television.

Goodwill

"Goodwill" is the term used for the valuable list of various business accounts and responsive customers you develop. This becomes a part of your company's actual value, and it is not uncommon to learn when a company changes hands that the goodwill amounts to half, or more, of the total asking price. Keep careful records of the names and addresses of your customers. In mail order this is no problem; and for many service jobs it is also quite simple, but in various craft and other retail-type operations, where the customer shows up in person and carries the product away, obtaining this information requires extra effort, since it is not a necessary part of the actual transaction. This may explain the popularity of charge accounts among retailers. Having the customer's name and address makes it possible for you to alert him to special sales and events. A Guest Register is often used to acquire such information, but it is better to ask the customer's name and address, and copy it directly on the sales slip, because the Guest Register is often ignored, and because the sales slip will identify not only the customer but his purchase.

And keep records, photographic, if possible, of every job you do. Writers keep carbon copies of their work, why shouldn't bricklayers have photographs of every chimney they build?

Your Advertising Message

Unless you are a skilled graphic or psychological artist, and even if you are, you should probably keep the message as simple and direct as possible. If recorded for TV or radio, the name and address of the business should be repeated—repeated twice if possible—and the voice that makes the offer ought to be relaxed and unhurried. Do not let your commercial message give the impression that you've just moved your used car lot to town and will be selling cars there for at least a week. A slow, easy approach will help encourage the trusting attitude necessary among good customers.

On the printed page, the same principle applies, except there's no need here for repetition, so the ad can be even "cleaner." Be sure in all cases to rent sufficient air or page space so that your message can have this uncramped feeling. Even a small space can allow effective advertising, if you keep the message direct.

Send 25¢ for my new Catalogue
"The Finest in Garden Seeds"
Billy's Seeds, Lancaster, Pennsylvania

Leaving out just a few words can add the impact of a telegram. Consider the *visual* effect of your message, whether or not it includes an illustration.

CATALOGUE
25¢
"The Finest in Garden Seeds"
Billy's Seeds, Lancaster, Pennsylvania

Special Sales

Special offers are a good way to draw customers, and they give a focal point and special timeliness to your advertising. Just make sure the special offer doesn't cost you too much in lost profit, and be extra sure that you can keep the promise your commercial message makes. A minimum of words to describe an offer with wide appeal works best. "All Lawns Mown in February Half Price! Other Yard Services Too!" "Ten Percent Off Everything, April 8–20!"

If you can afford to discount your entire stock you're likely to draw more customers than if you limit your sale to specific items; further, limiting the sales to specific items requires that you have a sufficient quantity of those items in stock. If you make special offers on certain items, include a phrase like "while supply lasts," or be prepared to offer disappointed customers "rain checks" which entitle them to the sale discount as soon as the product is again available.

Remember that the primary purpose of advertising is not so much to sell your product or service as it is to draw the customer to you. Once he meets you and sees what you have to offer, the need for advertising disappears. In mail-order businesses, the equivalent of this is enticing the customer to order your catalogue, or make a trial order. Douglas and Jackie Eichhorn, who succeed very well in the antique business, explain that it is never necessary to "sell" a good antique. The same principle applies to all goods and services in quality-starved America! The trick is in letting the customer know you're there, and in keeping the price down so he'll give you a try.

While this sort of consideration may cost you a few dollars in immediate profits, you will gain friends for your business, and you will be striking a blow at the shins of chain businesses which are usually too busy cranking the register to learn about their customers, much less to take an order, which *would* be a way for them to get names and addresses, if they were interested in goodwill. They prefer to swamp our mailboxes each week with messages to Occupant.

"Organic?"

In less than 50 years, America has led the world to a unique marketing situation: the word "Organic" is stamped proudly upon a limited, few products in a few of the most-thoroughly stocked grocery stores. The dangerous implication here, beside the scarcity of natural food, is that "organic" is some sort of magical ingredient/property you add—like chemicals. The product is usually overpriced, and may eventually cease to be organic at all, while the price remains high and the packaging imitates the "organic look." I have met organic farmers who no longer label their produce "Organic," even though they wouldn't dream of using chemicals on their crops. "Our reasons for growing organically are ecological, not commercial," Toni Attmore told me. These growers have found that the public is wary of the word "Organic," because it suggests higher prices and suspicious claims!

Doing With or Without

Most self-employed people have discovered ways to keep the overhead low so that they can market their product or service at a competitive price. Richard and Evelyn Fatigati list as their biggest business mistake hiring an advertising agency to make up a mail-order ad for them; when the bill for $1,000 came they were

shocked, especially because they had decided the ad was impersonal and, for their purposes, unuseable. But their legal responsibility was to pay the fee.

Certain professional fees may be unavoidable, and in the case
of lawyers' and accountants' services, can save you money or
prevent costly mistakes. But with advertising agencies, for
instance, it is probably wise to rely on the artistic instincts of
someone who knows you and your business, rather than on the
costly and impersonal service of a place that just cranks out commercial messages.

Similarly, if you want a leaflet printed up, you are likely to obtain better results, at a saving, by contacting a friend with access to
a mimeograph, than by hiring the job out to a printing company.
Unless, of course, that printing company be one similar to Allan
and Cinda Kornblum's, where the management is concerned with
obtaining unique and suitable results. Without personal rapport,
how is the printer going to understand your needs?

If you decide to design and prepare the printed message yourself, you will save considerably, the ad will reflect your mood and
spirit, and you will be assured that no printer can accidentally im-
pose a typographical error. All this presumes that you will take the
message you have prepared to an offset printing service where you,
the customer, provide the master image that can be duplicated as
many times as you wish.

One form of free advertising that many small-business people
overlook, either because of modesty or shortage of time, is the
"human interest story" about their business they could provide to a
local radio or TV station, or give to the local newspapers. The less
overt "salesmanship" in such a presentation, the more likely it is to
attract customers. The approach here is to share your own enthusiasm for your business with the general audience, using anec-
dotes where possible, and explaining the differences between
myth and fact. I think here of John and Colleen Calhoun, goat
farmers, who have dedicated a lot of energy to improving the
image of the goat in America. "People say goats eat anything,"
laughed Colleen. "They're the most fussy animal there is; they
refuse to eat off the ground—they're naturally browsers, not
grazers—and they'd sooner go thirsty than drink water that has so
much as a speck in it. Just because they happen to like the flavor of

the glue between label and can, they have a reputation for eating tin cans." Colleen went on to explain a campaign some goat farmers launched at Expo 1974 to have a gimmicky giant mechanical goat removed. It had been constructed to encourage visitors to dispose of their trash properly. "Drop the cans and bottles and papers into the dumper and this big goat would eat it," explained John. "They said they couldn't change the display—it was too costly!" The Calhouns recognized that such a story makes a more memorable media presentation than would a point-by-point review of the inadequacies of cow's milk, or a more commercially oriented message. As a matter of fact, most of the interviews in this book demonstrate this technique. These people are positive about what they do, and by conveying that positive feeling they are able to advertise without hounding us as big businesses often seem to do.

Finances

Probably the biggest single mistake made by people starting their own business is to underestimate their operating and living expenses while overestimating early financial returns. Especially in the crafts, the tendency is to expect immediate returns on the investments required; craftsperson after craftsperson told me: "Don't make the mistake of thinking you'll be supporting yourself by the end of a year or two. It requires *at least three years* to discover the market or to be discovered!" Good promotion might lower the waiting time, and no one should "wait to be discovered," even though *good promotion takes time away from production.*

If your self-employment involves a crop rather than a service or nonperishable product, you might well consider how many years it will be before that crop is selling at your intended peak-rate of production. For instance, while a service or craftsperson can have relatively "instant" peak-production, agricultural self-employment requires years of patient effort before the returns begin to equal the investment. In such activities as winemaking and Christmas tree farming, the first five years can be virtually income-free. During such lean years, the options available are either to work out at a full- or part-time job, or to take a loan and devote full-time energies to getting your business on its feet as quickly as possible. A fortunate few people do not need to choose either option because they start their business with money they've had stashed away somewhere.

Wealthy self-employers sometimes work with a disadvantage, because for them, the luxury of being able to absorb financial failure removes a large part of the incentive necessary to make a small business work. Rather than envy the folks with the trust funds, sharpen your pencil and make a realistic appraisal of what your financial needs will be. You will want to make careful, expense-by-expense itemizations, for each of at least your first three years. Make such an appraisal without estimating potential or probable income: remember here that you are merely figuring what your gross expenses will be.

Making Projections

Among the most common "mistakes" listed by the people who responded to a questionnaire I mailed about self-employment, was "being too idealistic." This translates, roughly, into "unbridled optimism," usually of the sort that is necessary, yet dangerous, to any major self-employment project.

Someone who expects the worst isn't going to take even the first steps toward bringing an idea to reality. But all too often, the brilliance of an idea bleaches out all the hazards that line the way to success, as the sun hides all other heavenly bodies until nightfall, and the inspired optimist takes out pad and pencil and calculates the projections that show he simply cannot lose!

"Never use the best-case scenario when assessing the possibilities/opportunities of the business you're considering," wrote Mike Keiser of Recycled Paper Products. "Always assume the worst—if you can make it under those circumstances you have a 50–50 chance (because your projections are probably *still* too optimistic!). And remember that time is your most important personal asset. You simply have to plan on working 60 to 70 hours a week, no matter how small you plan to keep a business that's going to provide your support."

Money

People who lived through the Depression, and those who have suffered its woes vicariously, know about "security," and many have dedicated their lives to insuring it to their families. Almost everyone younger than 50 has important adult figures in memory who have held to "secure" positions to provide the important cushion, sometimes at a terrible personal sacrifice. The collapse of many of these positions during recent years has led to important changes in many lives. The terror of being "laid off" has motivated many people to set up their own small business, often with the benefit of a financial cushion earned in different times.

When I think back on the sixties, when a large segment of the student population was equating Capitalism with piggery, I remember the uncomfortable dependency these students had on their "Capitalistic" parents, whose tuition checks kept them in school, out of Vietnam. In some ways, this generation fulfilled its own prophecy; a number of student radicals have turned 30 and are now earning handsome incomes within the system. The evils of Capitalism have been refined in their minds. The system is okay, except, in its emphasis on competition. Or does competition manifest itself exclusive of the system?

Is it the equation of money with greed that often clouds money matters with embarrassment? Poor people often pretend they're not, and rich ones sometimes try to hide their wealth. I have trusted the statements of the people in this book, although I have met a few self-employed people who are reluctant to disclose certain financial matters. "One of the attractions of having a small business is you're in control of the accounting, and that way it's quite possible to hide some of your income," one craftsperson told me. While some of the information from people like this might be useful, their overall approach is unhealthy, and manifests itself through nervousness at being caught, if not through genuine guilt.

One is tempted to say that small-business people are more honest than big-business people, but this temptation derives from stereotypes of fat cats vs. skinny people with dirty hands. So even though I have tried to be candid about those who conceal real income, we should probably consider all figures as approximately representative.

People with the healthiest attitude toward money are those who regard it as a tool. A few, lucky individuals are able to regard this tool with a minimum of emotion. One friend of mine uses his extra money to buy good rugs, usually Persian rugs that need repair. He repairs the rug and enjoys his possession. The brick walls of his loft are covered with rugs, and so are his floors. I was afraid to step on them, especially when he told me some are worth as much as $1,500! "Don't be silly!" he said. "They're made to be walked on. They can take it. When I buy a rug I'm paying for all the hours and hours some person dedicated to making it. That *time*, not the rug, is what has value." Two or three times a year, he wedges three or four rolls of rugs into the back of his old VW and drives them into New York where he sells them at good profit, buying more that need repair.

The Illusion of Fast Money

In almost every case, the person who goes into a self-employment venture with quick-money attitudes is doomed to failure. While "get rich quick" may be the Great American Dream of the first half of this century, it is indeed not one of the realities of the century's second half—even the government is dead set against such nonsense, as federal tax forms show—short-term gains are taxed at twice the rate of long-term gains. Because of this phenomenon, self-employed people are wise to consider the decision of Ross McBurney, a Christmas tree grower, who won't sell a tree that is younger than five years, because "after five years it's taxed as a capital gain rather than income." Does the same principle apply to wine? To antiques?

Researching this book, I found only one person whose motive is acknowledged to be fast money. It is not incidental that he enjoys the process of earning this money, and works at least 100 hours a week! Ironically, he is among those people I met whose chosen style of living might be considered excessively simple by others in this book.

Motivation and Time

My neighbor, Gerald Weihs, who has started an herb business, characterizes three types of "independent" small-business people. "First," he says, "you have your trust-funders. For them it's no sweat to spend all day doing their thing, because paying the bills is no sweat. They don't need to worry about a market, even. Next there's those people who start out with a gigantic loan, and spend their first 20 years in business working to pay the interest.

And finally, there's people who try to do it entirely on their own. They buy a lot of food stamps and live pretty close to the bone."

Given such diversity of circumstance, it may be surprising that with only one exception, the self-employed people I talked with cited not money, but the activity and/or product of work as their biggest source of motivation. That is hard to believe, until you realize that the average full-time self-employed person spends 80 hours a week to earn what he once made in 40. So it is necessary to find joy in the work, if not in the fact that so little time is left for life's other pleasures.

Mrs. Hazel I. Diaz Pumara, of Diaz Handcrafts, puts it perfectly: "Any self-employed person should have an abundance of energy, especially if he is both manufacturer and salesman. If your motive is getting away from a boss, realize that to profit you will have to make demands on yourself that no boss or employer could demand. Without rigid self-discipline one can easily develop a potentially dangerous life-style, unbalanced in favor of too much work, and too little recreation, with the excuse that one's work is also one's relaxation."

This aspect, the management of time, is very important. When you are working on your own land or inside your own home, you do not have the physical separation from home that is normally experienced in the eight-to-five situation. Separating family matters from business matters can be a significant problem when there is no bus to catch, no boss to make the decision. For me, as a writer, part of this problem has been solved by constructing a very small shack in the woods, convenient to our home but far enough away that going to it means putting on a coat in winter.

How Much Do You Charge?

So many variables come into play with pricing your work that no formula will satisfy every case. The biggest consideration is the value of your own time, determined by your experience and how much money you need. When experience is not sufficient to equal need, then need must be reduced while experience grows. This is the choice most people in this book have made. If you live simpler, you can devote more time to your work—and plow more money back into the work too.

One of the biggest mistakes you can make is to undervalue your own time. Remember, it isn't just the time you spend in the act of performing your work, but in arranging for sales, in delivering, in cleaning up, in general pondering. Somehow, a lot of self-employed people, because they do not come home at 5 P.M. and turn it all off, get into the bind of working 60-to-80-hour weeks for subsistence pay. Often, this is the result of simply underpricing their work by a few cents the customer would never begrudge a "quality" product.

Assume, for instance, that you are a cabinetmaker, producing 10 cabinets a week. The cost of materials per cabinet is $50. Your average time per cabinet is six hours. *You are working a 60-hour week.* Have you priced your cabinets to allow yourself a weekly wage or an hourly wage? Have you allowed yourself "overtime" pay for the 20 extra weekly work hours? A small difference in retail price can mean the difference between subsistence pay and a really lucrative business. In the accompanying chart, a 100-percent increase in labor cost, which would mean the difference between an income of $15,000 or $30,000 a year, results in only a 37.5 percent increase of wholesale cost. The effects of this are doubled, alas, by the retailer's profit, but note that the retailer can pay your highest labor rate and still show a profit selling at your lowest suggested retail price.

Expense and Income Chart for
Cabinetmaker Working a 60-Hour
Week at Three Different Labor Rates,
Making 10 Cabinets a Week

	Fixed Costs	Labor	Wholesale Price per Cabinet	Retail Price per Cabinet
$ 5/hour	$50	$30	$ 80	$160
$ 7.50/hour	$50	$45	$ 95	$190
$10/hour	$50	$60	$110	$220

If you write up a chart similar to this, make a realistic and all-inclusive estimate of the "fixed costs," and balance this figure against the variables of production output and what you will charge for your labor. Such a chart, as simple as it is, will often reveal where small alterations in procedure can make a big difference in whether the venture succeeds. For instance, figuring the above chart's findings over a one-year (50 week) period, we see that the cabinetmaker who calculates 20 hours of labor at an overtime rate, working a 60-hour week, realizes $22,750 net profit per year, as opposed to $15,000 for the person who does not figure overtime. And for supertime, the annual income is $30,000. The point is to realize that labor costs, your real source of "profit," are a lot less consequential to the customer than they are to you.

Juggling Figures

A neighbor of mine in East Fairfield who once wholesaled toy horses for about $15, of which $12 went for materials, began to tire of building toy horses. So he calculated that, if he were to sell at a retail price of $35, he would have to make only one toy horse for every seven he had been producing before, and realize the same profit.

Juggling figures is especially important in the early planning stages, but the importance of this imaginative mathematics cannot be emphasized too highly, even in the mature stages of a small business. Whenever an opportunity arises to reduce overhead, you have a chance to improve your profit margin, or reduce the cost of your product, or both.

In the five years since Mike Keiser and Phil Friedmann started Recycled Paper Products in Chicago, their tiny business has grown to the point where it really has ceased to be a "cottage industry"—they have 20 full-time employees. "We've always worked out of near-tenement environs," they write, "paying $1 per square foot when the competition is paying $4–$6 per square foot. Saving on rent also becomes saving on fixtures, furniture, and equipment to some extent. And once the spirit of cheapness is established, accessories like autos, clothes, and first-class travel aren't as important as they once seemed. We could have plush surroundings and the related accoutrements but we'd be into our bank a lot heavier than we are now, and it would only increase as we grow. There's no flexibility in debt—right now we could experience a 50 percent drop in sales and still make money. Our debt/sales ratio is under 10 percent."

Keeping Books

Accounting is essential to any business, yet it is the factor most often overlooked by people who have started on a hobby basis. Because many self-employed people did not learn business as a part of their special trade, and because, at first, it wasn't necessary to keep books when they decided to turn their speciality into a primary source of income, they're at a loss.

The one universal rule is to keep a written record of every transaction. The variety of methods for organizing this mass of material is one of the frightening aspects of "business." All those numbers on all those lined pages in book after book are not only confusing, but too dull to learn about. I won't attempt a long, complicated journey through the many options that are available no further than your nearest library, but here provide one, simple, workable method of keeping books. As far as I know, it works in any given situation, and as long as you maintain the discipline necessary to record every transaction, the results will be clear, and those figures on the page will tell a story of real interest.

Everything in Triplicate

Numbered forms are available at any good stationery store; the carbon paper is already in place and a box of 1,000 costs less than $5. So your cost per transaction for having a clear record, is about half-a-cent. One copy of this form, preferably the original, goes to the customer. You keep the other two copies. File one alphabetically, by name of customer, and file the other chronologically. In this way, when the customer's name comes up again, you can turn to his file and know immediately what he bought and when. His file gives you an interesting profile of his specific interests and needs, and might be quite useful in certain advertising situations. The file will also provide you an instant reference regarding the customer's reliability when it comes time for payment.

The chronological file tells you exactly what business you did on any specific date, and with whom.

Customer's name should appear at the top of such a form, and be sure this information is legible. If you are a traveling farrier, for instance, this sort of bookkeeping is going to be more troublesome than a feisty horse, because it's no simple matter to write legibly, leaning against a truck after shoeing four horses in 90°F. heat with flies buzzing your nose. "How do you spell your name again?" Indeed, if your business is a service, try to write up as much of the customer's card as you can when you take the order, in advance of the work. Keep a clipboard, a couple of good pens, and a supply of forms in your vehicle, have similar facilities on your desk next to your telephone, and half the battle is won.

Beneath the customer's name is his address and phone number. Except in the busiest of retail operations, like a supermarket, it makes good sense to obtain this information, at least in your initial transaction with the customer. (See the chapter on "Promotion" for more information in this regard.)

Below the customer's name and address should appear the date, and below that, a description of the actual transaction. This will be the customer's bill, and it should show clearly the amount due, and whether that amount has been paid. At the end of each business day, you should file your two copies in their appropriate places.

Next, you should establish a checking account in the official name of your business, and keep that account wholly separate from any personal use. Some people even recommend establishing a business account at a bank different from the one used for other matters; I favor "shopping around" for a bank that wants your business account, and demonstrates that desire with friendly service and good banking advice.

With a business checking account established, you can key your monthly billing and accounting activities to the arrival of your bank statement. For this reason, the actual date the statement arrives may be important to you, and you should not hesitate to make this a factor in choosing a bank. Presuming your canceled checks and the notations in your checkbook give you a double record of all business disbursements, the monthly balancing act will serve as the best time to get out your double record file of all sales, and enter both receipts and disbursements in your business ledger.

You should bear in mind, if the bookkeeping procedure ever tends to bog down, that the records you keep are an actual asset to your business, and the better they are, the more complete they are, the greater their value in the event you decide to sell your business. This principle was demonstrated memorably to me when I met Marianne Stewart, a candlemaker, who was selling her tiny business in Mount Vernon, Maine. Asking price for all her equipment and a healthy inventory of wax was only half what she wanted for her "goodwill," which is an accepted means of acquiring a royalty for your hours of keeping good books!

Taxes

"The best way to figure income tax," a lawyer once said, "is to take every possible deduction you can prove, even if you're not completely sure it qualifies. If the IRS complains, you may be disqualified, but chances are your deduction will be allowed."

The real trick of keeping taxes low, then, is to keep a careful record of every penny spent on business. Remember that, to the extent you use personal property for business, its depreciation and operation are tax deductible.

Many people are not sure whether their activity qualifies as a legitimate "business." Therefore, they are reluctant to keep any records, or to consider the possibility that by claiming a "hobby" as a business on their tax form they might be able to enjoy considerable tax advantages while they switched their income base from a regular employee situation to independence.

Art and the Law, a newsletter from Volunteer Lawyers for the Arts, recently published guidelines, based on legal precedent, that show business status is relatively easy to prove, *even though you lose money at that business activity and deduct its loss from your other income!* I found this information reprinted in *CODA*, which is a writer's newsletter (see "Bibliography" for more about both publications), and while the guidelines which I gratefully reprint here are based on the case of a free-lance writer who, let's say, loses $500 a year because he can't sell his novels, they would apply equally to any somewhat self-employed person.

According to the article, until 1969, one could deduct just about any personal loss to minimize tax liability from real income.

But the law was tightened so that "the difference between a business and a hobby lies in the demonstrable intent to make money. So the tax-conscious writer should arrange to make *some* writing income each year and keep it in a separate bank account.

"But in the absence of income, the intent to make money may be shown by your answers to the following questions." If you can answer "yes" to all or most of these questions, the article states, you should be able to survive a tax audit easily.

1. Can you show that you are recognized as a writer? Any publication, regardless of quality, will help.
2. Do you write regularly? Keep work records, and try to show at least four hours a day.
3. Can you show you have earned money in past years through writing? Tax returns of previous years would substantiate this. Showing writing profit for two of five past years would "greatly strengthen your position."
4. Is your secondary job low paying? To help prove you can't afford expensive "hobbies."
5. Are you keeping work separate from pleasure? ("An unprofitable reading tour to the Fiji Islands may cause some suspicion.")
6. Are temporary losses necessary for your work? Some novels just take years to complete.
7. Are your expenses reasonable?
8. Do you keep expense records?
9. Can you show your non-writing job is of secondary professional importance to you; i.e., that you are a writer not simply for the tax deductions it offers, which are:

Acceptable Tax Deductions, Using Writer for this Example:

- Upkeep and depreciation on a portion of home or apartment used for writing, or full rent on studio space used exclusively for writing;
- Upkeep and depreciation on car used for travel for research or to readings or workshops;
- Travel and lodging expenses in connection with a literary project, reading, or workshop (i.e., 15¢ a mile is now allowed for gas and oil);

- Typewriter repair and depreciation (usually one-fifth the original cost will be deductible each year, if the machine is regarded as having a five-year life);
- Paper, office supplies, and stamps;
- Business phone expenses, or a proportion of home phone used for business calls;
- Subscriptions to literary magazines, publications used for research, reference books;
- Membership fees in writers' associations (also helpful in establishing "professional" status);
- Insurance on manuscripts;
- Publicity items, such as flyers and photographs;
- Gifts and flowers limited to $25 per recipient, who must be business-related;
- Commission to agent;
- Fees for secretarial, legal, and accounting services;
- Entertainment of prospective editors or publishers ("Accurate records *must* be kept detailing the place, people involved, why they serve your business purpose, and business topics discussed");
- Copyright registration fees.

The key to all tax matters is to know your liabilities, and to meet your obligations, but to be sure you do not contribute unnecessarily. One good way to do this is to hire the job done, keeping accurate records for your accountant. After he's done it for a couple of years, you can copy his methods and tally your own.

Whenever a question comes up, you will probably find that the people at your local IRS office are very willing to be of assistance. And, perhaps surprisingly, the assistance they give will be in the interests of having you pay no more than your fair share.

Sales Tax

Sales tax is a means used by most states to raise revenues. Anyone starting a small business should inquire whether his state law requires that he register with the local sales tax bureau. Toni Attmore, of Turquoise Trail Herb Farm, calls the sales tax a "business privilege tax," and refuses to pass the cost on to her customers, paying the actual New Mexico percentage from the income of selling herbs.

Regardless how you raise the money, most states will want you to turn over a small percentage of your retail sales, and while the money may not be all that much, a certain amount of paperwork is made necessary. In cases where you sell to libraries or schools, where a tax exemption is in effect, no sales tax is involved.

"There's one obvious benefit of registering with sales-tax people," writes Elaine Gill, of The Crossing Press. "Once you have a tax number you can use it when purchasing business-related items to avoid *paying* a sales tax. Particularly in printing, where we use a lot of paper, this represents a big saving."

Professional Help

Bankers and Loans

"Of all the people who come to us for loans, I would say the so-called 'artist type'—that is, the creator of jewelry, pottery, or whatever—is probably harder to evaluate than anyone else, until you know he can sell his stuff." These are the words of a bank executive I know, who has worked with a Burlington, Vermont, bank for many years. I had shown him a partial table of contents for this book, asking his recommendations for someone who has a good idea, but no capital.

"The loan officer's biggest problem is to get an idea of whether the project is going to sustain life. So any proven sales record should go with you to the bank, so you can demonstrate that you have practical experience so you can say: 'I *know* I can make money with this.' Even though it is harder to make a loan to someone without capital, I'd rather see experience than a lot of collateral. Good management is the key to business success, and some guys can't find out how to lose money, and some can't find out how to make it.

"For this reason, we also look for an interest in the real nitty gritty of the proposed endeavor. The guy living with it as well as working with it you somehow feel is more likely to succeed than the guy whose books aren't quite up to date, or who needs an accountant even before he's got the loan. That type of person is probably less motivated than someone who has obviously participated in all aspects of the organizational work.

"It's very important to be obviously established in the community. In other words, it's a bad idea to invest capital in a strange town. But if circumstance has it that you are new in the community, you can establish credit quickly in the time-honored way of borrowing money you don't need and paying it back on time. A small loan, no more than $500 for a month, for which you'd probably have to put up some collateral, wouldn't be too expensive.

"Or, if you have credit established with another bank, you can always write an officer at that bank for a letter of introduction. Or the new bank can make a phone call to inquire, if you request.

"Otherwise, as far as getting established: open an account, hopefully with some money in it, and make an appointment with a loan officer. Remember that the big risk with small enterprises is their lack of established substance. The banker doesn't want to see some gypsy performance that'll disappear next week.

"Again, creative people, as distinguished from business-people, are very leery, as a whole, of partners, and they tend to feel a financial partner isn't really part of the business. Your trash hauler here is probably pretty good at basic economics because his success relies on business judgment, whereas people involved in the arts can be 'successful' in terms of aesthetics, but helpless when it comes to business. So, in every case, it is wise to regard your banker not as an adversary, but as a *partner*, and to value that partnership because you probably can't do without it.

"Someone just starting a business has the whole struggle of getting it up to speed before the money runs out, and time and patience are critical. And then, once it is in full swing, comes the question of expansion. At any time like this, whenever you are facing a critical decision, it's a good idea to make your banker an advisor, and go over your plans with him. He's pleasantly surprised you're not after a loan, and happy to help you see through your rose-colored glasses.

"Needless to say, if you are going to consult your banker as a partner, you should shop around a little to find someone you like. Some bankers will require so much red tape that their advice isn't really worth the time. But there are creative bankers, too.

"Really, the best advice I can give is never to get behind in payments, because not only does the bank get worried, but it costs you time with weekly statements, rewriting notes, and protecting your rear.

"And the guy who thinks he's dealing with the enemy when he goes for financing should reconsider the situation objectively."

Obtaining Grants

A grant can often mean the difference between floundering along at amateur level for years and quickly developing a process that may eventually be capable of returning a profit. Especially in the arts, it can mean the difference also between turning out marketable mass-appeal work and experimenting with forms that do not have such immediate saleability. Grant money is made available through the federal government and state arts councils, as well as through large foundations and corporations; anyone who needs to "buy time" for the development of an artistic, crafts, or research project is eligible for such money. The biggest question is *where to find it, and how to apply*.

When it comes time to filling in the grants information form, you should emphasize those aspects of your project that are most in keeping with the grant guidelines. A young printer whose father works as a consultant to agencies seeking grants told me: "Reword what the grantors are giving the grant for as your proposal. And if you're ever in doubt, phone them up. Let them hear your voice. Or better, go and see them. And never, but never, lose your temper with an arts council secretary!"

Ron Hays, Video Grantsman

I talked with Ron Hays, a 31-year-old videoartist who lives in Boston, and who, after university training and three or four successful jobs in television production "lost motivation for the commercial thing. I came to see my boss one day and said 'I just can't do it anymore.' And she said, 'Yeah I know it, I'm really sorry.'

"The problem became, how could I create a life-support

system both professional and personal that would support me in the work of my choice—the visualization of music and feelings— which to the corporate state was a pretty far-out thing. It wasn't a product, it wasn't a refrigerator, it wasn't a service, it was something entirely new. I had to learn where the sources of money were to support what was, essentially, a process of experiment and learning."

With the help of a friend, Ron wrote up a proposal in association with WGBH, the educational television station in Boston, which was receptive to the idea of Ron's using station facilities "in return for 'obligations in print'. Work there provided me the craft and skills leading to *Prelude*." (Ron's half-hour visualization of Wagner's prelude and "Liebstod" from *Tristan und Isolde,* conducted by Leonard Bernstein).

It is because of *Prelude* that I was able to meet Ron Hays. I was in Boston to talk with Jock Gill about free-lance photography and Gill just happened to have a job that day making a Polaroid

Ron Hays

print, suitable for poster-sized enlargement, from *Prelude*. Hays met us at WGBH late Saturday afternoon, when the pace at the station is extremely slow. As Jock set up the camera and took a few test shots, Ron screened *Prelude* for us, and the abstract color splashes created by Ron and other visual artists worked in astonishing contrast and blend with Bernstein's conducting. The effect, though diminished by the small television screen, was not unlike that of Kubrick's *2001*. I could see how a project like this would easily require the many months of solid conceptual and artistic commitment Hays put into it.

"Having established myself in a broadcast institution dedicated to experiment, I then encountered the problems of how to relate to the institution and remain valuable to it on its terms, while at the same time fulfilling my artistic obligations to myself and the proposal that I had made.

"I was cutting film on Gloucester fishing upstairs, while I was producing my own noncommercial video feedback on the first floor. And really kind of having a ball. I mean there were times when I couldn't believe the difference between third-floor and first-floor activity. But I realized how unique and temporary the situation was.

"Because of *Prelude*, I learned how to approach the best creative side of myself. I learned how to raise money. I learned how to write about my project so I could talk people into it. I learned the procedure of application, learned who to go to, learned how mostly to communicate my idea in a credible fashion, and learned that without the image script, without a budget, without an application, I wasn't worth beans. And mostly without a choice to make a commitment to doing those things which were the requirements for getting to the final vision, I wouldn't have gotten anything done at all.

"There is a very important factor in obtaining grants which sometimes makes me feel very futile for people. They don't have a sense of how much they're worth. I intuited how much the project was worth, and somehow I evolved the idea and the piece and its execution based on how much I knew we were worth.

"I assessed the sources and the potential for receiving their grants, and I wouldn't have dared ask the National Endowment for the Arts for $50,000, for instance. I knew the structure that implies $10,000 might be possible for an individual artist, but any-thing much bigger must be a project involving many people.

"More and more I was learning that foundations don't want to give anything more than $7,000–$10,000 to an individual artist. They want to give it through an institution because they trust the institution's administrative ability. It's tax exempt and it's ap-proved. They have accounting sheets they can see.

"Also, if I'm going to relate to an institution, that institution has to know I have certain rights. I learned from my relationship with WGBH what rights the institution expects to have. I learned that learning about my rights is also part of a current event that is now evolving. It's not just me, it's happening all over the country. I walked into a university the other day, and the professors were talking about the exact same thing. *Who owns the copyright?*

"Who has rights to it? Who can use it? Who can make money from it? How much? And what in the future is going to insure you in print or a handshake that the contract or agreement is going to be adhered to? And I realized the next time I went into an institu-tion I wanted to make sure that it was set up and understood. Not purely from my standpoint, but from *both* of ours."

Hays reports that insuring his retention of rights to projects completed with the assistance of grant money took a lot of effort, and established precedents in some cases. "I understood that if I didn't start standing up for my rights and set a precedent, artists would continue to lose their work, then, Holy Tamale! off the presses comes a contract that in the future will be a form for all other artists that may, perhaps, protect their rights. I'm not interested in the money but in the investment I've made in my own creative spirit, and in what the money provides that will allow me to make more work, greater investments into that spirit.

"So there it is—the artist as businessman. And there is noth-ing wrong with thinking about it sometimes as business. The one comment that hurt me the most when I first started out here at WGBH was from a very ensconced videoartist who came up to me and very cynically said 'How's business?' And now I'm going to go back to him and say 'Business is really good; I've really learned my lesson.' Because that's the only way that I'm going to be able to provide myself with the ways and means to do more of what I want to do."

By this time, four hours after we'd entered the building, Jock had shot two dozen stills from *Prelude* as Ron painstakingly rolled the tape forward and back through the machine, often by hand, very slowly trying to find just the right stage of a particular image for a photograph. Earlier, Jock and I had been discussing the relationship of art to business, and Jock added at this point: "Artists living in a period have to accept who the principal patrons are. And in our day and age the principal patrons are the big money boys who are either blatant capitalists or newly reformed ex-capitalists. And they understand business. If they can't understand you, they're not going to stick their necks out. If it had been a thousand years ago, we all would have been Catholics, you know, and relating like mad to the Church.

"A couple of Fridays ago I put on a tie and paid a visit to the international department at Polaroid. After I showed them some samples of the synthesized Polacolor 2 images that Dennis Purcell and I have been making, they gave me a generous supply of film, and mentioned the prospects for an exhibition in Europe. The point is that many people hesitate to present themselves as anything but the dusty artist, and it never hurts to meet someone on their own, perhaps slightly formal and bureaucratized, level. I know in photography, particularly in art photography, that some people think talking about money in the same breath as Art and Photography is just practically dirty business."

The conversation was winding up. Ron added an important point, one that is supported by Elaine and John Gill at The Crossing Press, and by just about anyone else I know who has received grant assistance. "A lot of people in the foundations are rich, beautiful, inspired human beings who are there for no other purpose than to aid and abet the artist. They can and should be approached as human beings, and just as fallible as anyone else."

"Don't be afraid to phone them if you have a question," is Elaine Gill's advice.

"The other thing," added Ron, "is an understanding of the institution that is offering the grant. How it operates. In contemporary art, where so much of the equipment is so expensive, concentrate not on owning but *having access*, grant money that will buy you the all-important access to the technology of your medium. Learn where the materials are and how to get to them! Also, don't let anyone call you a sellout for taking commercial work. I did a department store commercial on the Dalton computer about three weeks ago in North Carolina. I didn't care if I did it, even though everybody came in and said, 'Oh, selling out, aren't you?' 'No, I'm learning more craft. Give me the money, and I can put that in the bank account. That helps me pay Jock here to make photographs.' That's what it's all about, it's all interdependent and cyclical."

In the hallway, as we were leaving, Ron summed up the steps by which he arrives at a figure, and presentation of his needs to a patron. "I budget on a very practical scale what I need to live on. A weekly amount of dollars that is necessary for me to live comfortably. That's roughly $200 a week, but right now I'm allowing myself only $50–$60 a week. I eat in, take public transportation, sold my car and ride a bike, and I've moved to a part of the city where I can pay less rent. I know I am going to get the money I need only by going out and thoroughly investigating the requirements: personal, physical, creative, artistic, and technical, and by figuring the business and accounting. It is necessary to make a model of the vision, with script, budget, personnel, credentials for yourself and everyone else involved, and the entire presentation should be proportionate and accurate to the scale of your vision."

Contracts

The very word sounds harsh, dangerous, sharp. It's nearly 80 percent consonant. And while it seems to offer legal recourse to both parties, remember that the person who produces the contract is the one who has familiarity with it, through all legal ramifications.

Contracts seem to be particularly dangerous to free-lance people, especially to artists whose "freedom" may be their only tangible reward for the incredible amounts of insecurity they endure. So a contract, offered by a big company or by a comforting person with money to offer, is appealing: It offers security, and even more dangerous than that, it is flattering. It says, "Your work is worth at least this much to us."

I talked with a singer who has recorded albums with the biggest and with the smallest of record companies. She reports that some companies are honest, and some will ignore their contracted responsibilities. In one case, a church-based company sold its record holdings and the new owner, also related to a church group, sought to appropriate certain copyrights. The point is: Contracts have a way of getting "old" or "lost" or "misunderstood." If you are going to sign one, you had better be prepared to fulfill the obligations required, and to act as your own personal watchdog to be sure you get your due.

Ron Hays, the videoartist, suggests that one of the problems with artist's grants is the murky question of who owns what the artist produces under grant monies. This is a significant question, and again one that baits the flattery problem. "Suppose someone wants to give me X dollars to write a symphony, maybe something I've never been *paid* to do before. Okay, but one question: Who owns the symphony when it's completed? The artist, flattered and unwilling to seem ungrateful to the sponsor, rushes to sign the grant receipt form, and autographs away a year or two of his prime output."

Here's how to do it: You have entered the sitting room of a large walnut-paneled building where your patron has agreed to meet you at 3 P.M. for the signing of the grant receipt. (Or it comes in the mail with the check stapled to it and a note, "Sign one copy of this form and return in enclosed envelope"). Your patron enters from the other side of the room and shakes your hand warmly. You are offered a drink and refuse. You are directed to a small table, and the check is flashed before you with the actual numerals in large, red type. "You might want to review this receipt before you sign," your patron suggests helpfully, letting out a sigh of boredom and tapping his foot. Now is your moment; you accept the pen he is holding at arm's length immediately so his arm doesn't tire. You take the pen and hold it above the spot he has checked in pencil at the very bottom of the page, under his name, and just as you begin to squeeze the pen down over the empty space, jerk it back dramatically and in a calm, level tone, clearing your throat if necessary, ask: "Oh by the way, who retains legal possession of my work once the grant period expires?"

As Hays says: "Make sure the contract is understood not purely from *my* standpoint, but from *both* of ours." Or as Rosalie Sorrels advises, "Get a lawyer who specializes in your field. Have him check the contract, then be sure the other party's lawyer has checked it, and then take it to a third lawyer who isn't involved."

Of course, half the time a contract isn't even involved, or when it is, you're sure you can trust the other party. But if a contract is involved, be sure you aren't signing away more than you intend to.

Or as my friend Derc Bass once said: "I guess the joy of self-employment is minimum contracts."

Lawyers

I am fortunate to have a good friend for a lawyer. He is a friend first, which is extremely helpful. He knows the context within which I present my legal problems to him, and he cares about me, so his advice is well-considered. His perspective on law is very helpful. "A lawyer's outlook is generally one of cynicism and skepticism," he told me. "Law school training teaches you to disbelieve, or if not disbelieve, reevaluate all things you have taken as being truths.

"And there is one thing all of us have been brought up with in American society and that is a sense of optimism and the prospect of success for any given business venture. I feel that a large part of my job is to challenge a potential client as to why he feels the business will be a success in an attempt to give him a dimension of the possible loss or failure of the business itself. My hope is that he will be able to exhibit tenacity and aggressiveness in asserting his wants and business needs. There is a great tendency for people to want to say 'yes' and to sign their names; good lawyers try to get people to say 'no' if that is the realistic answer."

Recognizing my good fortune in not having to shop for a lawyer, I asked my friend how someone determines if a lawyer is needed, and how to find a good lawyer. "It's important to remember," he answered, "that lawyers tend to give the kind of advice that best serves the interests of their firm. An inclination is to get the client to involve himself in sophisticated legal mechanisms when they're not necessary.

"If a lawyer won't make himself available to you at any time during the day, even at home, I would say, as a rule of thumb, he does not have your best interests at heart. Lawyers are very busy people and they are often in court during regular business hours and very hard to get ahold of. I make a point of telling my clients, 'If you have a problem I want to know about it *immediately*, I don't care what the hour!' This can prevent further legal complication.

"It is vital that people know they are not bound by my business hours. If I can be advised *before* things are going to happen, *before the deal*, I can help. But if the deal is made without consulting me, I am reduced simply to a technician who reduces their commitments and agreements to legal terminology; i.e., a legal plumber. If I am consulted in advance of an agreement, I become a tactician and that's how the client is best served. He saves money, energy, and emotional trauma, and all the things people encounter when they disagree because they committed themselves too early, when they didn't say 'no' in time.

"In other words, a good lawyer will always make himself available to his client. His best advice to a small-business person is often given by advising that person what his legal risks actually are, and where those risks are likely to be exposed, and the likelihood of claims against the business. The lawyer also advises his client on the probability of such contingencies, and helps the client, if necessary, find legal protection from them.

"The lawyer can also be of assistance in tax matters, of course, but an accountant is usually cheaper and will do the job as well or better. As soon as your business is stabilized, you can figure your taxes yourself, on the basis of the accountant's methods of preceding years.

"With both accountants and lawyers, even though you no longer need their services, keep the relationship you've established with them, even if it just means a telephone call once or twice a year to tell how everything is going. Chances are you won't be billed for such conversation, and you may well get some good, free advice. Then, when and if your business or tax situation changes, your accountant and your lawyer are still there, aware of your situation, and personally ready to be of help."

Incorporation?

The only real value of incorporating is to protect yourself, with the business corporation, in the event that you are unable to repay a loan or cannot pay for inventory. A corporation is chiefly useful to those people whose business will require financial assistance or a substantial advance delivery of inventory. Even though the practical purpose of incorporation is to allow you to declare bankruptcy on behalf of the corporation, your supporters, possibly stockholders, may feel more secure in their venture if it is formalized in the name of a corporation.

While incorporation protects you from financial disaster, it does not offer shelter from liabilities where personal negligence is involved. In other words, a free-lance cab driver may incorporate his one-car business, naming himself as the sole employee. If the business is unable to pay the gas bill on the taxicab, the gas company may sue his corporation, presumably winning his cab, but not his color television or private fleet of Jaguars. However, the free-lance cab driver, incorporated or not, can be sued if he is involved in a traffic accident.

There are instances where incorporation can be a costly mistake. "When it came time to do taxes this year, we found that incorporation was not a well-considered move," writes Evelyn Fatigati, of Era, Incorporated. "Our business is so small (granted, we were expecting bigger things) there is really no need for it. If Era had been simply a small business and not an incorporation, we would have been able to write off our loss and get money back from the government. As it is, we have to swallow that loss and *pay out* taxes. Yuk!"

"Nonprofit"

A special form of incorporation, Nonprofit, is an important consideration, because it offers, where you can show that your business is not a money-making venture, certain tax advantages or exemptions. This does not mean, however, that you, as an employee of the nonprofit corporation, cannot receive a salary—personal profit, if you will. As opposed to a corporation organized for profit, a nonprofit corporation has no stockholders. Instead, it is owned by a board of directors, whose officers are liable for all taxes levied against the corporation, and who retain the power to decide your salary and even fire you from the business you started! So, in forming a nonprofit corporation, if you intend to rely on it for livelihood, be sure to choose directors who are sympathetic not only to your aims, but to your means, and to you as well! Further, some thought might be given to choosing your directors on the basis of "geographical distribution," which can effectively keep them far enough apart to prevent upheaval.

In the case of a corporation organized for profit, the stockholders (and there may be as few as one—you) have legal control. Check with the secretary of your state for the state laws dealing with the formation and management of corporations.

"Tax Exempt"

In the case of some nonprofit educational and some nonprofit medical organizations, a special type of nonprofit status—Internal Revenue Service Code 501, section (c) (3)—can be obtained which exempts the institution of all federal income and all real estate taxes, and offers the opportunity for contributions to that organization to be fully tax deductible. Anyone starting a school should definitely consider applying for a 501 c-3. Unfortunately, the government cracked down on the requirements for this status a few years ago, and a good lawyer may charge as much as $100 to help you establish 501 c-3 eligibility.

By the way, the assets of any 501 c-3 nonprofit corporation, in the event of dissolution, must be turned over to another 501 c-3. If you decide to close down your pottery school, you've got to give the wheel (if owned by the corporation) to another 501 c-3. You can't take it home with you on closing day!

Equipment

Almost any job can be made simpler "with the right piece of machinery," but obtaining equipment can be an expensive diversion from the realities of work, too. Specializing helps cut down on certain equipment demands, but can require sophisticated devices to justify the "specialization." As Jock Gill, the photographer, says, "Equipment that isn't being used ties up your capital while it depreciates. You should apply sufficient discipline on yourself so you don't become an equipment freak."

Tom and Nita Hafford are a young couple who started Tin Top Farm Pottery in Weatherford, Texas, three years ago when "alarmed at the rising drug problem in the large school our sons attended and concerned about the lack of clean water and organic foods in the city, we decided to buy a farm."

Nita writes: "We feel our biggest 'mistake' is undercapitalization. But you never have enough! Plus 'make-do' equipment. Most of the time it is better to save and purchase proper equipment than to improvise with poor-quality substitutes. Inventiveness cannot be denied but sometimes technology is preferable. We do save money wherever practical, e.g., we are formulating plans to use the power takeoff on our tractor to power a pug mill for mixing clay."

In general, it is wise to visit the shops of two or three people who are well-established in the business you are considering. Notice what machinery these people are actually using, and what pieces, if any, are collecting dust and taking up space. Needless to say, if you can find good-quality secondhand equipment, you can save yourself a lot of money, letting the first owner bear the brunt of depreciation. But be sure you can repair or find someone to repair any such "previously owned" equipment, and be sure replacement parts are available.

Heavy equipment is often the cheapest; a good place to find bargains is bulletin boards at universities, especially toward the end of the year, when the students are moving and can't find room in the back of the van for a printing press!

As videoartist Ron Hays points out, learning about "access" is often preferable to ownership. Some equipment is simply beyond the reach of normal budgets. Leasing, or obtaining grants to use, such equipment is sometimes the only answer.

Dick Holbrook's Theory of Multiple Use

Dick Holbrook has been in business for 20 years, working as a chef, as a small-hotel manager, as business manager for a small Vermont college, and with Appleyard Corporation of Calais, Vermont. With his wide background and variety of business experience, Holbrook's principal advice is "Multiple Use! The family car is used for business, the home and office are heated by the same furnace, etcetera!"

Holbrook's point makes sense from many vantages, and it is certainly worth the effort to plan a new business with an eye toward ensuring the multiple use, or sharing, of business facilities, so that expenses—overhead—are kept to a minimum. Of course, when the family car is used for business, when heat for your home is also used for your office, the proportions of those expenses incurred in business are tax deductible. If you do need to rent an office, think about sharing space, sharing a storefront, sharing whatever facilities or employees you need, with someone else—possibly someone whose business might attract customers for you.

Holbrook and Hollister Kent, director of the Appleyard Corporation, had worked on an idea that would fuse the dreams and possibilities among members of the tiny village at Maple Corner, Vermont, where Kent's mother, "Mrs. Appleyard," had written her famous Vermont recipes, which appeared daily in syndicated newspaper columns across the country. Kent, a city planner, convinced his mother that a small mail-order business would provide her busy readers with samples of her most painstaking recipes. "Such things as our chutney," Holbrook explained, "which must stew at a constant temperature for three days!"

Part of Hollister Kent's dream involved having neighbors grow as many of the vegetables and fruits and nuts as possible for the Mrs. Appleyard products, and the industry of this mail-order business could bring the community, now scattered daily by the 12-mile commute to office jobs in Montpelier, back to some semblance of the agricultural village it once had been.

Kent located Holbrook and hired him to help with the business and promotional aspects of Appleyard. And, at the time of Kent's death in 1974, plans were well under way, largely due to Holbrook's vision, to build a small restaurant. This would provide "multiple use" for the cooking facilities already in operation preparing the mail-order foods. Further, Holbrook envisioned a small cooking school, perhaps a hotel training program of sorts, so that the kitchen would actually serve three functions.

The Appleyard Corporation is alive and well in tiny Maple Corner, Vermont. Because the original idea has been through a number of interesting changes, this small business provides a lesson in adaptability and skillful management. Appleyard has survived a change of ownership and direction, retaining its vitality through a partnership of two, young married couples, who have benefited from Holbrook's planning for multiple use.

Other Applications of Multiple Use

The most obvious component of multiple-use potential, after house and car have been considered, is *you*. What can you do, what service can you perform that is related to your business, using its facilities, to help cover expenses? Can you teach your craft? Almost any craftsperson, or artist, or agricultural/gardening expert could give group or private lessons. Anyone with a speciality who has access to neighbors or a community where this special knowledge can be shared, should consider teaching.

Another "multiple use of the self," related to teaching, is writing. That you are now reading this page should prove the need for simple, clear-cut instructions and practical theory. "How-to-do-it books" are notoriously bad, perhaps because they are more often written by theorists than by people who really do it. Or by people who lack the verbal skills to communicate their experience.

Like Toni Attmore, herb grower and writer from Bernalillo, New Mexico, you may have a special point of view that contrasts with highly publicized myths, and you may feel an urgency to communicate your findings. Many organic gardeners, for example, know how much better their food is than the chemically grown foods at the supermarket. Yet among this large group of informed people remain vast areas of speculation and disagreement. To some extent, this disagreement reflects the variables of climate and personal experience. Unresolved disagreements remain; whether, for instance, garlic juice and picking bugs are practical alternatives to rotenone. "It's bunk!" claims Eliot Coleman. "The solution to the pest problem is not attacking the pest, but attacking the *cause* of pests, which is unhealthy plants."

Coleman's theories, the result of careful research in combination with experience, clash head-on with many traditional "organic" practices. Keeping careful records to substantiate and further develop his theories, Coleman writes up the findings as magazine articles with royalties helping bankroll homestead needs.

Likewise, Toni Attmore has seen a great deal of misinformation propagated by herb "specialists," whose books often make ridiculous and potentially dangerous claims for an herb's medicinal applications, and whose methods of harvesting and curing reduce "lovely, rich green leaves to the lesser qualities of yellow straw." Because her own experience has disproved so much published theory, Toni is now working hard on a series of information packets, and she is writing an herb grower's cultivation guide and cookbook.

Even if you don't consider yourself a "writer," going over the records, could you "talk" the story of how you got started and how others might learn from your mistakes into a tape recorder? Lewis and Sharon Watson built a house with stone, then wrote and published a book, *House of Stone.* They "have sold about $50,000 worth of this book alone in two-and-one-half years, all from our homestead base. About a third of this is profit." The Watsons, who call themselves "public school teacher dropouts," parlayed their unexpected profits by founding Earthbooks Lending Library.

To publish a useful and successful information sheet, you needn't waste time and energy trying to convince a commercial house to print your book—at least not until the book is written. You can mimeograph up the chapters—as they are written—and offer them for sale, by mail, through classified ads in appropriate magazines and newspapers. Remember that mail order works best when cost is *low*, and if you keep your chapters short and to the point, you can create a newsletter that you could sell for a dollar a copy or less. Better to sell 500 copies at 50¢ each than 100 at $2.50 each, because storage space is valuable and you'd rather have 500 readers than just 100. (See the chapter on "Small Publishers and Printers" if you wish to pursue this idea.) Consider approaching your local newspaper editor, who may wish to print your writing as a regular column.

Remember that although you may never choose to write about your business, the compilation of good records will provide the basis for a goodwill list, which can be sold with a business at considerable profit.

Working at Home

While using your home as your place of business has tremendous financial benefits, there can be important drawbacks. Separating family from business obligations is the most significant of these, as already described. One other regards insurance. If the nature of your business suggests an increased insurance hazard to your company, your rates could become almost prohibitive.

"Without doubt my biggest mistake was building my first shop attached to my home," writes Eric Bauer, the blacksmith from Fayston, Vermont. "The increased convenience was negligible and the cost of fire insurance became horrendous and prohibitive. There are advantages to having your business close to your home, but not under the same roof. In order to reduce my insurance rates to a reasonable level, minimize any hazards, and maximize privacy, it became necessary to have my business isolated from (but convenient to) my home."

Making the Jump

Many people dream all their lives about becoming independent. A few sketch these dreams, playing with ideas and figures, trying to determine whether there really is a chance for someone who gives up the regular nine-to-five scene. After the initial hemming and hawing, and the secondary elation that hits once a decision is actually made, the time that follows the act of change is likely to be as emotionally turbulent as the time preceding it. In some cases it can even be worse, because the financial instability involved in getting started compounds the emotional situation, which is aggravated by the discovery that the turmoil is just beginning.

Add to this the reality that almost every small business requires at least three years to break even and you see the makings of the closest thing to a postpartum depression known to man. "Our hardest problem in adjusting to working at home came with our three-year-old daughter; she just couldn't understand why I couldn't play with her all day," wrote Herb Griffin. "I was almost ready to take a job just to end that fuss. Also, about two weeks after I made the plunge the reality caught up with me, the guilt feelings, the fear of starving, etcetera, and I really got ill—moped around at half capacity for a couple of weeks before I could shake it." Griffin restores Model A Fords at his home in North Chichester, New Hampshire.

Whether you're going to be working at home or somewhere else, your new schedule and your new financial realities will require new energies of you and of your family. The more you involve your family in every stage of planning and actual work, the more easily will transitions occur. While children should never be rushed into responsibilities they aren't yet ready to accept, a change of environment might provide the ideal time to initiate some new habits.

But it is a mistake to enter any new situation with preconceptions about "how it's going to be," even though we all seem to be habitual victims of this sort of romanticizing. Plan carefully, then stay loose and adaptable! And, if you have children, don't make the mistake of predicting the effects on them of such a change. A move to the country, for instance, is not a universal panacea. Everyone involved should be allowed as much room as possible to experience the growing this is going to require.

What Your Friends Will Think

Even in the best of circumstances, friends are often negative when we show signs of changing our lives. This is probably because friendships tend to be based on the status quo, and when someone's life starts to change, our relationship with that person may be threatened. Likewise, in a family, there may well be people who are not living under the same roof, the proverbial in-laws if you will, who are critical, or fail to understand.

Barbara Foote, originally a city girl, wrote about her experiences on the farm. With their two small children, Barbara and her husband Jim returned to his family farm, in central Kentucky. Jim's family had been on the farm for years, but for Barbara it was a new experience.

"Many of the things we take pride in and want to put into practice here—things like milking and canning—hold no romance for people like the Footes who have been doing them for years. Alternative energy sources fall into this same category. Gerard and Mary have been stoking stoves for 30 winters at Basin Spring. It is not romantic to them at all, and perhaps I would feel the same in their shoes. As a result, we often seem to meet each other on common ground, but going in opposite directions. At these times, the best thing we can do for ourselves and those we love is to go our way quietly, setting our own standards and keeping our objectivity and sense of humor."

Larry and Karen Hines

Larry Hines, of Mountain Home, Idaho, had a civil service job as a meat cutter at an airbase, when three years ago he injured his back in a fall and had to give up his job. Rather than depend entirely on disability pay, the family began what they call "a diversified homesteading project" on the one-and-one-third-acre lot they live on in a mobile home. "Our first venture to earn extra income was simply to grow enough garden to sell a surplus and pay for our seed," wrote Mrs. Hines. "By word of mouth and a sign out front, we sold over $40 worth of produce, strawberries, and goat milk. This encouraged us, and that winter Larry processed game meat at home, and the return here was in the neighborhood of $1,000.

"Suddenly, we realized that we could really make a go of it on our own, and we now have a completely diversified homestead operation. We have orchards, grape arbors, and bees in the planning stages, and in the three short years since we started, we've increased our produce offerings, and have more calls than we can handle for custom garden tilling."

In spite of the fact that their new life suits the Hines family just fine, Mrs. Hines reports that "maybe it's isolated us from our age group—our friends don't always seem to understand.

"We're Latter Day Saints, and even though the Church encourages self-sufficiency, our friends can't seem to comprehend this sort of thing."

The Other Person

"Always be honest. I am always honest with everyone I deal with and I have found that this must be an exceptional trait as so many people I encounter are totally surprised by it." These are the words of an international crafts dealer, Ron Linker, whose Handicrafts International has become completely self-supporting after three years. "As a result, the people I deal with open up to me and in general much more good seems to be accomplished. The only drawback to this is that I expose myself to being ripped-off and

Larry and Karen Hines

taken advantage of, but I'm learning how to handle it, which is better than becoming less than honest with myself and the people I deal with."

In any business transaction you will be most successful if you are able to consider and appreciate the position of the other person. Anna Land, who started Down Home Comforters in West Brattleboro, Vermont, wrote a very helpful note: "For me, the most important thing I can do for myself and my business is be right-minded. I slip lots of times and get into feeling worried and woebegone, then one way or another I wake up and feel happy again. Meher Baba said it: 'Don't worry, be happy,' and he's right.

"If I spend my juices in worry I'll not have them for joy. I expect my business contacts, manufacturers, wholesalers, advertising people, to be human beings, and they are. Sometimes they need to know what I need, then they seem to drop the mask and come through as people."

I had a dozen three-year-old hens I needed to find a good home for because Janet and Ben and I were going on a long trip. I advertised in the local newspaper 'Fabulous Hens', and three people came to look, but wouldn't even take them for a gift. So I took my hens in grain sacks to Harold Allen, in Saint Albans, the man who sold me my first four chickens in 1971. Harold has a reputation for driving a hard bargain, and I remember being told I had paid rather dearly for the two hens and two roosters he sold me in that first tiny flock. So going to him with a dozen worn-out Rhode Island Reds was, I knew, sheer folly.

"I really don't need any," he said—a standard Vermont bargaining stance. I reached into a grain sack and brought out one of the hens, fortunately one of the prettier ones. He looked her over, scratching his jowl and shaking his head. He hadn't asked her age, at least, but the words of my first potential buyer kept ringing through my head: "Too old to lay, too tough to eat."

I don't like to slaughter chickens even if they are tender. The matter is complicated by a 'rather discouraging statistic: The average life span of a chicken left unharmed by predator and ax is 25 years! I had visions of trying to purchase passage for my family "and a few pets" at the airline ticket counter.

It looked as if Mr. Allen was about to say no, so thinking fast, I came up with an offer. "I'll tell you what," I said. "I'll shake the chickens out of these bags so you can see them all in a good light. If you like them a real lot, give me a dollar apiece. If you think they're just average, or below average, they're yours for 50^c a hen." I'm not sure he had ever been offered such a trade before, where he could decide, essentially, what to pay.

So he said yes, and I shook the hens out of the grain bags, he eyed them briefly, and gave me $12!

Maintaining "Contacts"

In legitimate small-business enterprise, maintaining "contacts" means taking a friendly interest in the people you meet during the day, and *taking the initiative* when it comes to reminding them that you have a service or a product that might be of use to them. It also means keeping in regular contact with your lawyer, your accountant, and your friendly banker, on an annual basis, with just a phone call, as a minimum. Someone who helps you write a mortgage, for instance, knows a certain amount about you and is presumably interested in your welfare. So it is just plain good business to stay in touch, on an informal basis, with those people who have served you—as well as those you have served— over the years. Some small-business people use Christmas for this purpose; I think April Fool's Day is a better time, because it is not normally associated with a commercial hustle.

In certain services, this sort of initiative means the difference between success and failure. Sarah Gallagher, of New York, wrote of her quilt restoration service: "Deep River's success really depends on the referrals by museums and retail businesses that carry quilts. Folks in need of our service generally contact one of the two. Thus, I maintain fairly consistent contact with the museum personnel in this city, and with antique and quilt shop owners by dropping them an occasional line or dropping in for a moment or two."

I am reminded of Mr. King, whose toy store maintained careful records on the birthdate of every child that entered his store, or for whom a gift was purchased. Mr. King always sent a birthday card, about 10 days ahead of actual birthdate!

A Family Business

Gordon Eichmann bought his father's printing business in 1948. "The business was organized in 1921, so there was a lot of goodwill behind it. It was the first lettershop in Boise," he told me, explaining that a "lettershop" is really an address-printing service that supplies retailers with mail-order access to specified groups of customers. Gordon and his wife, Verna, are assisted by three of their grown children. "The best advice I can give anyone in my position," Gordon told me, "is never try to tell your children how to do it. They'll always figure a better way. But show them how *not* to do it, so they can profit from your mistakes!"

Probably the greatest difficulty of a family business is the day-to-day and night-after-night proximity to the same people, and Gordon Eichmann's suggestion manifests the sensitivity he has developed after years of working in a business with his family. The people I met who have made a successful go at family businesses are people with this sort of sensitivity. The trust possible in a family enterprise is an aspect that enhances the desirability of working with your kin. Common also to successful family business is the kind of family devotion to being together manifested by the Usreys, whose worm farms are discussed elsewhere in this book. Every Christmas, all three of their family operations (worm ranch, retail outlet, and worm school) close down for two weeks so the whole family can retreat, Geraldine and Lloyd, their children, and the grandchildren to a rented cabin for some time together in a nonbusiness way!

The partners in yet another family business gave me this double-view: "The fights are worse, but the help is cheaper!"

Seasonal Business

A seasonal business sounds ideal because, depending on the length of the season, you are presumably free of work the rest of the year. But seasonal businesses have the disadvantage of being extremely hectic in-season, and they usually require a considerable amount of off-season preparation, maintenance, and cleanup. And what sense is there to maintaining inventory all year that is only used in-season? Further, the profits from these endeavors are rarely sufficient to last a year. "You get what you work for," and if there is a self-employment opportunity that allows the average person more than a few months' vacation a year, I haven't heard of it.

Sugaring is a wonderful spring ritual in many of our northern states whereby buckets are spiked to maple trees by hollow spouts that intercept the sap that rises through the tree when the first warm days come. This sap is boiled over a hot fire until 39 of every 40 parts have gone off into the atmosphere. Do it indoors and your ceilings will rain, your walls will relinquish their paper, and your long-abandoned houseplants will bloom. Many folks have dreamed of supporting a homestead on its sugar crop, then learned why dairy farmers who sugar in-season bother with cows and field crops the rest of the year. Yes, maple syrup typically sells for $10 a gallon at the farm, and yes, that gallon was once 40 gallons of maple sap. The work of cutting wood to feed the fire beneath the evaporating arch, the work of gathering and boiling the sap, and the unpredictability of any given year's sugar crop account for the high price of maple products. Once in awhile, someone who is well-established in a good sugar bush will produce a really profitable sugar crop, but most often maple sugaring is viewed as a good way to be out in the early spring air, enjoying a touch of midas fever as the water-like sap boils down to sweet gold.

Yet maple sugaring, like many other seasonal activities, offers itself to certain "multiple-use" possibilities whereby the tools for this operation might also be used for something quite different in another season. In Vermont, Eric and Francine Chittenden, as well as the people at Appleyard, take apple cider and boil it down into a most delectable, pure apple syrup, using a standard sugaring rig. Like maple syrup, apple syrup is easily packaged without need of any preservative or other ingredient. Someone with a good sugaring rig could thus harvest apples in their season, and run an improved chance of realizing a profit. Double use for expensive sap buckets in Vermont is often accomplished by using them to protect young tomato plants from late spring frosts.

The Day of Small Business

During the 1960s, the impersonality and the efficient coldness of chain businesses began to make themselves felt among millions of employees, and millions of customers who were fast becoming "consumers." The franchise system flourished in these boom years, but the real owner is still a thousand miles away and that fly in your soup was packaged last April.

As resources dwindle and costs climb, substitution and inferior quality diminish our respect for possessions. Things become "disposable," a big selling point in the 1970s. Imitation has become the key means of concealing substitution in the "goods" we take from mass producers. Some of the steel in my car is painted to look like wood, plastic is painted to look like steel, and what I thought was rubber on the bumper scraped off in places as only paint will do.

Traveling certain cross-country routes the tourist never has to ask where the toilet is, as long as he stops only at Brand X Motor Inn and Restaurant. Marketing, like television programing, becomes a cynical measurement of some electrically determined, lowest common denominator, and the consumer loses his sense of uniqueness and any respect at all for the marketplace, while our "needs" are anticipated and met in increasingly repetitive ways.

This terrible situation is reflected by the employees of large chains, people who have been plugged into certain rote positions where ingenuity and human intelligence are valued less than pomade. The result is a consumer rip-off attitude that prevails and is expected by the store's employees, and reflected by their attitudes toward the store itself. "As long as I don't lose my job," a cashier once told me, "I don't care what happens. If I see someone stealing that's not my business. I just want my tape to balance with the amount of cash in the till."

People tired of buying bad stuff from bored cashiers, and people tired of working at unchanging jobs for unseen profiteers, which is a lot of people, are going into business for themselves and doing it right. Compete with plastic and get to know your customers, keep it small so they can get to know you too, and ride the boom-tide return of personal service. If you like your work, your customers will too.

No get-rich-quick schemes have emerged, although I have looked for them. Even worm farming, whose promoters have been known to boast annual profit potentials as high as half-a-million dollars, requires constant, persistent attention and *work*. As Geraldine Usery of B's Worm Farm told me, "You go self-employed and the hours will be a lot longer. So you'd better like what you do!"

2.
FARMSTEAD
INCOME

A Start in Organic Farming

All advice in agriculture points to having the right piece of land, and worrying about other matters somewhat less; without the right climate, without the right type of soil, without a community that is supportive of the sort of farming you plan to pursue, how can you hope to produce, much less market, your crop?

Many people make the big jump from city to country life without really knowing whether the country will begin to meet anything beyond their emotional longing "for peace and quiet." Living in the country means a certain amount of inconvenience. Long waiting periods are often necessary before certain items can be ordered and shipped. Intellectual and social stimulation may be too infrequent for some people who rely heavily on peer contact and the amenities of city living. None of these matters can be taken lightly; if you are gregarious and a committed moviegoer, you should concentrate your search for farmland to areas that are close to a community offering what you need.

Without a doubt, before you buy a piece of land, have soil samples tested, to be sure it will support the sort of crops you have in mind. If possible, spend a night or two on the land, and visit the property in more than one season. You may discover, after buying, that your remote country paradise is smack-dab in the center of a midnight snowmobile club's Wednesday and Saturday route. Better that you buy land prepared for this than to be surprised after the deal is closed.

Visit the land during all seasons at all hours. Prepare a list of those features you want, and those you *do not* want. Make a point of checking your list of do-not-wants with both the realtor and the seller.

Do not settle for the answers of just one person.

WANT	DO NOT WANT
Good soil for mixed veggies	Frequent air traffic
Reliable clean water source	Loud neighbors
Supportive community	Chicken-eating dogs
Good house on land	Zoning that forbids hogs
Nearby lumber mill	High taxes
Good school system	Black flies

Some friends of mine, who started a school in a rented building, learned of a church for sale that was more conveniently located and larger than the space they were already using. They bought the church, in somewhat of a hurry, accepting a deed that strictly limited the land's use to purposes of schooling or religion. They soon learned that state law required an improved septic system, and that the land where the church was located drained so poorly that standing water was a problem in the proposed "playground" area every season except summer, which was when they had considered and completed their purchase.

A private contractor was hired to improve drainage and to install a proper septic system. Work commenced in early fall, just after the dry season had ended. The contractor rented two bulldozers and had to rent a third to release the others when they became mired. Worse, he accepted word-of-mouth permission to traverse an absentee neighbor's land with heavy equipment, ran up a rental bill of $3,500, and billed the school an additional $3,500 for materials and labor. The field still does not drain adequately, the absentee neighbor returned to find ruts in his yard and nearly sued the school, whose directors would have considered selling the building and lot were it not for the land-protection clause that so strictly limits its use, and therefore, its marketability. They have now raised funds to buy an adjoining five acres that are well drained, and will move the building there, where it will be free of restrictive covenants, in case they should ever decide to sell. Of course the landowner with five acres for sale was fully aware of the school's drainage and legal problems and inflated his price to scandalous proportions.

The best way to be sure you are buying what you think you are getting is to list all functions you hope the land will be able to perform for you, and then check them off one by one to see whether they are physically and *legally* possible. It is a good idea to hire a lawyer to run a title search on your property. Be sure he knows your aspirations in regard to the land, and ask him to review local and state zoning with you. If he clears the title and assures you no zoning hassles will develop, ask for his written guarantee and pay his tax-deductible fee happily. Remember that, like a doctor, the better a lawyer knows you and your aims, the better he can serve you. So if you find a lawyer who is helpful and sympathetic, be sure to consult him in all legal matters.

A Partnership?

Many people find the prospect of sharing the responsibilities and costs of a farm venture more acceptable than the idea of going it alone. Certainly, a partnership between two truly compatible families, for instance, might help conquer a lot of the drawbacks involved in country living. To name a few advantages: Cost of land and equipment can be shared; care of animals and crops can be shared—one family can work one month and take the next month off, for instance; and a partnership might help ease the problems of intellectual and social isolation. But before you rush out and agree to front $20,000 with your friend's cousin who wants to start a melon patch, listen to this advice from Howard Prussack, of High Meadows Farm in Westminster, Vermont: "From my experience it seems great at the beginning of a business to have a partner to share the work and hardships. But as time goes on and the business improves, many things surface and you begin to wonder if the partner is doing his share of the work. I believe a partnership can work out for the good, but for me, a partnership is the worst ship that ever sailed."

A partnership is a business contract and, no matter how good your friendship with your proposed partner, each party to the contract should be represented by a lawyer. And a contract should be demanded that covers all contingencies, not only for the operation and obligations of the ongoing partnership, but for the eventuality of its dissolution. If all partners have in clear ink before them the legal knowledge of the consequences for any given action, the friendship might be kept even if the partnership fails.

Herbs, Goats, Honey, Seeds, and Wine

Most successful small, diversified farms have been started one project at a time, beginning with that special crop or product for which the farmer has a special interest. In dairy farming, as in almost no other endeavor, the farmer is required to perform almost every conceivable agricultural operation to produce just one item for market. The dairy farmer must build and maintain fences, buy cattle and machinery, and he must sell the milk. In between these operations, he plants in springtime, cuts and bales hay three or four times throughout the summer, plows fields and spreads manure when he can find the time, harvests in the fall, and milks the cows twice a day, seven days a week.

Many dairy farmers in Vermont swear they'd never want to "get into" dairy farming; but born into it, they don't know another way, and a very grim agricultural battle continues. During a good season, with a maple operation in the winter, the really skillful Vermont dairy farmer with good land can probably net $30,000, with luck. The same farmer, with two bad seasons in a row, can easily lose such profits, and go into the red as well. And if his luck fails, things can get worse than that.

I doubt many of the farmers described in this book will make get-rich claims, but each has a special idea of how and why his speciality has found a ready market and provided the family homestead with partial, if not total, income. Among such specialties, growing herbs seems most attractive. Herbs are traditionally retailed in small quantities for high prices, so a relatively small crop can return substantial profit. As in many other successful self-employment endeavors, part of the trick is growing what the other local growers don't. If you look around and discover no one sells red peppers in your community, ask why. "Just can't grow them around here," may well be the reply. Such common folk wisdom failed to discourage Toni and Chuck Attmore of Turquoise Trail Herb Farm, who were told the climate in their valley in Bernalillo, New Mexico, wouldn't permit the growing of good herbs. Similarly, Christmas tree growers and worm farmers I talked with had ignored local advice, quietly experimented with a few of the "won't work" species, and then gained a rather splendid monopoly by succeeding where others had failed or been afraid to try.

Because goat's milk is low in butterfat, it is reputed to be far healthier for humans than cow's milk, and it is in fact the milk of choice for over 80 percent of the world's people! Colicky babies are known to be "cured" by goat's milk, and some children who cannot tolerate cow's milk, due to allergies, have no problem at all once their diet is switched to dairy goat products.

Goat farming has the advantage over a bovine dairy operation in the conversion rate of feed to milk, which is much higher for goats than it is for dairy cows, while land and barn requirements are much smaller. Further, goat's milk, if you have a market, brings a much higher price than cow's milk. Like all dairy farming, keeping a herd of milk goats requires regular hours, seven days a week, and the ability to perform a variety of seasonal chores.

Chances are that no market problems exist anywhere for good honey. Almost everyone recognizes it as being superior to refined sugar in every way. And, besides, isn't honey a trouble-free crop? Just set out a few hives in the spring and extract the honey come fall! It's a wonder the stuff is so expensive at the store, you think, until you've set out that first trouble-free hive. Although you don't have to milk bees twice every day, nor fence, nor weed them as you might with garden crops, a well-managed apiary requires nearly as much care as most other agricultural projects. Still, you can safely leave bees for a few days, whereas fully domesticated animals require daily care.

Next to herbs, the ideal mail-order agricultural business is seeds; if you have a few acres and a certain amount of success with garden crops, consider allowing some to go to seed and marketing that seed. At Johnny's Selected Seeds, in Albion, Maine, Joan and Rob Lee Johnston experiment with a large variety of garden produce, selling the seed from their best plants, and specializing in varieties with proven records for maturing early in cold northern climates.

Winemaking is an ideal home business if you have fields that will ripen the crops from which you intend to make your wine. Of course, if you already have a crop established, this might be one of those secondary projects, produced from your surplus. Herb wines are said to be good, and honey wine is, like goat's milk, frequently quaffed in the Bible. Grapes make good wine, for sure, but grape wine is only one of many kinds, and perhaps a fledgling vintner should concentrate on developing a wine where the competition is less established. Apple wine is a favorite among less-competitive wine varieties. In any event, experienced winemakers recommend that anyone considering a home wine-business first experiment with small batches of wine (15 gallons or less) to find out if the extraordinary demands of this precise science are suited to his temperament.

Vegetables

Howard Prussack

Howard Prussack grew up in Brooklyn. "In high school I began to wonder more about where our food comes from and what happens to it before it gets to our table. I began to read books about food and health and started eating what was considered 'health foods' and sort of romanticized about working on an organic farm. In the meantime I graduated from high school and went to a very intense commercial art school, The School of Visual Arts, in New York City. It was there that I saw that the end result of living in New York would make me go crazy. Money was king there and we were its servants, in varying degrees.

"So at the end of my first year of college I thought I'd go to the country, wherever it was." Prussack lived briefly in New Hampshire, "The state that every four years the politicians remember . . . in a funky old farmhouse where I learned a little of living simply and slowly, something a New York person doesn't know. I also learned of an organic farm starting in Vermont." A friend drove him to Vermont "with all my belongings, and I've stayed here ever since. That was five years ago. Since that time the people who started the farm left, and I took over the running of it. For the first two years I had a partner but now I'm on my own. I learn by doing mostly, and a lot from older farmers in the area.

"The farm now totally supports me. That includes my maple syrup operation, which provides about a third of my income. I

Howard Prussack   *Photo by Bob Griffith*

hope to make $12,000 this year." His major crops are standard vegetables and fruits, as well as Jerusalem artichokes.

"For the person starting out I would suggest that they work on a commercial farm for a few years and then decide. Try to do as much of your own work as you can. If you become self-reliant, you can cut costs tremendously. For instance, I built a walk-in cellar for under $400 that would have cost $2,500.

"It sounds close to impossible to start a farm these days, but it doesn't have to be. If you start out renting a few acres and using simple tools and renting your expensive equipment when you need it, you can earn while you learn. Keeping a good credit rating is also very important. Start with a small loan that you can handle and try to pay it back before it's due. Good credit is as much of a tool to the farmer as anything else and you should not be afraid to use it.

"Also, although the states seem to be paying lip-service to helping the small farmer and business, nothing is really being done yet, so don't wait around trying to get grants or low-cost government loans. Because if they do become available they will more likely go to those who already have something started and stable. So use your own juice and Do It!"

"The expenses in starting a farm today run from the ridiculous to the absurd," Prussack told me. "I do not own this farm yet, so I'm renting the land and the equipment: $25 an acre, and $300 plus all maintenance and replacement for the equipment. But the same equipment would cost at least $10,000 to buy new, and maybe more like $20,000. These are just the minimum equipment requirements for a 30-acre produce farm: medium-sized tractor, $5,000 to $7,000; rototiller, $2,000; cultivators, $600 to $1,200; seeders, $300 to $1,200." Prussack also listed a truck, manure spreaders, and spraying equipment. "And I've just spent $500 on seeds and onion sets and hot caps, and I'll probably spend another $700 on miscellaneous items before planting is over. I think it's best to put your money into the land, and slowly build up the equipment as your skill and knowledge increase, renting what you can't afford to buy."

Marketing fresh produce is accomplished in many ways, from selling to a trucker who collects produce from many farms and dispenses it to a distributor to throwing up a sign by the road "Pick your own fresh produce! Put money in the box!" The latter method, the "honor system," is fine for hobbyists with a surplus of produce, but somewhat impractical for the gardener who wants to make a living from his food.

"I sell as much as I can direct to the customer," Prussack told me. "My best days are when we go to the flea market. I've made as much as $350 in one day, though $150 to $200 is more the average. The rest of the week I wholesale my produce to local stores and co-ops.

"Some places I don't tell them it's organic until many weeks have passed and they see that it sells." The main point here is that the regular buying public has been too browbeaten by Madison Avenue claims. The word "organic," which in a better world would be superfluous, rightly represents a personal standard, but the use of the word in advertising can, and has been, corrupted. So grow it organically, and don't be afraid to admit that you do, but think carefully before you advertise your methods.

Any self-employed person will tell you that to be your own boss requires more of your time than working for someone else. In farming this is more true than in most activities. And during certain seasons, most farmers work 16 hours a day or more, seven days a week. The bigger the piece of land you're working, the more of your time that will be required during the crucial periods of tilling and seeding, harvesting, and selling. One good way to take the pressure off is to find people who can work for you on a seasonal basis. Eliot Coleman, in Maine, provides camping space and all the garden produce they can eat to a stream of people who give his three-and-one-half-acre intensive garden four hours a day throughout the summer. Howard Prussack, with 10 acres presently under cultivation, hopes to have several apprentices each season. "But labor will always be a problem," he admitted. "In the springtime 16 hours a day are not uncommon. I can't ask helpers to work that long because I know it's hard doing it for someone else."

Above all, Prussack maintained that the successful farmer has to enjoy his work, to love the process. "There's a lot of love involved in farming, because if you don't love the work, it becomes simply work," he said.

The Colemans' Organic Vegetable Farm

About seven miles off a paved road that leads from Deer Isle up to Penobscot, Maine, is a small community of families that live along the rocky coast at Harborside. I couldn't believe we were on the right road, as Janet, Ben, and I bumped along through potholes and dust; suddenly we came upon a beautiful five-foot-by-three-foot, hand-painted-and-varnished sign that seemed enormously out of place on such a remote road: "Sue & Eliot Coleman—Organic Vegetables." Backing up, because we had overshot the drive, I saw the sign was painted just as carefully on both sides. "Apparently they get business from both directions," I joked, looking on down the long dirt road.

We drove through a heavy grove of conifers to a parking area where three out-of-state and two Maine-licensed vehicles were parked. Three of the cars belonged to customers, we discovered, and two of the out-of-state cars were owned by people who were camping on the Colemans' land and helping with garden work at least four hours a day in return for camping space and a vegetarian's run of the gardens and orchards. The land was, until 1968, entirely wooded. We learned that as many as 14 helpers had been there at one time during the summer. But now, in mid-Sep-

Eliot Coleman

tember, the Colemans were down to a skeleton crew, with Michele, Frank, and David—all survivors of the entire summer—their only outside help. Eating lunch with them later, I could feel the ease of their relationship, and I felt among them a kinship that comes among people who work together through the many evolutions of the comings and goings of others.

As we walked from the parking area along a fabulous hedgerow of rose hips, I noticed the vegetable stand with only a few bunches of carrots and some tomatoes on a table with a weighing scale, cash register, receipt pad with carbon paper, and a blackboard with prices chalked up—comparable to those of regular grocery markets.

Coleman explained that the vegetable stand was so lightly stocked because he likes to let customers pick their own, fresh from the garden. "You know," he laughed, "we even get visitors who've never seen the actual plants that produce their favorite foods!" I admitted I was amazed they receive visitors at all, located seven miles off a remote highway.

"People are attracted here by the same things that lure folks to the supermarkets," Coleman explained. "The customer wants cleanliness and pleasant surroundings. In our case that means don't pile the manure next to the sales stand. And, we have that beautiful, colorful sign, which helps immeasurably. And . . . we have every vegetable available throughout its growing season which means, for instance, our customers know they can get fresh peas here in August and September as well as in July. We plant everything in succession, so we generally have a wider variety of fresh produce than the big stores. Word gets around if you provide good produce full season."

The Colemans live in a two-room cabin they built on wooden piers, using lumber cleared from the 40 acres they bought from Helen and Scott Nearing, their nearest neighbors, at the same price the Nearings paid 20 years ago. Like the Nearings, Eliot and Sue are willing to share a part of their life and its philosophy with people who volunteer to participate in the physical labors involved. Both the Nearings and the Colemans serve a good homesteader's vegetarian soup with crisp, raw vegetables at lunch to those who've helped with the morning chores. This sacrifice of privacy in the summer to accomplishment is probably compensated by what must be a long and lonely winter way out there seven miles from pavement without electricity.

"We're not interested in a wind generator," Coleman said. "After you've mined all that copper and smelted all the steel for a tower, you've used more of the earth's resources than you can ever repay through the savings of the wind system. I think such systems are really an artificial clinging to the wasteful luxuries we're trying to avoid."

Do they ever get the winter blues, I wondered, when outdoors the February winds are thick and there are only two indoor rooms for the two adults and their two young daughters? "No, we don't get them," said Eliot. "People ask about privacy, too, and I simply tell them we just all like to snuggle a lot. And if I'm reading and a lamp runs out of kerosene, I take that as a signal not to refill the lamp, but to go to bed."

Although their highly regimented and totally organic approach to gardening is similar to that of the Nearings, the Colemans do employ some methods that are not practiced on the Nearing homestead. For instance, the Colemans keep nine dairy goats, and use manure for fertilizer. Scott Nearing is heartily opposed to any use of animals or animal products. "It becomes a slave–master–slave relationship," Nearing told me. "The animal becomes your slave and you are responsible for its life and death." I asked if he and Helen had any other differences with the Colemans. "Not differences," he smiled, "but on occasion we do have disagreements."

Common to both homesteads is a reliance on the sea to provide what Scott Nearing calls "good healthy mulch for our provender." In practical terms this means that gangs of helpers from Colemans' or Nearings' are frequently seen after storms, down on the beach, raking up truckload after truckload of seaweed, which is a favorite mulch—especially in the potato garden. "In 25 years of using seaweed on my potatoes," Nearing told me, "I haven't seen one potato bug." He let out a long sigh. "But unfortunately, the mice like it under all that hay and seaweed"—in which he literally sandwiches the potato eyes, each with a handful of compost—"they find it quite a nice place to live. And take their breakfast, lunch, and supper there. Maybe even tea and a snack as well. They don't say."

Coleman argues vehemently against agricultural scientists who continue to ignore vital research areas, specifically whether healthy plants resist insects and disease. "I have hundreds of references and notebooks filled to overflowing with photocopies of pertinent literature," he says. "I think this is the most important concept in agriculture if properly understood."

Insects and disease are not the grower's problem, but rather are the symptoms. For Coleman, to use palliatives—whether chemical or organic—is to hide from reality. Three years ago, Coleman wrote an article, which includes this paragraph:

"Once you become determined to eliminate the cause of insects and disease rather than just mask the symptoms, a whole new world opens up. A plant bothered by pest or disease need no longer be a cause for dismay. The plant can now be looked upon as your co-worker. It is communicating with you. It is saying that conditions are not conducive to its optimum growth and that if the plants are to be healthier next year, the soil must be improved."

Eliot, who grew up in New Jersey, and Sue, who comes from Boston, knew very little about country living when they bought their land in 1968, and they like to reminisce about their early experiences. Some of their successes, including growing their biggest crops in first-year gardens, have been as surprising as some of the mistakes. "I remember our first year, when I took our old Jeep down to get Scott a load of seaweed as a surprise for his birthday, and I got the Jeep stuck. So I went to Helen asking to borrow the truck to tug the Jeep out. I didn't want Scott to know or it would have spoiled the surprise. Then I got her truck stuck too and we had to go and get help to free it. While I was returning the truck, the tide came in and drowned our Jeep."

Surely one of the reasons for the Colemans' success in their quest for independence has been their thoroughness in doing every job right the first time, and keeping their efforts limited to their real capabilities. In starting with a plot of wooded land, the kind of land which—if ever cleared—is usually farmed for nothing more than blueberries, the Colemans wisely limited the size of their garden to only a quarter-acre. The garden, and the income it fetches, has grown with every season. Their first summer of selling vegetables, the Colemans earned only $350, living on savings from Eliot's years of teaching. Their economic yield, after seven years, was $4,200 from three-and-one-half acres, which for them is just fine. Outside expenses are limited to gasoline, grains, sweeteners, and, right now, a new root cellar, contracted to a concrete firm— the only contracted project on their homestead.

The Colemans have been very lucky, acquiring land at a favorable price from people who wanted them for neighbors. Sharing a gardening and living philosophy with the Nearings, the Colemans could borrow ropes and ladders and other homesteading tools.

But this sort of luck is worthless without energy, careful planning, and a determination that Eliot and Sue quite obviously possess in abundance. Eliot is absolutely unyielding on the matter of planning and work. "Hell, luck is nothing more than the ability to make good use of whatever advantages are available," he said. "'Luck' is available everywhere. It just takes some hustle to find it." The Colemans *want* to be where they are. Doing without electricity seems to be a challenge rather than an inconvenience. And, as cheap as the land may have been, it was completely wooded. They faced a tremendous amount of work—clearing and stumping, spading and mulching and enriching—what is now three-and-a-half acres of productive garden with small house, enclosed vegetable stand, tool sheds, and barn for the goats.

When the success of the Colemans' farm was attributed to free labor, Eliot wrote: "Nothing annoys me more, when I lecture, than the 'professor of economics' type from the university who suggests haughtily that our farm could not survive without the free labor of our live-in students. I usually devastate the professor by replying that I suspect my profession would survive without students far better than his. But that is actually beside the point. What he is trying to discredit is small farming, and what I object to is using our example to prove his point. We are not typical. And the students are not responsible for the creation of this place. We are. We have worked here eight years and have run the apprentice program for only four of those. And very often now it ends up that I spend more time teaching them the job than it would have taken me to do it. Now the above is not to say that we don't end up by benefiting from the apprentice program. We do. Sometimes one of these kids is a whiz and more than makes up for all the bum ones."

Eliot Coleman is quick to discourage potential "off the land" gardeners. "Don't tell anyone I said this is the way to live," he cautioned as we were leaving. "It's wonderful for *us*, but I believe less than one person in ten is meant to live like this. And all it would take would be one person in a family who didn't like it. I'm afraid most people who have learned to live with comforts they take for granted really wouldn't be able to reduce their expenditures enough."

By trimming their outside expenses to a minimum, the Colemans have made sacrifices many people cannot face. Heating with wood, they have no fuel bill, except for kerosene lighting and gasoline to power their only power tools: a '48 Jeep (once drowned) with trailer, a nine-year-old Troy-Bilt rototiller, and a chain saw. They have no insurance of any sort. When Eliot was refused a reduction in the premium for their old Jeep ("I told the lady it won't go faster than 40 mph, and we never drive it more than 5,000 miles a year") he canceled the policy. "What I tell people," Eliot wrote after my visit, "is that they should go to the insurance company and plan all the policies they want, find out how much it will cost and then put that amount in the bank every month, quarter, year, whatever. I tell them the odds are heavily in their favor and that is correct." But he added, "Just because I carry no insurance, I don't tell people to do the same if they are not comfortable with it. I carry no insurance because I can't afford it."

Leaving the Colemans' homestead, pulling out onto that dirt road past the colorful sign, we suddenly glimpsed the sea, then dipped down the hill, past the Nearings', before looking out onto an even greater expanse of ocean. It was a gray morning in mid-September and I was ready to drive home. It would be a long day at the wheel, and I felt envious of the people at Harborside, with their easy access to the saltwater and its fantastic mulch. Then I realized we have the same resource at home—brought by seasons rather than storm cycle, in the goldening maple leaves less than a hundred feet from the garden.

In the rearview mirror I caught a glimpse of the Jeep, rounding a bend, with the trailer behind it: Someone out for seaweed. Wanting to see who was in the Jeep, I let up on the accelerator, but couldn't go slow enough to let them pass before they turned off, toward the beach, to get another load of their garden's favorite weed.

Herbs

Herbs 'n' Honey Nursery

Nancy Fisher and her family, at Herbs 'n' Honey Nursery in Monmouth, Oregon, have two acres of their homestead committed to growing herbs for sale. Interplanted among the herbs, which keep them completely pest-free, are the family's vegetables: not just a summer's supply, mind you, but the whole year's supply. Nancy is a firm believer in the healing power of herbs, and while she credits "all herb books" with helping her, she points to her childhood, and her mother, who taught her to grow and use herbs for health and good taste.

Nancy is clearly an unusual person, dedicated to work and discovering the wonders of God's kingdom as few people are. She follows a strict schedule, seven days a week, that involves rising at 4 A.M., and working two hours at filling orders and correspondence. From 6 to 8 she prepares breakfast and attends to cleaning and barn chores. From 8 to 3, Nancy works in the herb nursery and in the greenhouse; Mondays through Fridays, customers are greeted from 1 to 4 P.M. After 4, Nancy prepares the family dinner and lays the fireside. From 6 to 11 nightly "365 days a year," she sits by the fire "or at the kitchen table," dividing parent-stock herbs.

Nancy calculates that she puts in 14 hours a day, 365 days a year, "which means I don't even net 50¢ an hour in *monetary* gains. *But*, in spiritual gain and joy and inner peace I cannot put a price on the joys I have received. I have seen children made well with God-given herbs, sick people with sores become free of them, people from all walks of life have their path made a little smoother by a kind word or deed."

Nancy started her herb business when she noticed, shortly after moving to Monmouth, that few of her neighbors cultivated herbs. She started with 56 herbs, purchased from mail-order catalogues. She reports that she and Chester, her husband, only plant one acre, while the other lies fallow under half-a-foot of chicken, sheep, and cow manure, and spoiled hay. "We keep our outside purchases to a minimum," says Nancy. Ninety percent of the family budget goes to paying the mortgage on their 98 acres.

Herbs 'n' Honey, as its name suggests, also offers honey; it is sold by mail, at $3 per quart, f.o.b. Nancy was nearly driven from mail order when *Organic Gardening and Farming* ran an article on the tiny herb business in the March 1975 issue, offering a copy of their catalogue for 25¢.

In July, Nancy wrote the magazine to advise the editors that in the four months since the article's publication, the Fishers had received, and answered "each and every one of just over 11,000 letters." At this point, she resolved to simplify the mail-order procedure.

The Fishers' experience, where a special offer or unexpected break into public prominence stirs more response than the business can handle, is not uncommon. A well-placed ad might have netted the Fishers as much business as the *Organic Gardening and Farming* article. The point is, they were not prepared for the response the article generated, and they found themselves faced by the prospect of their business growing larger than their simple wishes. "We are unable to maintain our chosen life-style with the volume of mail-order business generated by the article," Nancy wrote in her July letter.

"In years past, we sent our customers a brochure-offering, which netted us thousands of handwritten letter orders which are nearly impossible to sort; and try finding the intended order in the

Nancy Fisher

midst of a letter! So this fall we designed an order form which is also our brochure; the customer simply checks off the herbs he wants. As far as the order itself goes, the only handwriting we have to read is the customer's name and address. Letters are written on separate paper, and we can answer them at leisure."

To handle the matter of questions through the mail, the Fishers printed up a sheet, which they enclose with their ordering list, which answers the most commonly asked questions. In addition, they have prepared a 102-page herbal book which they sell, postpaid, for $4.95.

Among questions answered on the free sheet, is how Nancy controls ants around her honey: "Common sea salt is sprinkled at the door jambs to ensure little ants will not cross into the room, no other ant retardant need be used to keep a honey room insect-free."

Terms on the accompanying order form are explicitly stated: "Minimum retail: 9 plants, mix or match, $11.25 f.o.b. our farm. Minimum wholesale: 36 plants, mix or match, $27 f.o.b. our farm." Beneath, in alphabetical order, the plants are listed, followed by blank spaces that form a column, with these instructions: "Please write in the space provided to the right of each herb plant, number desired. Please be certain your order totals multiples of 9 or 36."

In the past, Herbs 'n' Honey would ship all orders Air Mail Priority, having the customer pay an estimated charge in advance. But Nancy discovered this is a bad way to charge for shipping; too much paperwork is involved, and customers who live near pay way too much, while those far away do not advance enough postage. "Many, many, many organic farmers and nurseries and organic food supply houses have been forced out of business," she wrote me, "because of the impossible mountain of paperwork created by shipping with estimated shipping charges. *Please* tell your readers to state clearly the price of their products, and then state, 'f.o.b., our place of business'. They can pick up an f.o.b. shipping book free of charge at their local post office, which enables each farmer or nursery to list the daily shipouts and the post office writes in the amount of postage due. The shipper then pays the postage in advance and within the week (after arrival of the parcels to their destination) the shipper then receives the postage back. Since we have gone to f.o.b., we are many, many weeks ahead of shipping!"

Abracadabra

A small herb business could be set up for $15 or less. Abracadabra, (10102 Herb Road, Windsor, California 95492) a company that sells herb seed by mail, offers a minimum wholesale offer of 50 seed packets for 30¢ a packet. Suggested retail for these packets is 50¢ apiece, so it would be possible to start plants from seed, and have the seed "pay for itself" as you learn the business, and gradually expand. In her book, *26 Easy-to-Grow Herbs and How to Use Them*, Mrs. Philip Foster recommends that beginners avoid the challenge of starting perennials from seed. She recommends, further, that plants be ordered from the *nearest* nursery, saying, "Plants which must be shipped from a distant nursery, usually arriving in poor condition, are a wasteful, costly, and often disappointing beginning." Mrs. Foster recommends five herbs, in particular, for appearance, borage, burnet, lemon balm, chives, and lovage; and she recommends five favorites for flavor: basil, parsley, sage, thyme, and sweet marjoram.

Oak Valley Herb Farm

I visited Oak Valley Herb Farm, in Camptonville, California, where a dedicated group of young people have set up a marginal business that involves buying herbs to supplement those they forage and grow, and mixing them into delightful blends for teas and smoking mixtures. Selling on a wholesale basis, they mix and label pound and half-pound bags, which are broken down and repackaged by dealers and co-ops. The Oak Valley people recommend that when a product is packaged, the colors on the label should be compatible with the intended use, or effect, of the herb. Marketing for their products has been hampered by a local health department ruling that their labels and promotional literature may not suggest their products' specific medicinal values. So, while their tea mixture of peppermint, chamomile, mullein, skullcap, passion flower, catnip, wood betony, hops, valerian, and lobelia (which they market under the name "Naturally Numb") may well have sedative properties and provide effective relief seven times faster than the leading analgesic, they can't even point out that it is "reputed to relax and ease pain of headache."

Steven and Colleen Jeffré, Turiya Schoolnik

A great deal of controversy among herb growers rages between those who believe herbs are culinary additives that can be dangerous when applied to medicinal uses, and those who believe that certain herbs, taken in the proper combination, are safer and more effective than the drugs currently approved by medical authorities. A good compromise would require all manufacturers of drugs, and producers of herbs, to label their packages "believed to aid in the relief of . . ."

In the meantime, while they are refused freedom to advertise their product's supposed medicinal values, herb growers are free to follow federally established, tobacco-industry precedents. Plainly stated on the package, the following message would surely satisfy all parties concerned:

> WARNING: Health officials have determined
> NATURALLY NUMB is not an
> approved remedy FOR HEADACHE!

Perhaps, the last two words could be printed in capital letters, with red ink!

The Herb Chalet

Dorothea Noback, 55 years old and a veteran of "about 35 years" of experience with herbs, started her small organic herb business in Hartland, Wisconsin, only a year ago. "I knew I was an expert in the field," she wrote me, "and there were no experts in the selling end of herbs, only charlatans. And it was, until I entered the field, impossible to get everything one wanted at one place of business, so I decided to provide that service.

"And as soon as I went into business I discovered how much I didn't know." But with the help of a daughter who is majoring in retailing and merchandising at the University of Wisconsin, a son who is her lawyer, and a husband who taught her basic accounting, Thea Noback established a home business that, she said, "with proper administration could totally support my husband and me after retirement."

Mrs. Noback estimates the total cost of setting up and operating her one-year-old home business at $6,000.

Licenses and sales tax permit	$ 12
Inventory, plants, stock	4,000
Furniture, display cabinet	500
Transportation, freight, postage	750
Labels, pots, soil, flats, stationery	200
Advertising	150
Printing and photocopy costs	530
	$6,142

The only renewable expense is printing costs for the mail-order price lists, and Mrs. Noback said she learned to cut printing costs drastically by preparing her own advertisements and price lists, which she duplicates by photocopy or offset printing.

"Some businesses need high foot or auto traffic to succeed," wrote Mrs. Noback. "Mine does not, people seek me. In locating a business, determine the best location for selling your product. For me it works that our home can be my place of business, which not only reduces the threat of robbery and vandalism but permits one to take advantage of IRS tax savings when one allocates expenses to home and to business." Locating the business at home, she believes, "is the only way small businesses can survive."

Even though The Herb Chalet has been in operation just a year, Mrs. Noback is concerned with the number of hours the business requires: Depending on the season, she works "One-hundred-and-five hours a week at the most, and 50 to 55 at the least. My husband averages about 20 hours a week. Our main problem is help: I cannot afford to hire someone and pay Social Security and unemployment insurance, and without help I cannot expand as necessary." Like many small businesses, Mrs. Noback's is one that seems to be hindered by a combination of government agencies. For her, in particular, Social Security and unemployment are known cost-blocks to expansion. A further problem, for her, is that her community has developed since she moved to Hartland, and new zoning regulations threaten her business.

Dorothea Noback

At present, one possibility the Nobacks are considering is to open another herb business. "Prospects this year were so good my daughter, who will graduate in June, plans to join me and open an herb business closer to Chicago, where the market is greater. We may run two businesses concurrently for awhile but ultimately there will be only one business with two people actively engaged," she said.

"If we can encourage two other daughters to donate time, why the business should really grow. We'll look for a building in which she can live and sell. It's the only way an herb business can make it. We'll have gardens there where I can do on-the-spot lecturing as I do here at my home; we'll also expand into selling bulk spices and herbs—fresh and dried. We also expect to go into wholesaling, especially the unique and lovely herb teas and potpourris. My one year has taught me not to be afraid of business, but also not to overextend our ability or potential."

As with The Herb Chalet, where Thea Noback lectures and leads tours of her gardens, the folks at Oak Valley Herb Farm schedule weekly Saturday herb walks, in season, and almost every other herb business that features retail sales, whether at the farm or mail order, takes pride in opening its gates to visitors. Needless to say, if the hours of such visits are not limited, you can be drowned in a trickle of people; far better to establish specific hours, so that your home and gardens are not continually disrupted by onlookers. Scheduling a regular "herb walk" is a good way to attract customers at a time that is convenient to you.

From there it's really up to the grower—herbs will sell themselves if they are displayed attractively. This can be done cheaply and easily in small plastic bags, stapled to a display rack, or more elaborately, herbs can be marketed in hand-thrown urns, as special gifts.

By the way, most herbs will grow in just about any sunny, well-drained garden location. And don't take up much space. And scare away most insect pests, so as Nancy Fisher does, you might plant your vegetables among them.

Turquoise Trail Herb Farm

Toni and Chuck Attmore have a 10-acre strip of old land-grant property and a 270-year-old adobe house a mile above sea level in

Toni and Chuck Attmore

the desert outside Bernalillo, New Mexico. Chuck, who is 52, met Toni, 48, when they were both studying geology at the University of New Mexico. Chuck served with the paratroopers during the Korean War, and now receives a military pension, retirement pay after 26 years of active duty. "I don't know whether anybody could just start up a business like this without any other income," he told me when I visited their farm. "Maybe with national advertising, well-placed, and a good mail-order response you could. The best aspect of the business is that you don't need a lot of dirt. Some herb plants offer 10 or 15 harvests per season. Basil, for instance, the more you cut, the more it grows!"

Toni Attmore is quick and to the point. I asked her to recommend herb books and after listing a few she said: "Most of the good herb books are written for the East Coast, you know. And many of them overstress the medicinal qualities of the herbs, some of which can have toxic effects." The East Coast climate, explained Toni, is not as severe as that which Turquoise Trail faces: "One hundred degrees for two weeks straight, with constant winds and no rain in summer, and it goes below zero in the winters."

To succeed in their business, the Attmores have been imaginative, observing, and hard working. Their time is pretty much committed to the work. Toni told me how they started growing herbs. "We asked neighbors who said, 'Oh, no herbs can grow here,' and we wondered why. The climate seemed right, except herbs need shade from such constant sun, and watering. The herb books, written for the East, were all saying 'full sunlight and little water'. Even under a tree here you get as much light as on the East Coast."

According to Toni Attmore, so much misinformation about herbs exists, some of it dangerous, that a book is needed to set the record straight. Which, by the way, she is writing. "One herb that is reputed to be an aphrodisiac was called 'lad's love', or 'maiden's rue'. The name has since been changed to 'old man'!"

Among dangerous herbs, sometimes used in teas and medicinal potions, Toni lists rue, pennyroyal, and tansy. "Contrary to the books, tansy does not repel grasshoppers from the garden, but attracts them like crazy. And nasturtiums, we've found, pull in black aphids.

"Since we've planted the tansy," Chuck told me, "we haven't seen any lions and tigers out there, so at least it's good for something. Tansy will repel flies and ants, but it is toxic to livestock and humans. It should be labeled 'For External Use Only!'"

Turquoise Trail Herb Farm has been in operation only four years, although the Attmores have owned the house and land for nearly fifteen. Toward the end of his military years, Chuck began fixing the place up on weekends, and looking toward some retirement scheme. "When Chuck was stationed in Germany, neighbors would knock on our door to ask what smelled so good, and I began giving cooking classes. We've always grown at least 50 varieties for our own use, and when we first moved here, we simply couldn't locate a dependable source of the herbs that people were saying couldn't be grown locally."

And so, when they "went commercial" four years ago, Toni and Chuck had experimented with more than 300 herb varieties, and were successfully growing more than 100. By now, they offer 200. They also sell plants, which, Chuck told me, are "the real money-makers," and two of Chuck's specialities, garlic and Indian corn, "our other two cash crops."

"What we're trying to do here is start a service for the shops that are just screaming for Indian corn. There's lots of land here going to waste, but no one seems to want to go to the effort to grow it. The old-timers ask me, 'How much are you asking for a ton of your corn?' and they can't believe it when I say: 'Thirty-five cents an ear!'

"If you want to make some money in produce gardening, look around the community. Everyone's growing cukes and tomatoes, but what about garlic, what about shallots? Around here, garlic grows wild. It's considered a weed. My neighbor, next door, buys garlic from me, saying, 'Your garlic is terrific!' And he's got half-an-acre of it growing wild!"

The Attmores are sad about the implications of why their produce is so heavily in demand. Toni has noticed that people seem reluctant or unable to work for themselves. "Food stamps and welfare seem to have killed people's self-respect and initiative, which may explain why so few people here are growing their own. The young people want to 'get back to the land', but when they see there's work attached to it they go back to the city!"

"We lent some land to a group of young people," Chuck said sadly. "I plowed it and they came out and planted it, and then the weeds began to grow up all around, and when they finally came by again, about two months later, to harvest, they wandered around in their patch for about half-an-hour looking for their vegetables. And do you know, it's almost funny, but they were ticked off, as if somehow they'd been cheated!"

The Attmores have had ample opportunity to expand their operation through big orders with large distributing concerns, but they believe hand-processing to be the only way herbs should be treated. "Some of these businesses want to buy herbs by the bale," Toni explained. "And you know, herbs have got to be very carefully tended or they lose their vitality. We are as much in the business of teaching people how to grow, harvest, wash, and dry their own herbs, as we are in herbs. 'Herbs should never dry in the sun,' 'herbs should never hang in bunches' are two, important lessons most people have not learned. The sun bleaches the herbs, and herbs in bunches cure unevenly with the center of the bunch spoiling.

"It's the oil gland in the herbs that gives them their essence. Herbs should be green dried or else they're no good. And they shouldn't be crushed or broken, but kept as whole as possible. So, you see, the branches have to be stripped by hand, or else the leaves get broken to bits," she said. "And herbs should never be crushed with mortar and pestle; just break them between your palms right before use. The warmth of your hands will bring out the oils.

"Everything's gotten so big, but the nature of our product demands that we stay small. And we've found peace of mind—and that is one of the greatest assets of our work—knowing our product is the best we can offer."

Toni and Chuck admit that one other factor helps them retain their resolve to be small. "It's unreal," Toni said. "The governmental bookkeeping you have to go through just to hire someone part-time. I can see why farmers go into this big combine thing because it's big business—we don't have time to do that sort of bookkeeping."

Just as they believe that small is the only feasible size for an herb business, the Attmores have found that doing their own marketing allows complete supervision of their product's storage and its selling price, as well as direct contact with their customers. Like Herbs 'n' Honey, Turquoise Trail was jolted by unexpected demand when *Organic Gardening and Farming* mentioned that the tiny operation offered a small booklet and catalogue by mail. This kind of public exposure, and the results, pretty much prove what Nancy Fisher and the Attmores claim: The market for good herbs and solid information is more than adequate. The Attmores rushed to press with a new catalogue and, like Nancy Fisher, sought to answer many of the most commonly asked questions with a mimeographed information sheet.

The Attmores' mail-order business has expanded to the point that printing is a major cost. The neatly mimeographed catalogue features five pages of herbs, with brief descriptions and price: "Unless otherwise noted, each plastic bag contains eight grams and an insertion sheet giving some background and suggested uses for the enclosed herb. An alternate of packaging is in hand-thrown stoneware jars, nontoxic glazed, corked and also containing an insertion sheet." The hand-thrown jars cost more than the herbs, but provide an inventive marketing idea for someone who wishes to use herbs as a gift item. In addition to the mimeographed catalogue is a printed mail-order form, which folds into its own self-addressed envelope. Additionally, Toni has written seven information sheets, which sell for a dollar each.

Mail order is a big portion of their business, but the Attmores enjoy weekend flea markets where they set up regularly, for good profits and repeated contact with a growing number of customers, who seek them out not only for herbs but for herbal advice. "We keep the price as reasonable as possible," Chuck said, "just selling packets of herbs for 25 to 50 cents, and those quarters and halves just seem to add up." During a recent six-month period, with just weekend sales, those flea market quarters and halves added up to $4,600!

"The flea market is a fantastic thing," said Chuck. "It has everything and your only commission is payment for space. Here, it's located at the parking lot of the state fairgrounds. The state takes half of the $3 fee, and the organizer takes the other half. About 500 tables typically set up, and while the head flea says he doesn't know how many customers he gets, we've estimated it at 9,000 to 20,000 people a day."

"So you can imagine what a good market that is," said Toni. "We've talked to professional fleas and they feel it's a bad day if they don't make $400! Of course, the local merchants are getting a little upset, and recently the IRS has been out checking on licenses."

"We got descended on by the guys in the horn-rimmed glasses, but we keep books and have the nursery licenses," laughed Chuck.

"In Europe," said Toni, "there's plenty of flea markets. In the United States, the farmer's markets take 15 to 20 percent of your sales, even though you're doing all the selling. We consider the flea market to be the last place where an American grower can get to know his market and show a profit."

I asked Toni if all growers at the flea markets do as well as they do. "They could," she answered, "but you need a personality to sell, you can't be a clam. If someone shows a little interest in your display, show some interest in him; a conversation will raise the curiosity of passersby. Then if you keep the price down, your herbs will sell."

Surely another component of successful marketing is enthusiasm, which Toni and Chuck possess in abundance. Toni is an active proselytizer for the proper care and use of herbs, and she has appeared on TV and radio talk shows, and frequently speaks at local garden clubs. "This is really all the promotional effort we need to make," she said. The Attmores are typical of self-employed people who believe in their product: "There could and should be at least one fully stocked herb farm for every metropolitan area," they told me. And, like most other small-timers, they are more than happy to share their knowledge.

To save money, they keep their imaginations and eyes open for bargains. Among major expenditures have been the purchasing of army-surplus camouflage netting, to shade their herbs, and the acquisition of three railroad refrigerator cars, which are heavily insulated, equipped with ventilation controls, and make ideal storage and drying "houses." Chuck and Toni plant through black plastic, which eliminates a lot of weeding, raises soil temperature five Fahrenheit degrees, and catches pools of water which attract the birds who eat the bugs that aren't naturally repelled by the herbs.

This imaginative perspective carries over into every aspect of their farm, where very little of anything has a chance to go to waste: Even last season's leftover Jerusalem artichokes, starting to sprout, are packaged and sold at the flea market as sets. Chuck keeps his ears open to hear what's in short supply at the local markets. This year, he has planted not only 11 miles of garlic, but ordered 1,000 horseradish roots "because, for some reason, there's a shortage of horseradish around here."

"Of course, as in any agricultural endeavor, there's a lot of unromantic work involved." Chuck calls stripping herb leaves off their stems "idiot's delight. I'll be drinking an organic beer, watching television, and stripping plants or breaking up garlic cloves. Just because it gets dark outside, the farming doesn't stop."

The Attmores use manure from a nearby dairy, and old hay and sawdust for compost. And they keep turkeys and chickens— the turkeys because the young poults, allowed to run free among the herbs, provide excellent grasshopper control. "But once they get big, you've got to bring them in," said Toni, "because their big feet will trample the plants."

To some extent, the Attmores have been disappointed with some of the more widely used organic methods of insect control. Toni believes that companion planting works in small, home gardens, but that in large, commercial operations, it is clumsy and inefficient. "Also, I definitely do not go along with the biological controls. Importing creatures that are not native to the garden can upset the natural balance." One of the Attmores' crops, garlic, is planted in early fall, "so that the weeds will work for me," Chuck explained. "They provide shade and help retain moisture in the soil, and when the garlic is ready for harvest, in July, the weeds haven't yet gone to seed."

After an extensive tour of the gardens and two relaxing cups of herb tea it was time to go. As we were pulling away, I realized I had seen only one mechanical tool to keep their six producing acres in action, a garden tractor. So I leaned out the window and asked if they used other machines. "Everything else here is jackass power," Toni said.

"I didn't see any mules," was my reply.

"We're the jackasses," Chuck laughed, and waved. "Come again next time you're out this way."

High "C" Goat Dairy

Anyone who's ever kept a goat for a pet can tell you how difficult, if not downright ornery, this stubborn creature can be.

> The trouble with a kitten's that
> It eventually becomes a cat.
> But once a goat, always a goat.

Goats are extremely social animals, they are incurably curious, and they're natural climbers. Such qualities, blended into one agile creature, make it a difficult animal to fence. Once out of its designated area, the goat likes to climb, and there's little you can do to keep it off the lawn chairs or a neighbor's prize convertible. Without something to climb, the goat is likely to turn its attention to a shrub or newly planted fruit tree.

Fencing goats doesn't have to be a major problem. The difficulties a pet owner encounters should be somewhat different from those of a small commercial operation, which, if set up properly, eliminates such basic problems. Goats can be trained to two-strand electric fencing, with one wire low and the other very high; they can also be fenced with wooden slats or wire mesh, at least 48 inches high.

One other disadvantage of goats, a matter requiring regular maintenance, is that goats' hooves require monthly trimming. If the hooves are not trimmed, they will "double over" and cause lameness in the goat. Trimming is done with scissor-like trimmers, a hoofing knife, or a sharp pocketknife; the goat stands for it best while eating about 15¢ worth of whole grains. Some people say the hooves trim easiest after the goat's been browsing in wet grass, just as your toenails are easier to cut after a warm bath.

If you can build a fence and don't object to the 10 minutes per month, per goat, hoof-trimming requirement, this might be the most sensible type of dairy operation you can go into; goats require a minimum of space, and the return on feed is far better than that offered by dairy cows. A good milking doe, according to Colleen Calhoun at High "C" Goat Dairy of Meridian, Idaho, will give a gallon of milk a day in return for about 35¢ worth of feed. That gallon of milk sells for $2.45 wholesale, in Idaho, but it's been known to retail as high as $10 a gallon during the off-season winter months in San Francisco.

Colleen's husband, John Calhoun, 47, wanted to supplement his truck-driving income, and so the Calhouns started a veal calf operation five years ago, on their 15-acre parcel of land 12 miles from downtown Boise. Before long, the Calhouns had purchased a milking doe, because goat's milk is known to cure calves of scours. As they learned more about the healthful properties of goat's milk as a replacement for cow's milk, the Calhouns' herd of dairy goats grew until "one day we found ourselves hand-feeding 100 veal calves and hand-milking 60 goats. We couldn't even find time to say hello to each other," said Colleen, "and we knew we had to decide between calves and goats, and the goats won hands-down."

The Calhouns are presently milking 125 to 130 does, and feeding a herd of about 250; they have 18 bucks. All male kids are wethered (castrated) four or five days after birth and sold before they're six weeks old for meat or as pets. All kids are separated from their mothers at birth; bucks are bottle-fed goat milk until they're about three months old, does are bottle-fed milk for about four months. In addition, the Calhouns provide a full grain-and-hay diet from birth. "If they grow fast enough, they can be bred at eight months. The only variable in raising goats is time. Pound for pound, the feed ratio to milk won't change. What *will* vary is how fast the doe is ready for breeding. The more you feed, the sooner she's ready." As we talked, Colleen washed pint pop bottles, then filled them with goat milk, and fixed rubber nipples on top.

John and Colleen Calhoun

"The real problem with a goat dairy," said John, "is labor. In spite of the very favorable feed-to-milk conversion rate, it takes six goats to produce as much milk as one cow, so you can see it requires more work. We use a regular milking machine with two of the teat cups blocked off. Colleen puts in 12 hours a day, and I figure with my 8-hour trucking job, which is when I get my rest, I put in a 15-hour day. We employ two part-time helpers, but during kidding season, one of them works pretty near a full 12-hour day."

"If the day were just a little longer," laughed Colleen. "For instance, there is simply no better ice cream in the world than that made with goat's milk, and if we had time we could produce more ice cream than we do. And the yogurt market hasn't even been touched yet. Cheese too. But all these products require new equipment and time."

High "C" Goat Farm is the only licensed goat dairy in Idaho. The Calhouns have found a ready market for their milk, and for the buck kids whose meat, called chevon, is extremely popular among the Mexican, Spanish, Oriental, and Greek people who live in the Boise area, near enough to drive to the farm.

The Calhouns are extremely positive about their venture. Their fondness for goats is genuine: Colleen brings the newborns into the house when they still require hand-held bottle-feeding. "Did you know that 70 to 80 percent of the world's population drinks goat's milk?" she asked. "I only wish I'd known about it while my children were still small. Families will come to us because their young child wakes at 2 A.M. screaming with colic, and we'll say, 'Here, try some of this,' and give them a quart of our milk, and they'll be back the next day for more, saying, 'You know, this is the first time he slept through the night.'

"And yet goats have this terrible image in the United States. They're supposed to eat anything, according to the myth, and since unwethered bucks do have a distinct odor, all goats are reported to stink. Never mind that in reality a goat is the fussiest of the barnyard creatures when it comes to eating. A goat won't take *anything* off the ground. They're browsers, not grazers!"

In spite of the highly efficient conversion of feed to milk, a goat dairy, like other types of farms, is not usually a big profit business. "There's no big profit for any farmer," said John. "It's all in accumulations. We plow the money back into our breeding stock, or into new buildings. We want to build a 20-by-50-foot nursery for goats now." The Calhouns claim a dairy license is not difficult to obtain, but that a large investment is required for a bulk tank and bottling machine. John says having a good potential market is essential for the new goat dairy. "With a cow dairy you can know in advance how much milk you'll sell on a given day. With a goat dairy, the market is an unknown, so starting a goat dairy generally requires a lot more guts than brains!"

For High "C," Colleen reports the biggest marketing problem to be keeping enough goat milk in stock for the winter months. To insure a steady supply of milk for their regular customers, the Calhouns freeze a certain percentage of their milk during the summer months. To do this, they simply fill four-gallon containers with three gallons of milk, and take it to a freezing plant where it's quick-frozen and stored until they need it. The milk is then thawed and bottled in smaller containers, and sold at the regular wholesale price.

The Calhouns handle all their business operations, from breeding their own stock to milking the does, processing, bottling, and marketing the milk. Three years ago, they constructed a large A-frame that they use as a salesroom. Almost half their sales are right on the farm, but they deliver milk on a regular schedule to health food and grocery stores. At the farm, if you're lucky, you can find a quart or two of goat's milk ice cream; at a dollar a quart it is a bargain.

"Many people can't tell the difference between goat and cow's milk," said Colleen. "Of course there are reasons why good goat milk is so sweet. Worms are one of the chief causes for off-flavor, so we apply worm medicine, twice a year to all the mature members of our herd." The Calhouns report that the most efficient method of worming is to avoid pills, which goats are often reluctant to swallow, and instead employ a caulking gun, loaded with paste. The Calhouns use thibendazole, in accordance with a veterinarian's recommendations, and "no other chemicals at any time unless the animal is down and almost dead," said Colleen.

Except for necessary worm medications, High "C" goats are raised in strict accordance with organic principles. The Calhouns purchase a special dairy mix that is custom-blended for their herd, without urea and without antibiotics. The grain must be top quality, and cannot be musty, Colleen told me, "or else they turn their nose up. I'm convinced that good milk flavor is more a matter of management than anything else. We've found that good alfalfa hay and organic grains keep them from pasturing or browsing on growth that might spoil the milk."

"And," John added, "whatever the goats won't eat, we just feed to our calves."

The Calhouns keep a mixed herd of registered purebred Nubian, Toggenberg, Alpine, Saanen, and American LaMancha goats. They also upgrade their herd in accordance with American Dairy Goat Association standards. During summer, "when we have the time," they show their goats. Colleen said this is a particularly good way to obtain professional opinions on a herd, and to cull goats that do not show superior qualities.

One other valuable source of information for the Calhouns has been their state veterinarian, who, they report, worked seven years in Argentina, "He told us," Colleen said, "that in Argentina, a major beef-exporting country, the people are permitted to eat beef only once a week. The country's major source of meat protein is the goat!"

Johnny's Selected Seeds

At 26, Rob Lee Johnston has a thriving, four-year-old, mail-order business, specializing in seeds developed in his trial gardens in Albion, Maine. Under the incorporated name of "Johnny's Selected Seeds" Rob and his wife, Joan, conduct organic seed and crop research, offering each year by catalogue a wide variety of vegetable seeds selected especially for their ability to germinate and mature quickly in the brief northern New England growing season. "Of course if it does well this far north," Johnston told me, "It's probably going to do even better south of here!"

When Janet, Ben, and I arrived, Joan greeted us at the door and explained that Rob was in the barn with an inspector for the Bureau of Weights and Measures. "Last year they told us our seed packages need to specify the weight of seed enclosed, and he stopped by early this year to be sure we remembered. Then Rob took him out to see our pear tree, and now they're down at the barn trying to fix the pulley on our tractor."

We had arrived at lunchtime. Rob and Joan shared their hearty lunch of raw vegetables, cheese, and bean soup, and Rob told me how he started in the business. "Even in high school I was interested in farming of one sort or another. I went to the University of Massachusetts and studied sciences, but I was restless in college, and left after two years." Rob explained that for the next three years he raised oriental vegetables on a New Hampshire farm, and marketed them in New York and Boston.

Four years ago, Rob moved up to a farm in North Dixmont, Maine, where he was offered the use of land and buildings in return for maintaining the farm and watching over the owner's pig. As his mailing list began to grow, Rob was developing trial gardens and better and better seeds, season by season. With the help of his friends, he soon had 20 acres of land under organic cultivation. Then, two years ago, he met Joan. They found a sturdy, spacious old farmhouse with a good barn on 65 acres in Albion, close enough to North Dixmont that the business could straddle the two locations while Rob and Joan set up the new place. In July 1975, Johnny's Selected Seeds, Incorporated was founded. Four stockholders have provided the resources for the business to expand, with an attractively printed catalogue that is mailed out to 10,000 mail-order customers, and four paid full-time helpers "in season," January through May.

"The toughest season for us is the fall, getting the inventory straight and the catalogues prepared for the coming season," Rob

Rob Lee Johnston

explained. "We're a really conventional seed business in that respect: the second half of one year is considered preparation for the first half of the next year. You're always working half a year ahead of yourself." Rob had invited the inspector in for lunch, but he had declined. The pulley on the tractor had been removed, and, as soon as lunch was over, he had to drive to town for a replacement pulley. He invited me to ride in with him.

As we bumped along in Rob's aging pickup truck, he explained that after only four years in the business, it would be nearly impossible to offer a complete list of homegrown, and therefore indisputably organic, seeds. For this reason, he supplements his seed offerings with imported seeds and seed contracted to local organic gardeners. "In some cases, the land has not always been farmed organically, and our growers agree to grow our seeds in the 'purest' areas."

One of the biggest problems in seed production is insuring that pure strains are kept far enough apart that cross-pollination doesn't result in hybrid seed. For this reason, even though 20 acres would seem sufficient to supply an abundance of seeds, Rob is fortunate to have two separate pieces of farmland, and contract growers within the neighboring communities.

Rob believes that homegrown seed is almost definitely superior for local gardening conditions to seed that is produced hundreds of miles away for general conditions. For this reason, he attempts to offer a majority of nonhybrid seeds, so that his customers will be able to allow some of their plants to go to seed and thus "complete the cycle, growing from their own seed, plants which are adapting genetically to the unique garden situation.

"You see, the big seed houses hire Ph.D. breeders to produce a strain no one can copy, such as Burpee's hybrid muskmelon, which will attract gardeners who will probably buy all their seed from this one company, year after year, because that's where they get the good melon seeds. Of course, the plants from those seeds being hybrid, will not reproduce faithfully, and you have to go back to Burpee year after year."

The prevailing atmosphere among small-time seed growers seems quite different from that of the major companies, which, Rob said, often contract their seeds from Western growers. Rob's catalogue encourages customers to grow their own seed, and offers to answer any questions.

In an article in *Organic Gardening and Farming* (January 1976), Rob explained the benefits and methods of saving seed. He stipulated that the home gardener should use standard varieties, not hybrids, and to be sure that cross-pollinating plants like cucumbers, corn, carrots, and squash, be kept far apart from any of their siblings. Self-pollinators like tomatoes and lettuce, he wrote, can be mixed within a single garden without jeopardizing the purity of the seed.

To save the seed of tomatoes, cucumbers, and melons, Johnston recommends carefully spooning the seed of mature fruits into nonmetallic containers, and keeping them at room temperature for two to four days, stirring twice a day, so that fermentation will occur, turning the pulp into a thin liquid. Fermentation not only cleans the seed, but "acts to destroy possible seed-borne disease." Seeds are then washed in cold water, and everything that rises to the top is discarded, including floating seeds, which are hollow. Washing is repeated several times and then seeds are set out to dry in a sunny window. Drying requires at least two days, and seed may be stored in a cool, dark place in airtight containers, or stored in the freezer. Lettuce seed is saved by allowing the plant to flower and "fluff," then pulling the plant and hanging it to dry. Lettuce for seed should be started early in the season. Carrots are wintered over, either with heavy mulch or by harvesting and storing in a cellar, then replanted the following spring. During their second year, they flower and go to seed. "When the greenish color disappears from the seeds and branches, the plants should be cut above the ground and further air-dried. In small quantity, seed can easily be rubbed off by hand," Johnston wrote. Corn, beans, and peas can be left to dry on the plant. Johnston recommends retaining parent seeds to check against future generations for size, plant type, and other characteristics. Scattered throughout the 50-page catalogue are notices: "Trading seeds is a lot of fun. We really enjoy hearing from gardeners and trading homegrown varieties. Let us know what you've got, or send it along, and we'll swap you one of our good things in return." In a prominent spot at the end of the catalogue, Rob and Joan have listed "Other Seed and Plant Sources" with the names and addresses of four organic "competitors."

One of these is Edward Lowden, an 86-year-old breeder and grower from Ancaster, Ontario. Rob spoke of Lowden with great respect, and I wrote him to ask his advice for someone starting a small seed business. In a handwritten letter that arrived by return mail, Edward Lowden wrote of his lifelong devotion to organic gardening. "From the time I was able to get around before kindergarten days, the love of the land, plants, and animals was very strong in me. If my parents were away and wanted to bring home something to my brother and me, most likely it would be a plant or a pet for me and candy or a toy for my brother. When I started to work for myself I went as far as necessary and worked twice as hard for half the money, so I could be on a farm rather than take a city job."

Lowden's father had lost his farm in Canada's depression that started in the 1870s and lasted into the 1890s, and young Lowden grew up on a rented farm, learning by observing, season after season, the "strictly organic methods used by my ancestors for generations and taught to me largely by my father, with some variation according to my own experience. I did try chemical fertilizer once when an O.A.C. man working for me thought we would get better crops. When the check lot without the fertilizer appeared to be clearly better than the lots with the chemicals, I experimented no more with it. So far as we know, none of our approximately 200 acres on five properties has ever had chemical fertilizer on it. I have more than 25 acres of absolutely virgin soil and many more acres that have not been cropped much.

"I figured it was cheaper to buy good land than to fix up worn-out soil." A firm believer in rotating crops, as stipulated in the Bible ("In the law of the land which God gave to Israel, the land was to be rested every seven years") Lowden wrote, "I believe it is possible to overfeed soil, or throw it out of balance, just as it is possible for us ourselves to overeat on an unbalanced diet. The secret of good crops is good seed, or plants, planted in soil suitable for that particular crop and then properly cared for. I am persuaded that most of the land on this continent is being worked far too much." Lowden's beliefs are based not so much on hearsay and biblical decree as on actual experience, and his catalogue amply documents his findings.

Having located the necessary pulley, Rob and I were driving back to the farm. Rob explained his philosophy that a good seed company seeks to provide those varieties that have been dropped by the bigger companies in favor of hybrids yielding more and larger vegetables. His catalogue offers early strains of hard-to-find old favorites like JACOB'S CATTLE and MAINE YELLOW EYE beans, GOLD STANDARD, LONGFELLOW FLINT, and COUNTRY GENTLEMAN corn. "At present, we're field-testing 70 different cabbages, 70 carrots, 150 beans, and at least 30 cauliflower, Brussels sprouts, and broccoli. We have well-separated cornfields, and we hand-pollinate our breeding plots," he said.

"Of course quality of seed is foremost, but service is what people see first, so it is equally important that your mail-order operation be efficient and fast." We passed a chicken farm, and Rob explained to me how many of his neighbors support themselves raising chickens. "Everything is supplied to them by the parent company," he said. "All you have to do is build the barn, using company plans, if you like. They deliver day-old chickens—started poults—and feed. All the farmer has to do is put the feed into the tray and collect the eggs each morning before the company truck arrives to take them to market." He adjusted his cap and fell silent.

For a few miles we drove without speaking. Then, just before we pulled into his shady farmyard, Rob summed up a few of his observations on small business. "The real problem is growth," he said. "You don't want to expand too fast. I find it's important to recognize your limitations from the very beginning and not to let business get ahead of you.

"The business itself is really a barometer of your own personal condition. You have to understand what you want, then know how to get it and be willing to pay the emotional price. To do any one thing really well, there's a big price to pay because you have to forfeit doing some of the other things you like." He paused, then added, "I think everyone has days when their life seems kind of hollow, no matter how good their work is."

Back at the farmhouse we found Janet and Joan with Ben and Joshua, enjoying a bright mid-September afternoon sunburst. Joan told me that one-fifth of Johnny's Selected Seeds mail-order business is right in Maine. "The rest is pretty much equally spaced across the country, with about 40 percent in the Northeast." Advertising works fine, she said, just as long as you're prepared to handle whatever the results may be. The Johnstons have placed advertisements in such garden-oriented magazines as *Organic Gardening and Farming, Mother Earth News,* and *Horticulture.* Their biggest expense, aside from the cost of machinery and land, has proven to be printing and postage for their catalogues and payroll for seed packers during the winter.

Four years after going "full time" in Maine with his own seed business, Rob Lee Johnston reports that Johnny's Selected Seeds, Incorporated, is providing him and his family total support. That isn't to say he's getting rich with money, but he is working, like Edward Lowden, in a tradition that mixes the knowledge and the actual seed of growers from all countries, and many centuries.

Driving further east that afternoon, Janet and I marveled at the dedication and patience such work must require, waiting season after season for a piece of land to come into balance, while generation after generation of seed slowly adjusts to local conditions. Janet laughed, remembering something Joan had said about Rob. "Sometimes he'll get this faraway look in his eyes, and when I was first getting to know him, I'd think he was about to say something romantic. And I'd say, 'What are you thinking?' 'Well,' he'd reply, 'if we move the beans next year to where the corn is . . .'"

Honey

"We are a couple who chucked their overpaid federal government computer jobs and are finishing up our second year as Bradford County, Pa., beekeepers, operating 200 hives with plans for 500. Our previous experience with bees, honey house construction, and rural living in general was zilch, but I think we're going to make a good go of it. And what's better is that we're in love with country living and feel better than ever before." So write Curt and Jeanne Morgan, the beekeeper-owners of Hanlon Hill Honey Farm in Bentley Creek, Pennsylvania.

Entering its third year of operation, Hanlon Hill Honey Farm now consists of 400 hives and will, "barring a total crop failure," gross $18,000 in 1977, with operating expenses of $3,000. The Morgans wrote me that they were attracted to the honeybee business not only by its rural character, but by the "minimal size of capital required (in comparison to other farming occupations); 'modularity' of the business (enables one to start small, learn, and increase as capital and knowledge permit), and suitability to the geographic region we were considering moving to."

Getting started is the most expensive and time-consuming aspect of the bee business, and during their first year, they both worked long, full-time days. "Once we are established, I think six weeks each in spring and again in fall will be the only times both of us will need to work full time," Curt said.

Their actual costs in establishing the business:

Pickup truck	$ 3,500
Honey house	4,000
400 hives × $50	20,000
Extracting equipment	1,500
	$29,000

"One could get by on less by fabricating equipment, hives, catching bee swarms and making 'increases' (dividing the hives), using an existing building for a honey house, etcetera, and once set up, you can operate full time on very little, possibly $3,000 a year, to cover all expenses."

The Morgans, both in their early thirties, say they learned beekeeping "the hard way." Oh, a neighboring beekeeper "helped" the first year, in which 18 out of 25 hives died. "Only when I stopped listening to random advice and took short beekeeping courses at Penn State and O.S.U., and worked with professional beekeepers in Texas and Florida, did I really start to learn," Curt said.

Curt cited the amount of time required in setting up as a major cause of bee failures. "Those who hold 40-hour-a-week jobs might run into two or three rainy weekends in a row at a critical time, and their bees would suffer. I've been lucky in being able to devote full-time labor to setting up."

Reporting that "inspection of honey-processing plants is nonexistent in most areas," the Morgans are able to perform all phases of processing and marketing their honey without special licenses or inspection. As for marketing, they wrote: "We believe with the time and money to invest in a full-time operation (those who do it part time always seem to remain just that), knowledge of bees and the equipment to produce quality honey (not just glorified sugar syrup), it is impossible to fail in the marketing aspect, given a good location and products with widespread appeal. Selling good honey takes no particular skill, and those retailers who sell our honey take 25 to 50 percent of the profit off the top for themselves, while it's our sweat and knowledge that is responsible for producing the stuff in the first place."

Another honey operation I know of is run by a mildly eccentric 80-year-old who lives in a room of the oldest house in his tiny hometown in upstate New York. The rest of the house, filled with dusty relics, is falling in. I promised not to disclose the man's identity or the specific town where he operates a seductively tourist-oriented honey business. But, if persistence or luck should help you find him, he'll sit you on the edge of his bed and bring out five-gallon jar after five-gallon jar of various shades and flavors of honey, and tell you the benefits of honey from sweetening teas to cataracts. "Put it right on the eye," he says.

"The government heard I was making honey wine and some inspectors came, and now they want to tax me every which way," he complained.

This honey man keeps his hives in distinct areas of the neighboring farms, and thus realizes wildly different varieties of honey. As he spoon-fed me tablespoon after tablespoon of strawberry honey, then God's honey and apple honey, my throat began to tighten and my head started to throb with the sweetness in what I later learned is known as a "honey rush."

I requested smaller quantities on the end of the large spoon, but he seemed to double the size of each offering, and I finally learned to nip into a small amount at the end of the spoon and return the rest. "The point is," he had told me earlier, "as in everything, don't be greedy. People want to know how to have the best honey and I tell them that, but it's my only secret I'm ever going to share. You have to be willing to put the hives far apart and to learn where the best places are." He laughed, and began to show me his postcard collection. His guest book for January already showed 36 people, and today was only the 12th!

"It's all right to have these visitors," he said. "They help keep this room warm." We gathered around a small kerosene heater. Outside the snow was three feet deep. "I don't make much honey. And I only sell it if you promise not to resell. I can sell it for a dollar a pound, but I don't want anyone increasing the price. Have you ever made honey wine?" he asked.

"Sure have," I said proudly. My throat was still a little tight from the sweet invasion.

"What's your recipe?" he asked.

"Well, I usually take a gallon of honey and add five gallons of boiling water . . ."

"Vinegar!" he scoffed. "All that water! I make mine quart for quart. Had a couple of girls here before Christmas and one of them was in theater at college. She wanted a little taste of mead, so I gave it to her, and she said 'Why this isn't very strong,' and so I let her have another cup. Pretty soon she wanted another. Then her cheeks started to get a little red." He then tapped his pipe against a brick on top of the heater. "She missed her rehearsal that night, I was told."

I would have outright asked for a taste of that famous mead, but the lesson on greed was already so well learned that I shook my new friend's hand, signed his guest book, and promised not to let his secret out. He walked me out to the car and made me promise to mail him a postcard from some exotic place.

The honey man's approach to the business is quite different from the Morgans'. Honey is a full-time occupation for him, but he lives on a shoestring, tacking old equipment back together year after year, and hiking distant hillsides on old legs.

The Morgans are interested in a more efficient production business and recommend "*not* cutting corners." They told me, "One *can* buy cheap equipment, use inferior building materials, paint, etcetera, but these will require quick replacement and do an inferior job in the meantime. The costs we have listed should set us up *for life* in the honey-producing business—thus the low operating costs. But you've got to have sufficient cash, knowledge, and desire to see the enterprise through to a profit-making condition. As we're constantly told, it takes time to establish one's self and one's reputation. It takes time for people to realize you are there and what you have for sale is good."

And finally, in learning about bees, the Morgans put a lot of stock in "well-thought questions to *knowledgeable* beekeepers. And the attitude, don't do *anything* to your honeybees unless you are absolutely certain that what you're doing is right: Ninety-five percent of the time the bees are perfectly capable of doing what's best for them. Your *interference* will be just *that*."

Winemaking

With the proper amount of self-discipline and a favorable political climate, winemaking can be a profitable and satisfying small business. Because federal regulations allow the making of up to "200 gallons" for noncommercial (home) purposes, many amateur winemakers supplement their regular incomes by quietly retailing a portion of their "home-use" surplus to friends. The going price is $2 a fifth, with the customer firmly instructed to rinse and return the bottle if he expects further access to your homemade wine. Make sure never to sell a wine for more than it is worth. If a batch should flop, it certainly doesn't qualify as part of your 200-gallon limit, and it should be served to unexpected guests before it has aged at all. Any wine that is offered for sale should have been allowed to age at least a year. A wine that tastes awful at three months can be downright pleasing at the end of a year. Such a wine is often too good for anything but saving if it makes it past the age of two.

Anyone seeking to bring his home wine business out of the closet should first investigate what state and local regulations control the operation of a small winery. In some cases, the cost of a license is minimal, because farsighted legislators realize that winemaking is a legitimate small-business opportunity that should be encouraged as a means of promoting local agricultural commerce. In other cases, costs will be prohibitive, and the would-be vintner must either maintain a small, clandestine operation with discrete customers, or move.

In some cases the cost of all licenses, federal, state, county, and local permits, totals less than $300 a year. State tax is another extreme variable. For instance, a gallon of wine produced in California (where 80 percent of all U.S. wine is produced) is taxed a penny by the state. In Massachusetts, a gallon of wine is subject to a 40¢ state tax! While such a tax is not absolutely prohibitive, it's a mite discouraging. Consult a lawyer or the local extension agency to learn the regulations for your locale.

Anyone who succeeded in determining that the political climate was favorable to a commercial winemaking venture would then be well-advised to consider the prospects for growing or obtaining the fruit. While grapes are the fruit of choice for nearly all commercial winemakers, there's no good reason why someone with a few hundred pounds of surplus honey, for instance, shouldn't consider producing mead. A cider mill could (and probably does) have a reliable setup for hard cider or apple wine. An avocado grower could perfect an avocado wine, just right with rich desserts.

The actual figures I present here come from grape wine producers, Tom O'Grady in Farmville, Virginia, and Jerry and Kathy Forest, who have a home winery in Buckingham, Pennsylvania. The figures can be adjusted by determining the amount of principal ingredients and acreage necessary to grow them, and substituting this amount for the figures below. One other possibility, for someone with limited desire to grow the wine crop is to buy it, in large quantities, in season. Hence, one winery, located without cropland, requiring only four walls and a roof, could produce a variety of six to eight wines, year-round.

The cost of establishing a vineyard will vary tremendously depending on the actual cost and condition of your land. But assuming you have fertile, well-drained soil where a test crop of the proposed fruit has flourished, you could start with one acre and add an acre a year to production until the operation was in full swing, with the following averaged costs as a guideline:

600 vines per acre @ 50¢	$ 300
200 cedar or locust posts	400
150,000 feet wire for trellis	300
Fertilize and prepare one acre	400
First-year labor, 150 hours × $3 per hour	450
	$1,850

In three years, when the vines have matured, this acre of land will produce about three tons of grapes, depending on the type of grape and local conditions, and the grapes' value is about $400 per ton. Thus, the annual harvest from that one acre, after three years, is worth $1,200 on the market, less harvesting and delivering costs. By the way, figuring 175 gallons of juice per ton of grapes, we see that the one-time cost of establishing your one-acre crop will yield 525 gallons of juice per season, enough to produce an encouraging 2,625 fifths of fine wine.

The labor cost is included. You must establish a dollar value for your labor. By all means do so, and include the labor cost in your final estimates. The amount of time per year, after the first year, is estimated at 50 hours per acre. By the harvest of the seventh year, you should be "in the black" regarding your produce. But if you make wine from the third year's harvest (your first), you can reduce the length of time required to show a profit, assuming the wine is good!

		Costs	Receipts
First year:	Establish one acre of vines	$1,850	
Second year:	Maintain one acre of vines	450	
Third year:	Maintain and harvest one acre	650	$1,200
Fourth year:	Maintain and harvest one acre	650	1,200

The disadvantages of establishing your own vineyard include the uncertainties of weather and the high cost of gardening equipment. Tom O'Grady manages to farm his three acres of vines using a 16 h.p. Sears garden tractor with an array of attachments that cost him $3,000 complete. O'Grady, who spread horse manure and plowed under a crop of soybeans before setting out his vines, has had to spray his vines to control fungus diseases and milky spore disease. He recommends purchasing praying mantis eggs to control insects, and building wren houses and condominiums for purple martins, as an alternative to bird-netting and chemical insect control. The martins and wrens will not only gobble up insects, but, claims O'Grady, they will scare off the fruit-eating, red-beaked, W.C. Fields tippler, a varied specie of smaller bird, known to be as dangerous to the vineyards as an early freeze. Birds may also be controlled with an electronic squawk box, if you can stand the noise.

Fish oil is recommended as a spray to control the spread of fungus; this should be done during the dormant season. O'Grady wrote me, "If vines are planted in an airy place and located in a region with little humidity and small rainfall, much spraying can be eliminated. Figuring the worst, estimate that annual maintenance of the crop costs $300, and that harvesting expenses and trucking of an acre's produce costs another $200."

Winemaking expenses will vary as much or more than the cost of establishing a wine crop. But just for simplicity, let's assume that you have decided to purchase, not to grow, your main wine crop, and that you have purchased three tons of grapes, the amount you could have grown on one acre, at the going price of $400 per ton. The cost of juice, then, to yield 525 gallons of wine, will be about 50¢ per bottle. Allowing for accident, 525 gallons equals 2,500 fifths.

Cost per bottle of wine:

Juice	$ .50
Sugar	.05
Bottle	.15
Cork and label	.10
	$ .80

Assume that you have produced 2,500 fifths that you will sell for $2 each. One acre of land can thus yield $5,000, less $2,000 in annual costs, taxes, and overhead.

Barrels, a press, crusher, filter, bottling machine, corker, pumps, and hoses will cost approximately $1,500. (Tom O'Grady figures $15 per 55-gallon oak barrel, which he buys in quantity from a whiskey distillery, for example.)

As approximate as these figures are, they should help demonstrate that making quality wine can be an extremely profitable business, given the proper legal situation. But the greatest variable of all, not yet considered in this chapter, is your own ability and interest. Winemaking is a tiresome and tedious process, somewhat like photography in that any number of variables can result in happy or disappointing surprises and are never known until a lot of time has passed. Because not everyone is lucky or patient enough with the fates that determine a wine's quality and ultimate saleability, you should procede in winemaking one tiny step at a time, making it, waiting for it to age, tasting it, testing the product on friends. If they come back, and if you've enjoyed your labors, consider the winery. If you've enjoyed your labors but they don't come back, you can always sell vinegar.

The Cold Hollow Cider Press

Eric and Francine Chittenden are neighbors of mine, full-blooded Vermonters who met while Eric, 34, was in the merchant marine, and Francine, 25, was still a student. Eric's father has had a successful cider operation for many years, but when Eric started thinking about some farming operation that would allow him enough income to give up his lucrative merchant marine job, so he could be with Francine and their daughter, Eliza, now three, his first idea was dairy farming. "We bought the farm the summer of 1973," Francine told me. "After 10 days of experience with a small dairy, we knew that kind of farming wasn't for us, so we decided to try growing wheat. You may remember the flood of that summer, which washed out our wheat."

"Someone came into the house," said Eric, "we were just moving in, and said, 'You know, this is the worst rainfall in 20 years.' And the old farmer who had sold us the house was in the kitchen and he said, referring to the coffee cans scattered all over the upstairs to catch the water leaking through the roof, 'Can't be the worst rainfall in 20 years. Those cans upstairs aren't half as full as they were last week!' "

Eric's next idea was a plan for cutting and retailing firewood. "I figured, the one way to make money on firewood is to reduce the number of times you've got to handle it. So I had this plan where I'd take pallets into the woods, and cut the wood, block and split it all on the spot, and stack it on pallets, by the cord. Then, with a

Eric, Francine, and Eliza Chittenden

forklift, after banding the pallets, I'd load the wood onto a delivery truck, a cord at a time, and drive it directly to the customer." He let out a soft chuckle. "But then I cut my own firewood and that cured me of the idea of cutting anyone else's. Next I bought a complete sugar rig and discovered that the glory there far exceeds the ability to make a living."

By this time, the Chittendens were somewhat discouraged. After a year of repairing roofs and old water lines, they had gone through the expensive and discouraging processes of discovering three or four different agricultural endeavors were not for them. They began to question whether they'd made the right decision when they moved up to Bakersfield and bought the 300-acre farm. Eric still had his seaman's papers, and he planned on a six-month return to the merchant marine starting in December. Meanwhile, they ran across a used cider press, rotting away in an orchard, that they were welcomed to haul away, which they did.

Three hundred dollars later, they had entirely replaced the hydraulic system, cleaned or replaced all rusted parts, replaced rotten boards, and supplied their press with new cloths and racks. They next went to work on the old dairy barn, taking out the gutters, and pouring a new floor, repainting, and tearing down a neighbor's horse barn for decorative paneling. (Francine was eight months pregnant at the time). "We hired two friends to help us tear down the barn," Eric said, "because our neighbor's conditions were that the job be completed in three days and that every nail and splinter be taken away from the site."

By this time the Chittendens were fairly sure they were on the right track. The work was hard, but at least they felt that here was an enterprise that couldn't be washed out by rain and that promised profit equal to the glory of the work. "We wanted to put together a cider mill where visitors could watch the entire operation," Francine told me, "all the way from the whole apple entering the building to the cup of fresh, sweet juice."

That was in 1974. Throughout the summer they worked, and they opened in the fall with a minimum of advertising, simply hanging their large, beautifully hand-carved sign, in front of the farmhouse that fronts on Route 108, a well-traveled road that connects Enosburg and Bakersfield with Jeffersonville. "There are very few cider mills in the area anymore that offer custom grinding as we do," said Eric, "and I'm not sure where such accommodations for seeing the whole operation are offered. Our very first day we were packed!"

The Chittendens hadn't expected such a flow of business and had cautiously bought only enough apples to keep the mill busy until December. Eric went to sea for the winter months, while Francine tended Eliza and the house, and they planned by mail for the coming 1975/76 season, which turned out to be a bumper-crop year for Vermont apple growers. It convinced Eric that the mill would be wholly self-supporting by the end of 1976, and that his days of packing off to sea were nearly ended.

Just as that 1976 profit was finally rolling in, an objective appraisal of their parking situation in Bakersfield, along with prohibitive zoning regulations, helped them decide to relocate. In the spring of 1976 they went hunting, and by summer, Eric and Francine had found a suitable place 35 miles south along Route 100 in Waterbury Center. They refurbished an old barn there, just as they had done in Bakersfield three years before, installing their press and bottling equipment. By fall, they were operating, with increased business, in their new location.

A large part of the Chittendens' success has been their ability to deal with large numbers of visitors on weekends. On weekends, they offer "custom grinding," whereby customers are invited to bring their own apples to the mill. The Chittendens report that this is very definitely a nonprofit aspect of their business, even though they require a minimum of 12 bushels of apples (enough for at least 40 gallons of cider). Customers often underestimate the number of containers that will be necessary for their apple cider yield, and Eric has a handy supply of 5- through 55-gallon barrels, as well as plastic gallon jugs, which he sells. The charge for custom grinding is 35¢ per gallon, and in view of the amount of time given to each customer's individual load of apples, it's quite a bargain, indeed.

"We also sell other paraphernalia," Eric explained, "anything to do with cider." Corks, barrels, and jugs are on display in the old dairy barn, along with the Chittendens' newly acquired, "modern" (10 years old) hydraulic press. "And we sell local crafts here, as well as a limited amount of organic produce." Free samples of cider are always available and have probably helped the Chittendens sell as much cider as their fast-growing reputation.

"We do all our own delivery," Eric told me. "And if any of our cider doesn't sell, or is ever returned by a dissatisfied customer, we take it back. Not everyone offers the grocer so much leeway. Guaranteed to sell; that's what we tell them."

What about cider that's returned? "We put it into the vinegar barrel," said Eric. "It takes a little longer to make but it sells as well as the cider does. This is a great business, because there's always the by-product you can make from your mistakes."

"But mistakes rarely happen," Francine interjected. "The most important aspect of cider making is to get it cold as fast as possible. The cider enters our bulk tanks at room temperature, and within half an hour it's been cooled to 33°F. The same afternoon, the cooled cider has been bottled and loaded into the delivery truck for Eric to drive his route." The Chittendens have already developed over 200 retail outlets for their cider, including all northern Vermont, and a few outlets outside the state. In their second season in the business, Eric and Francine, with one full-time hired man, pressed 20,000 gallons of their own cider, from apples Eric bought on contract during the summer, and 8,500 custom gallons.

The Chittendens have developed two supplementary products, pure apple cider syrup and apple cider jelly, both made simply by boiling apple cider in a maple syrup evaporator and pouring it into jars when the proper density has been obtained. No sugar is added and the apples provide their own pectin for jelly purposes. Cider boils down into syrup in an 8:1 ratio. A concentrated product like this could help make the distant city markets a lucrative reality. Francine reports that apple cider jelly retails in New York for up to $1.99 per 10-ounce jar. Wholesale price is 95¢ a jar.

Eric lauds Vermont as a state where cottage industries are still encouraged by tradition and a climate of mutual help. "But one day, probably," he adds, "some laws will be written that will change it all. So much is stacked against the small business in this country. For instance, insurance. As soon as we opened a commercial endeavor in the old barn, our fire insurance shot up unbelievably. And this was after we removed all the old hay and broken-down machines and replaced the frayed wires that are agriculture's biggest fire hazards. And who pushes for the excessive insurance and sanitary regulations? The big businesses, that can afford to meet the specifications!

"But so far, Vermont has held out in favor of the small business. The dairy industry is the only one I know that is heavily regulated here. For all other products, the stores exercise the control. And for the most part," he added, "the regulations the other states have come up with aren't always in the best interests of the public. In some instances, by demanding that plastics be used instead of wood, because plastic is 'more sanitary', they've even gone so far as to replace the old with unknown, and possibly cancerous, properties!"

Eric and Francine have considered starting their own orchards, but at present they believe the business is as big as they can handle. With the advent of their apple jelly and apple syrup making projects, they have uncovered a whole new area for themselves in marketing, and a lucrative and favorful one at that—and their method of forming the syrup or jelly is identical to the old-fashioned Vermont way of storing cider over the winter without having it "turn to something else." Boiling down the cider may well turn into an off-season enterprise, and help keep the distant New York market a reality, because so much more of the product can be profitably driven the distance.

In almost all ways the Cold Hollow Cider Press is a good example of native Yankee ingenuity. The Chittendens arrived at their chosen form of self-employment after examining a number of possibilities without giving up. They scouted around for all different sorts of opportunities, and whenever a bargain came up they took it on, keeping their initial investments extremely low by fixing up badly neglected equipment. Once they found an operation that was truly to their liking, they sank their whole efforts behind it, and at present, with the business in all ways a major success, they are investigating natural by-products to supplement their staple crop. They knew they liked to work all along; doing what was the only thing they hadn't figured out.

Growing
Christmas Trees

Growing Christmas trees is a particularly good idea if you have land that might be of marginal use for other crops. Christmas tree growers, who supply an ever-increasing number of evergreens each year, point out that theirs is an ecologically sound crop. "One plastic Christmas tree that lasts a family 40 years has still done more damage to the environment than the harvesting of 40 trees in 40 years," one enthusiastic grower told me. "Especially here in California these trees are helpful in purifying the air, and the professional grower replants after harvest, so the idea that Christmas costs the country 90 million trees a year is pure bunk!"

Ross McBurney, Retail Grower

Growers explain that there are two primary methods for selling trees. "Choose 'n' cut," the principal retailing operation, requires that the grower be able to provide parking space and ready service, as well as saws that won't "get lost" during the three critical weekends preceding Christmas. In California, the Christmas Tree Growers' Association issues a helpful quarterly bulletin to its members, which shares information and advice. Ross McBurney, who runs a choose 'n' cut farm in Cedar Ridge, California, advocates the "reservation" system for choose 'n' cut, wherein the customer visits the farm in October or November to choose his tree. The tree is then tagged with the customer's name

Ross McBurney

and dabbed at the base with bright fluorescent paint. This dab of paint, he explained to me, helps reserve the uncut tree during the Christmas retail rush, when nonreserved customers may inadvertently wrench the sold tags off these prime trees. McBurney's workers always check a tree for paint before the tree is cut. "When a reserved tree has lost its tag, we always blame the kids for messing with the tags, which saves the customer embarrassment."

McBurney, 69, is a retired insurance agent who began growing Christmas trees when his son, Bob, started a few for a 4-H project in 1954. Bob is now 29, and with his wife Carla, has moved back to land that is adjacent to the family tree farm, where his father is presently retailing more than 800 trees a year off two-and-one-quarter acres that are currently being harvested. "This will be doubled in four to five years," McBurney said, "when the full four-and-a-half acres are producing." McBurney nets between $5,000–$6,000 a year on his trees. He explained that trees over five years old are taxed on a capital gains basis, which makes a healthy difference over an operation where the tax base is shorter term.

McBurney's one recommendation to growers is to plant species that require pruning during a short, critical period, all in one area. "Other than that, nobody knows how to raise trees," he told me. "Everyone has a different idea on how to do it. Very few growers raise Silvertips around here because they're supposed to require 6,000 to 7,000 feet of elevation. Well, ours do quite well at 3,000 feet! The forest people said, 'You can't raise Silvertip at that elevation,' so we went ahead, just playing around, and now we just about have a monopoly on Silvertips!"

McBurney said he no longer needs to advertise, although last year he spent about $90 on classified advertisements. "My only advice to someone who's thinking of this business," he said, "is they better like work. I see a lot of retired people who come out here and say 'Oh, he's making $16–$18 a tree' so they go to work like crazy, and clear and plant and then let the whole business go to weeds because they can't keep up with the work. It's a situation where you simply have to take your time, and build the business step by step. We hire help and are able to pay $3–$4 an hour and provide a campfire and meals so that this is a very popular place for young people to work."

Peter and Juanita Browne, Wholesale Growers

While gross income from a retail operation is typically twice that of a wholesale operation, profits may be no higher, after the added expenses of hiring seasonal cashiers and helpers, and acquiring as much liability insurance as you can get to cover your business in case a customer slips on a snowy trail or misses with the saw. Wholesaling requires that the grower actually begin marketing his trees in late spring, arranging to have them picked up on a specific date, usually in November. His responsibility is typically to harvest the trees and have them stacked at the roadside, although other arrangements can, of course, be made. The advantages of wholesaling are especially obvious to growers who do not wish to open their croplands each year to hundreds of well-meaning people, all in the Christmas spirit.

Peter Browne, 49, is such a grower. He and his wife Juanita, 47, have 23 acres in California's lush Grass Valley. They bought in 1963, planted their first Douglas fir trees in 1965, and in September of 1973, Pete quit his $30,000-a-year aerospace executive job, and the Brownes moved from busy Sacramento to the quiet of their farm. So far they have cleared and planted eight acres, with about 2,000 trees per acre, spaced on a four-foot grid. Although they are very enthusiastic about Christmas tree growing, the Brownes point out that theirs is a crop that requires a lot of patience—and time—before the money starts coming in. But Peter Browne is an unusual man, and he researched the business thoroughly before making his decision to leave his executive position. The Brownes knew they wanted to try something agricultural, so their first step was to determine the local market to see what sells and what grows: "These two things have to go together," Pete stressed.

Juanita, who is a free-lance writer, explained that their farm provided an income last year of less than $1,500. "If all goes according to plan, we should have the farm completely planted in six years. We should then make about $15,000 gross income from the sale of our trees each year." Until then, Pete has formed a construction company, and Juanita carries on as "part-time free-lance writer and a full-time gardener and preserver. Our two sons take care of our laying hens, and are expert tree planters and pruners."

On the table in front of us was a small gourd that had been

Peter and Juanita Browne

hollowed out. Juanita laughed when she saw me looking it over. "We try to find a use for everything we grow," she said. "Did you know that sunflower stalks make a wonderful frame for a kite? The boys and I made a terrific kite with a few stalks and some newspaper, then we tied that gourd to the tail, and I had some wild flower seeds I wanted to distribute, so we tucked them into the gourd for a ride!"

The Brownes' Christmas tree farm has benefited from this sort of individual thinking. Although they are anxious to hear the advice of local experts, the Brownes have not been afraid to experiment, and Pete has kept a thorough record of the procedures involved in setting up a Christmas tree farm, which he outlined for me.

"Rainfall is very important," he told me. "Here, for instance, we get 50 to 55 inches of rain a year, but none at all from May to October, so irrigation is essential. And the soil cannot be too rich, or else the growth on the trees will be too rapid and spindly. We do not fertilize our trees; no one has yet shown that fertilizing works. Nor do we practice chemical weed control, as some growers recommend."

The Brownes' first step, after obtaining their land and determining the existence of a market, was to hire a bulldozer for clearing the land. "Our experience shows you should clear down to mineral soil," Pete told me. "And, if you live in an area where irrigation is necessary, you must plan the irrigation before you plant. And, also, plan the road system before you plant. The road system should serve as a firebreak as well as your only economical way to transport the trees."

The Brownes don't believe in crowding their trees, and although many growers claim to raise as many as 2,700 trees per acre, the Brownes believe 2,000 is a more realistic number, especially if one allows for irrigation and roads. "Irrigation is such a problem," Juanita told me, "that I'd recommend someone just starting out try growing trees without it; if the trees have a survival rate of 80 percent or better, irrigation probably won't be necessary." One of the greatest causes of transplant failure, the Brownes said, is exposing the roots to the air. "Any exposure longer than 30 seconds can be fatal," Juanita said.

"You should look around and see what native varieties grow well," said Pete. "And obtain your seedlings from local growers, as close to your farm as possible." The Brownes have obtained most of their seedlings from California's Division of Forestry State Nursery, paying $30 per thousand trees, or $60 worth of seedlings per acre.

Of course, the cost of the seedlings is the least of the grower's investments. Clearing the land and the labor during the next four years of keeping woody brush from competing with the young trees are a major part of his work. Then, during the trees' final three years before harvest, they require annual shearing to obtain a desirable shape and density. Six to eight years after being transplanted, the tree is finally ready for sale. "Even though the shearing takes about a minute per tree," Pete told me, "when you multiply that times 20,000 trees a year, it makes up a lot of minutes.

"And, because we wholesale our trees, there's the extra work of cutting, hauling, stacking, counting, measuring, and helping load the truck. But for us this was preferable to facing the prospect of 3,000 to 4,000 cars a weekend, providing parking, rest rooms, maybe a fire and hot coffee, and most important of all, insurance in case some clod cuts off a foot instead of a tree."

The Brownes have found that the best advertising for their wholesale operation is the California Christmas Tree Growers' Association "Wholesale Guide," and they also recommend classified advertising, "no later than September." A lot of advertising might be aimed at special interest groups that would sell the trees to benefit their organizations. The Brownes sell a lot of trees to Boy Scout troops, the YMCA, and local service organizations. "It would be profitable to contact such groups with individual mailings," Juanita added. "But so far we haven't needed to. We keep an up-to-date list of people we annually invite to a choose 'n' cut party. This is really a nice way of maintaining some personal contact with your customers and if you want to open your house and farm once a year, it's a fun way to do business. I should point out that even though this is a party with old friends, we don't give the trees away. And I could write an article on how many times an orange can go through mulled wine!"

"One other bit of advice to wholesalers," said Pete. "Insist on a cash deposit of at least 20 percent at the time you take the order, and get the balance at the time the trees change hands, because trees are very perishable."

"And," Juanita added, "they're absolutely worthless on December 26."

The Family Worm Farm

Geraldine and Lloyd Usrey have been in worm farming "on and off for 27 years," according to Geraldine, a robust woman of 61. She invited me off the busy lot of their worm farm in downtown Huntington Beach, near Los Angeles, into the salesroom. Lloyd, who is 62, has been in marketing all his life. "A friend told us how great a market there was for worms," she explained. "In 1939, shortly after we were married—we were living in El Monte, the friend's wife and I were delivering 25 to 100 dozen worms a day to sporting goods stores in L.A. So we knew a market existed!"

During the following years the Usreys moved to Monrovia and opened a large retail operation that included 100 worm beds, a restaurant, and a grocery. "We employed 15 people, and when we finally realized it was all too much, we sold the restaurant and the store, and continued in business, just ourselves, as Jerry's Worm Farm. Until 1963, from 8 A.M. till nightfall, I packed and mailed worms all over the Southwest. During those 10 years, Lloyd was working full time for the Alpha Beta chain, and was developing a regular market through K-Mart.

"By the time K-Mart dropped us, we had developed new worm routes with many other discount stores, including Pay Less, Woolco, Grant Boys, The Treasury, and others. Never put all your eggs in one basket, is my advice! And don't be discouraged if you don't do it overnight!"

Presently, B's Worm Farm is a full-fledged family business, employing three Usrey offspring and their families. Alan, 33, and his wife Diana raise worms and rabbits and operate a thoughtfully diversified nursery in nearby Vista. They help keep Alan's parents in good supply of rabbit manure (best for worm beds) and they pack worm cartons for marketing at the lot in Huntington Beach. Alan has blended obvious inventive ability with the skills he learned at college studying industrial technology, and Peacefield Farms, with homemade worm beds positioned under the rabbit hutches, and an ingenious belt-drive worm-casting packaging machine, testify to his abilities.

Another son, Jerry, who is 27, has started B's Worm School, with an enrollment of 40 to 50 people each Saturday. The school is run by Jerry's Worm Enterprises, and addresses the major techniques of worm farming, emphasizing the value of different breeds of worms for plants, vegetable gardens, vineyards, orchards, and fishing. Jerry's Worm Enterprises has also located substantial markets for worm castings (in which, according to the Usreys, "everything grows best") through Alpha Beta, Pay Less, and nu-

Geraldine and Jerry Usrey

merous other chain and garden stores. The Usrey's 19-year-old daughter, Leann, who is still in college, lives with her parents and tends 15 worm beds at home.

"The biggest advantage of a true family business," says Geraldine, "is that we have full trust in our employees. We don't worry about theft, and we know that when a job is assigned it will be done. But there are disadvantages, too. We're all so busy we can't visit as often as we'd like, except over business matters. So every year, over the Christmas and New Year holidays, we all close everything down and rent a cabin in Big Bear where we can all be together."

Worm farming requires a minimum of space; essentially only that needed for the worms, and an appropriate amount of storage space. Worms are kept in beds, which are two to three feet deep and narrow enough so you can dig the worms out from either side, and as long as your lumber runs. Every three-foot-by-eight-foot bed comfortably houses 100,000 worms. Because worms live happiest in rabbit manure (though any kind of manure or compost, once past the heating stage of decay, is fine), the Alan Usreys keep rabbits directly over the worm beds. Worm beds, by the way, have to be "split" every three months, which is the average amount of time it takes a worm colony to double in size. (Something else they catch from the rabbits?)

While Alan and Diana Usrey's Peacefield Farms is one-and-three-quarter acres, the parents' city operation, with 26 beds, three sheds, and parking space, occupies only a 120-foot-by-200-foot city lot. Neatly visible throughout the lot, along crushed-gravel paths, are displays advertising many of B's Worm Farm products. Worm food, walnut meal, and worm castings are among the products available. And worms, of course, are also retailed here, selling at 75¢ for a pack of 60 red worms, or $40 for 10,000 for compost or garden. The Usreys also offer a deal for prospective worm farmers. For $400, they'll sell a three-by-eight-by-two-foot bed with 100,000 worms, including compost, fertilizer, and a 100-pound sack of lime flour, and throw in the six-hour course at B's Worm School free. Not only that, but they offer to buy worms back at $2 a pound!

The lot at B's Worm Farm seemed extremely busy for a Tuesday in early March. "People are getting their gardens ready," Geraldine explained. "A worm is so wonderful for the soil because he aerates, irrigates, and fertilizes.

"But business hasn't always been this good," she added. "We didn't start to pull ahead, and really make money in the worm business until about five years ago, when I finally started listening to my husband and we began advertising. That's when we started to pull ahead. You wouldn't believe our advertising budget now: $1,000–$1,500 a month!"

Hearing such an advertising budget, and seeing how busy the tiny farm was on a Tuesday afternoon in March, and rapidly calculating the rapid multiplying habits of worms, I smiled. Here at last, was the magic formula: low overhead business, good market, just remember to advertise! "Yes," Geraldine laughed, "it is a good business, but it's not like plucking money off the trees. And last week I spent $2,000 on worms alone. You have to have a market for that, and developing such a market isn't done overnight. And once you have those worms you've got to feed and water them. When you work for yourself you spend far more hours than if you work for someone else. You have to invest yourself in your own business. But this is the best way I know: Keep it small and keep it in your family!"

Given the high reproductive rates for worms, their ease of mailing and handling, fencing, and feeding, and the growing market for them, there's nothing I learned that would discourage worm farming as a profitable business in any part of the United States. Worms can be wintered over in the coldest climates, and protected and kept moist in the hottest places. The worm's feeding requirements are negligible, and he leaves "castings" more valuable than the feed he consumes. Worms like to fly, or even ride trains if they're packed properly, and it isn't uncommon for California worm farms to supply Vermont gardens and streams. Worms do have to be protected from their natural enemies, and the proper construction of bins is among the few agricultural precautions necessary for successful worm farming. Such requirements seem small compared to the fencing and sanitary chores, for instance, of a dairy farm.

Peacefield Farms, run by Alan and Diana Usrey, is a remarkably diversified operation, but worms provide a major part of the annual income. Diana explained that worms like manure, especially rabbit manure. "To put it another way," she said, "if you've got rabbits, you've got worms!"

Alan was facing a promotion last May at the grocery store where he was already putting in more time than interest, and he quit the job to devote his full-time energies with Diana to the farm. Three children, Tim, Tiffani, and Trina, help with the chores. Of course, Alan's parents, who really got them hooked on worms in the first place, market Peacefield fishing worms and worm castings, which Alan and Diana package and deliver.

Alan was away delivering worms, so I learned the Peacefield story completely from Diana. "We didn't really plan on it," she explained. "Alan's parents had been in the worm business for about 20 years, and they asked if we wanted to care for their guinea pigs and rabbits in return for half the profits. When grain prices started to shoot way up, and the market for rabbits dropped, a lot of rabbit growers went out of business. Except for those rabbit growers who keep worms, things have been pretty rough."

For the Usreys, what started as a very small enterprise has

Alan and Diana Usrey

grown into the family's entire livelihood. "It really is wonderful," said Diana, "because we share equally the indoor and the outdoor work.

"A man in L.A. ran a worm recipe contest. You have to remember that worms have quite a gizzard which means sand or grit, but if you run them through cornmeal like snails, or run cornmeal through them if you wish, they taste a lot like applesauce except not as sweet."

The Usreys find guinea pigs and worms to be seasonal enterprises, whereas rabbits and plants are all-year enterprises. The rabbits are sold as pets and live by the pound for meat. Diana says their plant business thrives because "you can grow anything in worm dirt." Out at one of the sheds she showed me a eucalyptus that was at least six feet. "That tree is just one year old," she smiled. "We started it from seed. Things grow really fast in worm dirt!"

Diana claims that the rabbits and the guinea pigs lose money, but that plants, worms, and their by-products more than offset the loss. "After we figured the books this year I wanted to drop the animals but Alan said 'Where will we get the fertilizer?' and we couldn't find a reliable distributor." And rabbit manure isn't cheap! Four dollars and seventy-five cents a yard, according to Diana. "The plants are just about all profit," explains Diana. "We just take cuttings, and we sell through Alan's mother at B's Worm Farm. To show you how good worm dirt is, once when Alan was working at the grocery, the manager was throwing out some dead-looking dried-out plants. All he did was water them and put them in worm dirt and they started growing again."

Worm dirt, or castings, is mixed with 25 percent peat and 25 percent vermiculite, which help prevent "packing." Diana showed me Alan's packaging machine in one of the sheds. Equipped with a small electric motor, it tumbles, measures, and funnels the completed mix into 325-cubic-inch plastic bags that are already printed with the family business message. Castings are sold through stores and at swap meets throughout Southern California.

Inside another shed are the rabbits, guinea pigs, and the family's flock of chickens. Diana explained that the guinea pigs are sold exclusively to pet stores, and that, because another rabbit grower is in the immediate area, she can sell any rabbits the pet store doesn't want to a buyer who comes regularly to her neighbor-hood. "Netherland dwarf rabbits," she told me proudly, "are the only money-making rabbit. Their popularity is growing especially among small-apartment dwellers. Did you know rabbits can be housebroken?"

The Usreys have diversified their family enterprise in many ways; they have a regular, small income from Geraldine's and Lloyd's farm, which pays them a dollar a dozen for packing worm cups. B's Worm Farm also provides a regular, retail outlet for all their products. Additionally, they sell worms by mail, and Diana says the market for worms by mail is extremely favorable. "We sell worms by the pound, about 1,000 worms per pound, for $9.95. We had to cancel our advertising at one point because the market was too big to handle." Now the Usreys buy and resell worms to insure that they always have an adequate supply. Diana recommends United Parcel Service or Greyhound or airfreight over the post of-fice. "They take better care," she says. "Use the new bags that are made now which allow air in without leaking. We used to pack in boxes that were waxed on the inside, but sometimes they would break or be crushed and worms don't smell good when they die. The post office would get really upset."

The Usreys' small homestead features a large garden, and they sell their surplus produce to neighbors. "One retired man from the mobile home park would walk over here every night to buy a couple of ears of organic corn, then go on to Colonel Sanders for his chicken." In addition to the storage and packing shed, the Usreys have built a double shed for the animals and a greenhouse. Thriv-ing in worm dirt are apricot, almond, nectarine, lemon, and orange trees, as well as plum, cherry, and loquat trees. One-hundred-and-fifty Christmas trees have been planted and a eucalyptus grove will be harvested for firewood. "We simply started with one thing, and added new projects as we got things under control," Diana told me. "Start small—and keep a reserve fund—that's my advice. *And* don't always believe what the experts tell you!"

A note from Diana Usrey arrived several months after my visit with an update. "I thought I would explain a little about the worm market nowadays," she wrote. "It seems many thought it was a get-rich-quick scheme and many have been burned by buying big and left with no market to sell their worms. In fact the market flooded a couple of times. And there have been a few people taken to court because they sold worm beds with 100,000 worms in them and come to find out, there weren't even 20,000. It's problems like that that have made many give up too soon. Worms have so much more going for them than just selling beds to people so they can grow them to sell to more people. For instance, we have expanded our potting mix made of worm castings and it is selling very well. And more and more people are beginning to see how beneficial worms are!"

As Nancy Fisher of Herbs 'n' Honey told me, "The earthworm count is the single most important thing in the garden!"

3.
CRAFTS

Producing and Marketing Crafts

The demand for quality crafts continues to grow, in direct proportion to public dissatisfaction with the cheap perfection of plastic merchandise. "It's no joke," Michael Kinney, a leatherworker from California, told me. "Some crafts factories actually incorporate 'mistakes' into their cutting dyes so the piece will look 'authentic'."

Many craftspeople live in college towns, where the student population provides a good market that is entirely replenished on a two- or four-year cycle, and where the college itself offers the possibility of studio space, the use of equipment, and the chance at an occasional teaching job.

Supplemental Income

Others have discovered the possibility of offering lessons, and in some cases, of opening schools, to supplement their incomes. One enterprising couple, Ed and Vickie Eberle, who manufacture high-quality wooden toys under their company name, Heartwood Toys, have opened a summer camp for teenagers, where they teach survival and homestead skills. The Colorado Outdoor Living Center, as it is called, is located right on their homestead in Hotchkiss, Colorado. It is the Eberles' "compromise" between full-time teaching and country living. "We had been teaching in an alternative high school in Los Angeles and running a wilderness encounter program for several years—rafting and backpacking,"

Ed wrote. "When we moved to the farm here in Colorado we wanted to continue to work with young people but not have a full-time teaching job . . . so the camp."

Ed said that he and Vickie, who work with another young couple during the two-month camp season, are able to keep expenses on the camp at a minimum. Even with their planned-enrollment of only 10 students in each of two $575 four-week sessions, their net income from the camp can provide up to 50 percent of their total income needs. "Our expenses are low because the whole emphasis in the program is to learn to become more self-sufficient—we stick to basic activities like gardening and canning and building—which are low-expense activities. Our buildings aren't fancy (total cost, $3,500 for main lodge and separate bunkhouse) and we don't offer high-risk items like horseback riding or rifle shooting, which would result in high insurance premiums."

Other craftspeople have found less-demanding ways of sharing their knowledge, though it is obvious that their summer homesteading school provides the Eberles with the kind of lucrative diversion they need from the tedium of production. For a craftsperson willing to demonstrate his techniques and discuss methods of production, almost all public and private learning facilities should be considered for supplemental income. You should also contact your state's arts council to inquire whether it might use your services as an "Artist in the Schools." The pay for such work, which usually involves a series of visits to three or four classes in a participating public school, can be as high as $100 a day.

To find part-time teaching work, make up a brief resume listing all teaching experience and exhibits and offering a program, on a per diem basis, that can bring a little outside zip to established programs at colleges and universities. Such part-time "academic" work is usually assigned on a basis of experience and ability rather than formal education.

Crafts Advocate

Among organizations assisting craftspeople, state arts councils are usually the most helpful in recommending the various possibilities. In Vermont, the federal government funded Terry Faith

Weihs, a self-styled "crafts advocate," for four years while she helped establish the Vermont Interagency Crafts Council, two state crafts centers, and "Craft Professionals of Vermont." Terry's principal goal, she told me, has been "to let the state agencies know how we can assist them through handcrafts." This positive approach has resulted in crafts being again regarded as a major resource by state officials, and used as a major aspect of public relations campaigns. "At this point," Terry told me, "it is possible for the craftspeople to move these organizations out from under state government auspices to a more independent and self-sustaining status."

Management

Jan Michael, 31, lives in Solon, Iowa, and has been a part-time guitar maker and repairman on and off for six years. Michael wrote that at one time, his little guitar business provided as much as half his family's income. During this time, he worked full time in his basement and his wife had a job downtown. Michael listed his biggest mistake as "not learning how to organize and run a small business to start with, and not organizing my production with a flow-chart where I could see exactly what was going on where, and how the operation could be streamlined by showing where a particular tool, machine, or fixture would open a bottleneck.

"I'm presently working a regular job, but if I were to go back to guitar work full time, as I expect I may again in the forseeable future, I would consider *very* seriously and pessimistically what:

1) I required to live on, until such time as the business could support itself;
2) What tooling was justified for efficient operation;
3) Overhead such as electricity, heat, etcetera;
4) Business expenses such as insurance, advertising, local permits;
5) Expendable supplies, sandpaper, etcetera;
6) Materials for starting production;
7) About 25 percent more.

"Things *never* but *never* work out as well as you hope and it's sure hard doing your best work when you don't know how you're going to meet that next rent, bank, car payment, or whatever.

Jan Michael

"It's not a bad idea to work part time at a regular job so there is for sure some steady money before you jump off the deep end. When you're certain it will fly, see about raising enough money. You can always pay it back if you don't use it and the interest charge is nominal, but just try going back to a bank and telling them you need a couple quid more than you thought you were going to.

"Figure out efficiency *first*. It's better to make clothespins efficiently for four hours a day and then work on your house, garden, etcetera, than to whittle them out for eleven hours and have to hire someone else to build your house and grow your food.

"Poor management is small business's biggest killer!"

Learning a Craft

Certain crafts are more-readily learned than others, and there are instances where being self-taught has real advantages. If you are lucky enough to live near other craftspeople who are willing to take apprentices, approach them with a *positive* indication of why you want to learn their craft. No one wants a half-committed bumbler taking up space in the shop.

Apprentice

Eric Bauer, a 31-year-old blacksmith from Fayston, Vermont, learned through the *Whole Earth Catalogue* about a course in basic forging operations and forge welding, run by Frank Turley in Santa Fe, New Mexico. "I went for a basic course of instruction and returned a year later to take an advanced course," he told me.

"I must emphasize that probably no method of learning can surpass a good apprenticeship arrangement. It is highly unfortunate that this system has gone by. The remainder of my learning my trade has come from reading everything I can get my hands on, and from visiting other metal shops and talking to other blacksmiths."

Self-Taught

Ross and Paula Simmons, 56 and 54, are full-time partners in Handspun, a 20-year-old wholesale and mail-order business in

Eric Bauer

Suquamish, Washington. When they made their retreat from the city, "we had no practical experience with sheep, and no knowledge of spinning. We learned completely by ourselves. No one else we knew was spinning, and the only book on the subject was then out of print. Being self-taught has a lot of advantages, although it makes for slower learning. But when you do get good at it, you have a style so expressively your own that it is easily recognizable as your own, not just a carbon copy of your teacher's work," Paula wrote.

"Actually, at first we tried goats, but they didn't really keep our pasture down, so we got into black sheep, starting with two old ewes. We kept the best of our lambs, and added to them by the purchase of a black Lincoln ewe from Indiana, and another from Oregon.

"I think the key to business success is to *stick with it*, stay in the same place, doing the same thing, so you build up a following. If you move around, you lose most of your customers every time you move. If you jump from one craft to another, you have a reputation as a dabbler, not a serious craftsperson.

"And be sure to keep track of every single penny of your expenses, so they can be deducted at tax time; don't let one postage stamp or roll of tape go unrecorded, or you lose money when you pay taxes, for you will pay tax on your total income rather than just on your profit."

Paula Simmons has also found writing about her craft to be a lucrative source of extra income. She has published a dozen articles in *Handweaver and Craftsman* magazine, and 11 in *Warp and Weft*, another speciality publication. "These articles have given us a certain amount of exposure among weavers and textile students," she said. "They have also served as a source of income, as I sell sets of reprints of my articles as how-to booklets." And the booklets, in turn, help promote Handspun.

Promotion and Marketing

Hazel I. Diaz Pumara and her husband, Sam, opened a small part-time crafts business, Diaz Handcrafts, in their home in Pine Grove Mills, Pennsylvania, 10 years ago. Mrs. Pumara makes real-flower jewelry, preserving flowers from her organic garden in clear casting resin. Under the same business name, Mr. Pumara manufactures working replicas of antique radio tubes, and custom-made, special-purpose filament lamps. Because Mr. Pumara has a regular job outside the home, Diaz Handcrafts has never felt any real financial pressures, but Mrs. Pumara's letter to me is full of good advice for craftspeople who wish to make more than a part-time living with their skill.

"The publicity-shy businessman *must* recognize the need for product exposure. Word-of-mouth advertising is good but not good enough or fast enough. One must take advantage of every opportunity to get public attention, no matter how it conflicts with personality traits," she wrote.

"I have accepted every invitation to speak at women's and church gatherings. When the Pennsylvania State University asked to film an interview for educational TV, I wanted to refuse but graciously consented because it would put my name and work before many, many thousands. That interview resulted in a TV interview with my husband speaking of his work in antique radio tube replicas.

"In April 1973, I was chosen 'Spare-time Moneymaker' of the month by *Ladies Home Journal*. My letter to them, written after weeks of interior prodding, was chosen from thousands. Their published picture and item provided sales and publicity which continue."

Consignment?

Mrs. Pumara said that her business started with "kitchen table experiments using $10 worth of resin and some fresh flowers. As my skill in handling tricky resin developed, my production increased. To continue with the craft meant finding a means not only to finance it but to dispose of the surplus. At first, consignment selling seemed the easiest way to get necessary exposure. The usual 33⅓ percent for consignment looked better than 50 percent for wholesale.

"In the beginning consignment served its purpose but we discovered that some shops do not have adequate financing, do not display one's work to advantage, have sloppy business procedures with slow payment, and often return work damaged by careless handling.

"We learned to visit the consignment shop before placing merchandise in order to assess the character of the shop and the owner and its clientele, thereby eliminating potential problems. The first person who offered to consign my work managed a discount salvage barn frequented only by bargain hunters!"

Mrs. Pumara is not alone among craftspeople in finding consignment the least-desirable, yet most-often-necessary, means of selling. While in some businesses, particularly in publishing, returned merchandise is virtually inescapable, the problems of damaged returns and slow payment—often a year or more after the item has been "placed"—are enough to discourage all but beginning craftspeople.

Wholesale

The major disadvantage of wholesaling is that it is the least-profitable method of distributing your wares, and that it often requires that you produce a large quantity of any given item. As Mrs. Pumara put it: "We prefer wholesale over consignment, but on a small scale. After one very large sale through an agent to a prestigious store on New York's Fifth Avenue, we have steered clear of large department stores. A craftsman, working alone as I do, seldom finds time or energy to mass-produce. Furthermore, wholesale prices do not compensate for the pressures involved."

Other craftspeople, not anxious to take on the work of retailing, simply establish a "wholesale price" in accordance with what they figure their time and materials to be worth, and offer that price, with a "suggested retail price," to anyone willing to take on the chore of distribution. The Eberles of Heartwood Toys, for instance, have prepared an attractive mimeographed order form and wholesale price list, which is distributed by a friend of theirs, another craftsperson who supplements his own crafts income by selling the work of others. He gets 20-percent-of-wholesale commission. While this means that the Eberles have to settle, for instance, for $20 on their toy farmhouse, which has a suggested retail of $50, it also means they are relieved entirely of marketing problems. They are, of course, free to mark their prices up in accordance with their dealer's commission.

Retail

"The ideal way to sell," according to Mrs. Pumara, "is to retail one's own work. One produces as much as comfortably possible and then sells it either at his own home or where the people are, at crafts fairs or shows. In my case, customers are seen only by appointment since seasonal demands of production require as many uninterrupted hours as possible during warm weather months." In this respect, Mrs. Pumara's experience compares with that of Michael Kinney, the leatherworker, and the Attmores, of the Turquoise Trail Herb Farm, and other retailers: unless you live right where the potential market is, i.e., on a city street, the flea markets and crafts fairs provide the best opportunity for retailing your product.

"Crafts fairs are so popular that one could spend the entire year traveling from fair to fair," wrote Mrs. Pumara. "However, they can be very difficult to manage without adequate help. We have wonderfully responsible younger friends who help to transport displays and wares and also man the booth. These same friends, craftsmen themselves, travel to other fairs, selling their own work as well as mine. This is the sort of mutual benefit association to be recommended for any craft venture."

Cooperation

Similar sorts of cooperation among craftspeople work with varying degrees of happiness, depending on the temperaments of the craftspeople involved. Wood 'n' Wheel Pottery in North Liberty, Iowa, is a successful example of this sort of arrangement. John Myers, a carpenter, rebuilt a barn on his family farm and rents studio and sales space to three other craftspeople whose work, chiefly pottery, helps draw customers. But Myers emphasizes the "independent" nature of many craftspeople and artists. It takes luck and work to make cooperative efforts a happy success.

No craftsperson I met claimed that crafts will ever offer a truly lucrative promise, and nearly everyone stressed that the first three or four years hold the nearly sure prospect of food stamps and disappointment when it comes to finding the market that *is* there, if only you can get to it. And all too often, the "money-maker," like the musician's hit song, is something you'll tire rather quickly of repeating.

Diversification

Diversifying relieves the tedium of production work, and extends the number of products you can offer. "Early in the business I realized that diversification was important to survival," Mrs. Pumara said in her letter. "Trial and error produced some very popular items as well as some absolute duds. My pressed-flower bookmarks and solid, clear resin bells are low-priced, boring to make, and the kind of money-makers one needs when other sales are slow."

"Have a line that's unique," Ed Eberle recommended. "All toy companies offer cars and trucks—we do too. But we also have several unique toys such as a zoo, circus wagon, and animal mobiles that are attractive, unique, and therefore excellent sellers."

"These little ashtrays I make," potter Rodney Tidrick told me, "sell for only a dollar each, but they take up spaces in the kiln that are too small for anything else."

Hazel I. Diaz Pumara summed it all up: "I advise that craftspeople hoping to make a living from their work have adequate capital and not plan to live on profits for at least two years. And, they should acquire a basic knowledge of business management and learn basic accounting.

"You have to accept the fact that self-employment is seldom the road to quick sufficient income, and that the compensations are not always worth the sacrifices. If your motive is getting away from a boss, realize that to profit you will have to make demands on yourself that no boss or employer could."

Self-Restraint

Mrs. Pumara continued, "Self-employment in a home industry is ideal for workaholics, but dangerous. Without rigid self-discipline one can easily develop a potentially dangerous life-style, unbalanced in favor of too much work, too little recreation, with the excuse that one's work is also one's relaxation.

"When one works alone, every business-related activity consumes excessive amounts of time needed for production.

Answering the phone, correspondence, receiving leisurely customers, packing and shipping, all are time-guzzlers. Labeling, picking, and packing before a fair can take a full day or much more. The management of time must be given as much or more consideration than managing finances."

And, I would add, all this overhead must be figured in when it comes time to determine a fair price to ask for your work!

Small Publishers and Printers

Book production is at once among the most challenging and versatile cottage-industry opportunities. In spite of the inroads on communication made by television and radio, print remains our primary communications medium. The history of printing is fairly dull for the long period following Gutenberg's revolutionary invention until the twentieth century, when offset printing began to open whole new possibilities. Suddenly, without the costly and separate processes of setting type and making special plates for graphic additions, text and illustration could be prepared and pasted together. Even hand-scribble could be added to top it all off. Virtually whatever two-dimensional object you can fit on the page can be handsomely reproduced, inexpensively, by the offset method.

The prospective publisher or printer should realize that not only has he two major types of printing from which to choose, but that the processes of making a book are so varied that he might wisely settle on just one specialty, and, like Al and Jane Wonch, hire himself out free-lance to other bookmakers in his area. The Wonches compose book pages in their home for a big publishing company.

Bookmaking can be broken into six areas: writing, editing, designing, printing, binding, and selling. Each of these categories can be divided; for instance, printing involves the composing of the page (typesetting) and the printing itself. Composing is the physical translation of the designer's plan, and for this reason a designer must be knowledgeable in the limitations of the medium faced by the composer.

Because the print industry is in the midst of so much technical upheaval, the times are right for acquiring "outdated" equipment, which is heavy and difficult to move, and therefore usually available very cheaply from shops that are converting from letterpress to offset, or going from old offset to a more sophisticated system. I know a printer who was offering a linotype machine and a large platen press for $75 each, discounted 30 percent if you'd haul away his paper cutter, which new government codes declared unsafe and illegal for use in a shop with employees.

Given sufficient space and a solid floor, you could, like Allan and Cinda Kornblum, outfit a letterpress shop with fairly good equipment for a song, simply by locating all the printers listed in the Yellow Pages and asking what old equipment they want to be rid of.

A more expensive, but less space-consuming and more trouble-free way to go into printing is to find a small offset press and an electric typewriter with changeable type fonts (such typewriters vary in cost and performance from a few hundred dollars for older but capable clunkers, to thousands for computerized composers, which offer the versatility of an entire print shop; investigate the possibility of leasing such a machine, or of renting time on one that is conveniently located).

If you do choose offset, you will also need either the equipment to photograph and make a master plate from the dummy page, or be near a shop that does such work. This is an expensive part of the offset process. Costs can be cut considerably if you're willing to settle for paper instead of aluminum master plates; paper has a shorter press life, usually about 1,000 copies, whereas metal plates last indefinitely and can be stored for future use.

The Crossing Press

John and Elaine Gill live on an old farm in Trumansburg, New York; at one time or another each of them has taught at the college level, most recently in the 1960s when they were on the faculty of Ithaca College, which is about 10 miles from Trumansburg. Cornell University is also in Ithaca, and the Gills have become, since their retirement from academia, leaders in what might be called the renaissance of tiny Trumansburg. Their farmhouse, which is also headquarters of The Crossing Press, has become a gathering place for local poets, actors, musicians, innkeepers, and other former denizens of Ithaca College and Cornell.

It has taken John and Elaine 10 years to develop their printing operation from the tiny one-man hobby it started as to the booming two-person enterprise that is threatening to gross $50,000 this year. "Just throw yourself in," is John's advice. "I started with an old typewriter and a secondhand Gestetner, which is nothing more than a hand-cranked mimeograph machine. And I did everything: typed the masters, ran the mimeo, folded and stapled the pages, wrapped and shipped, and kept the books. This was for my little quarterly magazine of poetry, *New American and Canadian Poetry*. Then I decided to put out little poetry chapbooks the same way."

John is tall and thin, with a gray beard; Elaine is a large, strong, almost imposing person with a hard gaze and an uncanny ability at formulating intuition: they are ageless, but I know from asking that they are in their late forties. Their two sons, Dan and Lor, are 17 and 14. "People start publishing houses according to the way they are," Elaine told me. "John's start was organic. In other words he made a book, he put together sheets of paper and he stapled them and he discovered ways to use a mimeo machine so that the show-through wouldn't matter, he folded the sheets so that they would go unprinted on one side, and he made the book and then proceeded to sell it. Other kinds of people would probably go at it differently. And arrange the selling first and make the book to fit the market. I see that there are different kinds of minds. Ours works this way. A book has to be organically arrived at, we actually literally make the book and then we start selling it."

"Sounds like a good idea," mused John.

"Well, sometimes I think the other way is probably better. The idea of marketing a book in your head first and then making the book is probably sounder financially. But I really can't see us doing that. Our books are not commodities, and I like to think it's what distinguishes us from other publishing houses. For better or for worse."

John looked up thoughtfully. "One of the things most important for starting in publishing is to have a sense of what it means to be an editor. Whatever it is you're publishing should have both glamor and integrity."

"Either that," added Elaine, "or you need considerable skill as a merchandiser, in the sense of knowing what the public wants. Either way would be all right, or a combination of the two, which is what John and I have. I usually know when a book has commercial promise. This ability, which is not the same as skill as an editor, requires that you define a market need and then find a writer to satisfy that need. To sum up, anybody can start a publishing house, but you need some capital, you have to have some idea of what you want to publish, or of what people will buy, and then you just do it."

John emphasized that The Crossing has evolved gradually. And that there are more than a few ways to run a press. "A completely different approach is fine printing, where you produce these really exquisite letterpress books, but that requires money for the good presses, and the fancy papers, and the time and patience and the *talent* to be a fine printer. Then you could sell to select buyers—a specialized market—for the craft of printing. But I think that would be very difficult.

"I wanted to learn to be a printer and so I went to the local high school and talked to the print teacher there and he asked, 'Do you really care how it looks on the page—do you want it exquisitely right? Or do you want people to read it?' And I said, 'I want people to read it.' And he said, 'Good. Stay away from letterpress and get into offset.' He focused me very nicely.

"And we quickly outgrew mimeograph; I wanted something a little more sophisticated, so I bought a used Multilith 1000 offset press and put it in the back room and learned the methods of offset printing. We were getting a little bigger, so I started to pay Daniel and Lor a penny for each book they collated. Somehow the rough-hewn look of books produced this way enhances their integrity. But certainly that doesn't have much to do with the marketplace as it exists in this culture where the present consciousness dictates that the product must appear glamorous and look sophisticated and beautiful and slick. So in one sense, because we were sort of rough-hewn and homegrown, we had to fight to get our way into bookstores and to find distributors."

John threw up his hands and invited me to the filing room where a telephone man was installing an extension phone. The

Gills had decided to offer a friend office space and a small commission for taking over the promotion of their books. John opened a large filing cabinet's lowest drawer. It was stuffed with legal-sized envelopes and larger ones; probably 25 pounds, in all, of poetry. "These are submissions for a regional anthology we intend to publish. I've already sent back all the ones I know we can't print. Now the job is to find the poems we do want. I suppose I've already rejected about three times as many manuscripts as are in this file.

"Finding the needles among such haystacks is one job. Publishing them's another. And then, finally, selling them is the biggest job. One of the most annoying things is how poetry gets condensed in the booksellers' minds. Right now there is a very annoying master list, issued by the American Booksellers' Association, of 'Books that Sell', that is circulating among bookstore owners. A lot of small bookstores obviously only want to give up their limited space to books that are endorsed by such a list.

"Anyway, there was a committee that made up a list of poets. I think four poets are listed: Denise Levertov, Robert Lowell, maybe Allen Ginsberg, and maybe Gary Snyder. And this was considered to be the list booksellers would use to stock books without taking any risk. Once I went to a big bookstore on Fifth Avenue with two of our anthologies, to ask if they'd sell them, and the manager said, 'Oh I'm sorry but poetry doesn't sell. Go away.' He was polite, but he didn't want anything to do with my product. So I looked for a poetry section in that store, and it was at the farthest point from the entrance, at a rear wall up at the second-level balcony, in a corner down on the bottom shelf. It took me five minutes to find this place that wasn't well lit, and I had to get down on my hands and knees to look at the poetry. No wonder it doesn't sell!"

"It's a hard way to make a living," Elaine said.

In spite of such difficulties, The Crossing Press does remarkably well, if my casual perusal of college town and underground bookstores is any indication. Elaine explained this as being largely due to "going commercial. In 1973 we became commercial. We decided to change, and we began with Lyn Lifshin's *Black Apples*, which was the first effort toward mixing physical glamor with editorial integrity. But it's very hard to change the image of a press. If you start out one way people will dislike changing their idea of you. It's somehow as if people maintain the illusion that they themselves can change but that others cannot. It's very hard to change the image of a business. We did it. It's been very difficult. We're successful now.

"In short we started using typefaces that look like typefaces to make books that look like books. And within two years we were commercial. We started using glossy cover stocks, and employing designers to help solve certain production problems. In our present evolution, this means that the only work we do ourselves is the work that involves editing and control of the master. In other words we either have the type set or we set it ourselves, and we employ a designer. But we do the actual paste-up of the master, which is like a collage, little bits and pieces that you plunk down on a piece of cardboard with rubber cement. We maintain strict control over this, and over what papers are used, but that's as far as we go. From there it's taken over by printers and binders. But we are the ones who must take the intricate pains with the details that make the difference between a professional book and an amateur one. And we maintain a very personal association with our printers. In other words, these people are our friends. And we have a real working relationship. And we all really sweat to have the product look good."

The Gills told me that federal grant assistance is very helpful to small presses. The National Endowment for the Arts and the Coordinating Council of Literary Magazines, as well as the state arts councils, provide subsidy funds for small presses that are engaged in printing literature. John said that grants committees are more generous with high-quality publishing efforts than with mimeograph magazines, for instance. "He who has gets: To get a lot of bread you have to look good, look as if your publication costs as much as you're asking for."

Fortunately for small press operations, you need no longer be recognized as a nonprofit organization to be eligible for public assistance. "The administrators are beginning to view such money as 'seed money'," John said. "The federal government subsidizes quite a large segment of American life, whether through military contracts, or through oil depletion allowances, or through sugar subsidies. So in one sense the government represents a very large portion of the profit-making economy. So why not in the arts? We certainly couldn't have done what we've done without such grants."

"It is important," said Elaine, "to act like the people who are giving the grants are human beings. And if you aren't learning what's happening with your application don't be afraid to phone them up and get to know them. It takes about three years for people to get to know you, but it's worth the effort. Because in the end they'll help you get what you need."

The Crossing Press has a well-organized bookkeeping system, which is simple and effective. Almost all business is conducted by mail, which makes careful bookkeeping a necessity. Elaine stressed that Book Rate is the only economical way to ship books, because there's no zoning involved in this mail classification. A book can be mailed anywhere in the country for a single rate, determined by its weight.

When an order comes in, the Gills check the credit of the customer in question. If it is an initial order, they request payment in advance; any order over $35 is automatically insured. John said that on occasion he has had reason to suspect that books reported "unreceived" were *not* lost in the mail. The only way to guard against such unscrupulous actions is to insure big shipments.

The order is received, credit is checked, and then an invoice is written in duplicate. Next comes writing up a mailing label, packaging the order, enclosing one invoice and keeping the other. The retained invoice is attached to the purchase order (or letter ordering the book), and then filed by number. Every order that comes in receives a number (the numbers are assigned in order, and the top purchase order in the file I saw was numbered 7241, which indicated that The Crossing Press had filled 7,241 orders since operations began).

This file is then cross-referenced with another file, in which customers are listed alphabetically on three-by-five-inch index cards that carry a running list of the books ordered by that customer and the dates of shipment and of payment receipt, as well as invoice number. This file, which by Elaine's estimate, contains at least 4,500 names, is divided into three categories: bookstores, libraries, and individuals. Big accounts, ones needing more space than that afforded by three-by-five-inch cards, go on four-by-six-inch cards. Elaine called this "a very simple bookkeeping system where anything can be traced. Beyond that we have to know how many copies of each title are sold in a given year, and this requires one separate file which we always keep up-to-date."

The Gills have found that unexpected reviews or mention in key publications can bring orders in surprising quantity. They published an anthology of gay poetry, *The Male Muse*, edited by Ian Young, which was the first of its kind. Sales bumped along at a normal rate for the first three years. "Then The Book People, a hip distributing outfit in Berkeley, included us in a four-page spread in their national catalogue and people started to learn about the book, and sales suddenly took off. Now it's about to go into a third printing," John said.

"But a much more typical sales figure for a book of poetry by an individual poet, is more like 1,000, unless he or she has a real national reputation. A first printing of any more than that would be really chancy. There are exceptions. Lifshin's *Black Apples* sold 3,500 so far, and we printed 5,000 copies of Alta's book, *I Am Not a Practicing Angel,* but that's because of the feminist market. It's a double market. And she gives lots of readings, which helps promote her books."

"Through a lot of work and sweat you can produce a beautiful book," said Elaine, "but where the work really comes in is the promotion and selling. We're now in the national catalogue for The Book People, and we work with wholesalers, and we also do our own mail promotions from here, flyers, catalogues, and we go around to book fairs, and we're starting to become more actively engaged with marketing through the help of this local person. In short, we use every method of distribution available. It took us eight years to get the poetry market figured to the point where we could begin to explore it to its fullest."

"It also helps," she continued, "that our books are finally being reviewed regularly in the *Library Journal*. Everytime you start something new, the market's totally different. We're starting now to understand something about children's books, and we have expanded our list to include original literature for children, such as *Walk When the Moon is Full*, by Frances Hamerstrom, and Joseph Bruchac's *Turkey Brother and Other Iroquois Folk Tales*. And this is natural for us, because poets write wonderful children's stories. Why not? They tell them to their children. And we've started publishing cookbooks too. With each new market we have different tastes, but we realize the potential of the children's market is at least four times that of poetry. At least. In other words a good children's book will sell 20,000 copies or more, at least, whereas in poetry a book would have to be really unusual to sell more than 5,000. What John said is true: 'It took about eight months of conscious application to the fundamentals of producing an attractive book. Discovering how to market is taking two years already and will probably take another three before we even know where we are. The biggest major reason is that it takes more than a decent-looking book to convince the wholesaler to give up precious warehouse space to your product. He's not taking any financial risks to carry your books, except in terms of his limited space. But to convince him in the first place, you need reviews. And to get reviews, to get reviewers to even look at your book, is a giant problem of public relations, which is another problem, altogether.'

"We're trying to solve ours by long-distance telephone conversations, tied in with letters and mass mailings. It's pretty lousy, because even after all this is done, and the wholesaler finally agrees to carry your books, you have to wait about another year before you're paid. But our books do sell, once we get them into the bookstores. It would be really nice if we could generate enough excitement at those necessary higher levels that we didn't have to go to all this sweat at public relations, which is a terrible waste of energy," she said. "I hate it."

John recommended three publications as essential to the small publisher. First is Clifford Burke's *Printing It*. Second is the *Publish It Yourself Handbook*, edited by Bill Henderson, published by Pushcart Press. Finally, he said, "Anybody who's starting a small press should immediately write to Richard Morris, Box 703, San Francisco, California 94101, and ask for the *COSMEP Newsletter*, and for their membership rates. They publish all sorts of helpful brochures and catalogues. And it's a democratic, populist organization."

"We've simply gone from one book to the next with occasional working for others and with grants, which were sizable only in 1975," Elaine told me. "It's a business where you could start for less than $500 if you were careful. We actually started with zero capital and no borrowing, but if you wanted to be profitable right away, you'd need more sophisticated equipment than what we used.

"You know," she said, eyeing me sternly, "I've seen a lot of small presses muddling, undefined, unfocused. They wonder why their books don't sell. I would urge that people be clear about who they are and what they're doing before they jump into this or any other business.

"It should be emphasized that while there are many ways to 'cut corners' in this business, none of it will help unless the published book is something that people will want and even have to have. And here you touch upon the intangible editorial sense of publishers, where taste and intuition tell an editor, 'This book is one I want to publish because I like and respect it—it is life-giving—and I think others (the buyers) will realize it when they see the finished book in a store.' And the publisher gambles that he is right. And he has to be right, most of the time, if he wants to stay in business."

Greentree Books

Vernon and Wendy Bender, of Sooke, British Columbia, started Greentree Books, "to make handmade books about practical subjects: gardening, beekeeping, goat raising, recipes, and a few impractical books of poetry." The Benders also offer a job printing service, and are "busier than we'd like to be with designing and printing tickets, letterheads, business cards, personal stationery, etcetera. Now our fame (and low prices) have spread to Victoria, where we deliver and pick up printing one day a week as well as deliver eggs, vegetables, honey, homemade peanut butter, and goat's milk yogurt." The Benders wrote me that they have a tiny natural food store on their property as well as a printing shop. "And sharing our nine beautiful acres are three goats and thirty-eight chickens."

"In summary," they wrote, "we seek here a mastery of a group of skills that will allow us to depend less and less on a distant technology for the things we need to live comfortable lives. There is so much to learn and it is so exciting to learn real, tangible skills that time has become a problem, time to simply sit in the garden or walk on the beach."

Magic Circle Press

Valerie Harms Sheehan, 36, started Magic Circle Press, a publishing company in Weston, Connecticut, four years ago. Valerie wrote that she had no formal training in publishing. Presently, the business "just breaks even, but I intend to have it show a profit in the next two years.

"The key lies in good marketing. Half my struggle has been to become part of a larger company's marketing program. In order to do that you have to have a track record, which I finally established." Valerie said that annual operating expenses for Magic Circle have steadily increased as the number of books undertaken each year has increased. Because she does not typeset and print Magic Circle books, her expenses are relatively high, but her time is free for editing, book design, promotion, and sales. By now, Magic Circle has expanded and diversified, so its list includes an anthology of poetry by women in prison, a book in celebration of Anaïs Nin, and children's books, including Ruth Krauss' *Little Boat Lighter than a Cork*, and *Diary of a Monarch Butterfly*, by Susan L. Thompson, with drawings by Sas Colby.

"My biggest business mistake has been to allow too much time to pass before collecting on unpaid bills," she said, echoing a theme I have heard from other small press people. "Several big customers eluded paying me because I was too kind, i.e., stupid." Anyone who runs a small press and seeks reasonable distribution terms is encouraged to contact COSMEP, and CODA, two small press organizations that maintain up-to-date information on cooperative distribution services and federally subsidized print centers where a publisher can have his books printed at a fraction of commercial rates. These books must usually be classifiable as "literature."

The Kornblums' Print Shop

Allan and Cinda Kornblum are a young couple who have bought an old house in West Branch, Iowa, just outside Iowa City, and outfitted a complete letterpress print shop for less than $1,000.

Pointing to the many commercial printers who are abandoning the "old-fashioned" letterpress for the more versatile offset printing method, Allan advised: "Pick a state and hit every small town and its newspaper and print shops and just ask everywhere if they have any old equipment for sale. It's still not too late if you can find these shops before the antique dealers do!"

"It's a good idea to buy equipment that isn't too far away," added Cinda. "Moving presses and paper cutters takes money or a lot of energetic friends."

The Kornblums' shop consists almost entirely of secondhand equipment. Their first purchase, a 10-inch-by-15-inch, chase-size Challenge platen press, which Allan said is "really all you need for setting up a small job shop," was located by friends. "I'd sent the word out among other printers that I was looking for a press and they mentioned they'd heard of one sitting at Community Auction, but that it wasn't being auctioned, and was waiting for a buyer. A mere $35 later, I was the proud owner of a half-ton white elephant. We dragged it onto a U-Haul, and from there to a friend's garage, while we looked for a new home for us and the press, because we were in the process of being evicted by urban renewal.

"We found a suitable house with a closed-in porch that had a strong floor, and we found a few strong friends who helped us move our new press again. Then I heard about a printer who was about to move and was selling duplicates of some equipment, and from him I bought a cabinet of 'furniture', the wood blocks that go around type, and many of the other necessary accessories to letterpress printing.

"We spent the first year or so of operation with only one typeface, a gift, in one size. It was enough type for book printing, but we needed variety for commercial jobs. We heard of a printer who had died, and his sister was selling his shop. We split the shop with another friend who didn't need all the weird type because he only wanted to print books. We also bought a paper cutter, and two little cabinets of ornaments and borders. With the purchase of that old printer's type, I had enough to do a moderately brisk business as a small job printer, although ideally it is good to have at least one typeface in roman and italic in 6, 8, 10, 12, 14, 18, 24, and 36 points, with a variety of display faces. After that, you can slowly add a bit here and there."

Allan Kornblum

Like Vernon and Wendy Bender, the Kornblums' job printing subsidizes their real publishing interest, which is poetry. To differentiate between their publishing and job printing efforts, they use two press names, The Toothpaste Press for poetry, and The Universal Letter for their printing business that promotes "Handset-Letterpress Small Job Printing" with a beautifully designed, carefully printed card.

The Universal Letter specializes in business cards, stationery, wedding invitations, "and occasional tickets." But Allan and Cinda have a long list of potential projects. Allan suggested that "anyone who wants to establish a thriving job-printing business" should consider printing wine labels, funeral and church programs, high school diplomas, and similar work, where individual appearance and high quality are necessary.

The Kornblums are always looking for interesting, low-cost paper. At one auction, Allan bought a few cartons filled with some yellowed old shipping tags. Then he approached the owner of a local antique store, offering a unique promotional message. The owner bought the idea, and he now wires his message, printed on the old shipping tags, to every piece he sells.

"If you want the work," Allan told me, "it's there. Print up a sample and take it around. Find paper that's interesting and cheap, such as the yellowed 'junk' I buy at auctions, old wallpaper, anything that's different and almost free. Keep a file of your customers, with samples from every job you've done for them along with their remarks."

John Franchot,
Story Street Goldsmiths

Anyone visiting John Franchot's retail shop, Story Street Goldsmiths, in December, will become immediately aware of one of jewelry-making's greatest disadvantages. Looking through the display windows, the Chrsitmas shopper can see two employees: a saleswoman and an armed policeman. "I only have him for the month of December," John explained when I visited him. "In December the contradictions intensify. That's when some people feel most desperate. Also, it's a form of advertising. The presence of a guard shows that we have something worth protecting.

"Security is a big part of this business, because crime is a big part of this society. And the business is a big part of my life as a goldsmith, so I take care. Even though the business is fully insured, I hire a guard to help prevent armed robbery. A robbery is like a rape—it's extremely bad for everyone's morale, including the thief's."

Besides a saleswoman and his December guard, John employs one other person, who runs errands and carries messages from the store to John's workshop. "I have never hired strangers," John told me. "These are people I know and trust. They're my friends, and this is the way I've always gone. In one way or another, it *has* cost me several friendships, but selling jewelry is very difficult. The jewelry has to be appreciated by the salesperson, and for this reason each piece requires specialized knowledge. When someone comes in to purchase a piece of jewelry, that person is looking for something that will act as an extension of his or her identity. This makes for demanding customers."

Even though his shop is located only a few blocks from Harvard Square, John sells very little of his work to students. "They can't afford it," he said frankly. "I sell to the intelligentsia and silent upper class. Harvard Square may be busy, but my store is normally very quiet."

I had entered the store and smiled at the guard, as I edged past him into the spacious showroom. The saleswoman was emptying the display cases and John, talking on the phone, motioned me to make myself at home. It was 5:30 P.M., and we had agreed to meet at the store at closing, and walk over to Cardell's for coffee.

"I'm not sure if I had it to do over that I would get into owning a store," he mused at Cardell's. "The initial growth period tends to be all-embracing, to the exclusion of everything else. The question is what is the most truly enhancing environment for my work, and what are the limitations of my activity? You have to do what you like to do, what nourishes you. It's a question of style and of discernment. Being out front with your own store has an advantage: It throws you into the mainstream, and is far less isolated than the wholesale business. But this is also its disadvantage. If you have any desire to make art, you have to ask how your work is going to live with other people.

"A piece of art must leave your own possession and go into someone else's life to continue its existence. The artist needs this feedback, though it is a cruel taskmaster, when translated into the idea of retail business."

I am often surprised to see artistic friends (who, when they were still supported by their parents, would sneer at the evils of Capitalism) coping, and sometimes at a handsome profit, with the marketplace. When Elaine Gill said that p. r. work and general distribution of her books is "a big waste of energy" in spite of the fact that she does it *successfully*, when John Franchot dislikes the pressures of compromise that "must be circumvented while striving for successful retailing," I begin to wonder how many artists end up making their art on weekends for the enjoyment of a few friends, and working 40 hours per at Giants selling the makings of a machine.

Franchot is skeptical of the usefulness of crafts co-ops, because in his experience they are often "fraught with idealism. There are so many political ideologies of 'how it should be' that it becomes difficult to accomplish actual selling and making. You can spend a great deal of time obtaining consensus on various political and aesthetic considerations within the co-op itself. While this is an interesting and perhaps valuable experience, it doesn't necessarily contribute in the least to either the personal development of one's art or the solution of problems inherent in selling and remaining financially viable. The continual conflict between personal ideals and the public reality of business in our society is the source of many impulses to close out some of the difficulties inherent in this struggle to create. Craftspeople in co-ops find various opportunities to 'ease the struggle', often at some personal expense. Or such is my view."

Disappointed with co-ops, seeing little hope for personal growth while working on a wholesale basis, John decided to open his own store. "One of the realities of a retail business, and of my store, is that it can change very fast. I'm sure by the time these words are in print, the form of my store will be very different. One of the reasons I work so hard at this is to know that quality, which is like sailing where the weather is always changing, is an attainment: being able to control your life. I believe one of the essences of small business is the opportunity to work at the limits of your capabilities and retain the capacity to keep things in order. This can be thought of as a chance for a particular kind of manifestation of harmony."

John Franchot is 30 years old. He has owned his store for five years. He started in California as a silversmith, working wholesale making what he calls "good jewelry that I was proud of" for three years. John explains that there is a difference between "good jewelry" and "precious-metal art," which is what he is now striving to produce. "In jewelry-making the forces of Capitalism come to bear very heavily. Every bit you give in quality comes from your own pocket because you're competing with the mass market, which involves low-cost materials, mechanical factory production, modern sales techniques, and high volume. I'm no longer interested in that sort of wholesale work. After three years of it, I realized I had three choices: 1) Give in and produce crap. 2) Stay *poor.* 3) Do different. There is just no room for adequate expression in the wholesale operation; the financial push kills your initiative. So I decided to open my own store and to pursue precious-metal art.

"There are two kinds of jewelry and two kinds of each of those. There is costume jewelry and there is art jewelry. In costume jewelry, there is either precious or nonprecious materials; in art jewelry, there is also either new imagery or old imagery. It is interesting that in the past several years, a certain group of artist-jewelers have turned to feathers and plastic, avoiding many of the hassles of precious materials. And certain galleries have encouraged this for their own reasons.

"An important consideration in jewelry-making is to be clear on your goals. Act in terms of the reality. You can work in costume jewelry with the goal of moving to art jewelry. Depending on which kind of jewelry you choose, your life activity will be very different."

Opening the store required an eventual capital outlay of $20,000, and John claims that "after five years, I'm satisfied. I've lived off the business for five years and have paid hundreds of thousands of dollars to those who have worked for me. I've gotten some possessions and taken some trips and gained some education. You've got to recognize that any real experience you have can be transformed to leading you somewhere you haven't been. If you have that knack your 'equity' is multiplied. Often people do not recognize this and thus they limit their spheres of experience. It takes effort to make a change. The $20,000 that went into the business is still there, in terms of the actual value of what I have, yet I know my experience to be of even greater value. But calling the experience part of my 'equity' tends to minimize its real value."

I glanced at my watch. I'd promised John I wouldn't prolong our conversation beyond his 6:45 P.M. appointment. "It's okay," he said. "I can be a little late.

"Jewelry is the easiest craft to sell, and the hardest art to sell. America as a culture is based on substitution. Anything of established worth is immediately replaced by something cheaper and of less value. Few can afford anything decent because what's real costs so much. This is the result of decades of hidden inflation. The substitute, which works almost as well, is so much cheaper. Everyone is surrounded by this abuse of Capitalism, and most of us have lost the ability to appreciate real value. In particular this has contributed to a transformation of the meaning of jewelry, so that most people can be fulfilled by costume jewelry.

"Another difficulty which is exacerbated by the workings of Capitalism in our society is the confusion between the exchange value (monetary) of the materials that comprise jewelry and the value of the aesthetic experience these materials combine to enhance. A drawing is evaluated wholly by aesthetics, it has no intrinsic value. But the value of jewelry has a double possibility of interpretation: Some people want simply the investment in the materials, while others like the experience of relating with a piece of art. Therefore the ease and difficulty in selling craft and art in jewelry!"

By now it was almost 7 P.M., and he shook my hand warmly, inviting me to call on him again whenever I was in Cambridge. "Just tell your readers that owning a small business is neither romantic nor exciting from the inside," he said. "It's only a mainstream activity, muddled and compromised, demanding and frustrating." Then he smiled, and said, "So what else is new?"

Michael Kinney, Leatherworker

"The key to financial success is finding and then specializing in a high-quality item where competition is slim. Then your worst problem is fighting the boredom and tedium of making that same thing, over and over." Michael Kinney is a 32-year-old Bay Area leatherworker, who specializes in three basic leather notebook designs, and can make as many as 80 notebooks a week. "Feedback tells you what's popular—but you can really get bogged down in the repetitiveness of satisfying that demand.

"After you get good at what you do, once you've figured out as many shortcuts as there are, still doing it all by hand, you reach a point of maximum production—you simply cannot increase your volume. But demand continues to grow, and you are confronted with a big decision: 'Should I go full-scale and hire assistants and buy a lot of expensive, production equipment?' If you take that step, you'll have to face the fact that what you're doing is being a businessperson and not a craftsperson, and your pleasure is going to have to come from running a business, not from handcrafting something useful."

We were in the small studio (about 20 feet by 28 feet) that Michael shares with another craftsperson, whose speciality is copper and glass. As the discussion progressed, Michael repeatedly tapped designs into rectangular pieces of leather that would eventually be dyed, stained, and bound into notebooks, journals, or address books.

"Presently I'm negotiating with a large New York store that wants to carry my journals, and the question I'm facing now is whether to enlarge or turn down their offer. It seems that in business there's an inevitable tendency toward growth—as demand increases, your enterprise keeps wanting to get bigger. It takes on a life of its own.

"This kind of freaks me out. I got into this kind of work largely for the freedom. I like not having to do anything I don't really want to do. But if I get into book production as a full-scale business, I won't be able to afford the luxury of saying no anymore. A further argument against expansion is that if you don't like working for others, what's the sense of having someone work for you?"

Kinney once worked as a free-lance copy editor for many publishing concerns, including *Rolling Stone* and *Not Man Apart*, and was "puttering" in leather, he said, as a hobby, while he supported himself by editing—"using my education, as they say," he added, smiling. "And I'd made a few journals for friends, and they started coming back and asking if they could get more for their friends.

"The editing work was drying up, and so I asked a friend who was selling jewelry on the streets what I needed to do to sell, and he said, 'Nothing. Not even a permit!' So I made a batch of journals, took them down to the street, and sold them all. I made $100 my first day!

"I'd never made $100 in a single day before, and conveniently forgetting all the hours I'd spent the week before, making those books, I decided this was really a great little business. That first year of selling books was somewhat haphazard, but very casual, quite easy. I'd make up a batch of books in my bedroom, and spend one or two days a week out selling them.

"Then things just started to grow. I discovered the crafts fairs, and found they were much more profitable and a more efficient use of my selling time than hawking on the streets.

"Slowly but surely I found myself spending less and less time selling, working longer at making the stuff, and going with a few, high-quality crafts fairs run by promoters I trust, who have come to know me and my work. If they like your stuff, they contact you for every fair they have, and these fairs can become your entire retail-sales market—just four or five big fairs a year, which is what has happened to me. And over the years, I've developed a pretty good wholesale business as well—usually making my initial contact with the store owners at one of these fairs."

He recommends leatherwork as a craft—or a business—that is fairly easy to start with little money. Overhead is extremely low. Michael shares the $60 monthly rent on his studio, which is in a former steel fabricating plant that is presently occupied by about 20 young artisans. The tools of his trade are few and inexpensive. "A good knife, a good straightedge, dyes, about $40 worth of hand-tools including edgers, groovers, cutters, a swivel knife, and a few stamping tools."

Although we'd only been talking for half an hour, Michael had already stamped, since my arrival, intricate designs into at least half-a-dozen "blanks." Looking them over, I noticed that a star was missing from an otherwise symmetrical pattern. "Oh, leave it," he laughed. "To someone, that will be a guarantee it's handmade. No kidding, there are big producers now who use stamps with errors intentionally built in.

"The most important thing to learn is about the nature of leather, about all the different kinds of leather, what each is suited for, and the difference between a good hide and a bad one. Leather comes tanned in many ways, which determine its properties and suitability for certain uses. Which is the right thickness? Which animal skins to use?" He recommends dealing with leather wholesalers or a shoe findery (so named because it supplies shoe manufacturers with leather and with metal accessories known as "findings") as the best sources of leather and reliable advice. "They know more and charge less than the people at the hobby shops."

Showing me a notebook he recently made that had a sculpted human foot inlaid in the cover, Michael recommended two books as especially helpful to the beginning leatherworker. "Both *Modern Leather Design* and *Brendan's Leather Book* emphasize getting away from traditional tooling and into more innovative possibilities. For instance, working with color and with inlays like this plaster foot. I'm making a series, which I plan to sell through an art gallery, of six 'anatomy journals', with inlays that include a cast foot, a nose, a breast, and more!"

Although he is basically a production leatherworker, Michael will admit to being a "bookbinder"—"if I'm trying to impress people. But generally I try to avoid custom work, like binding or repairing people's books for them, unless the project really interests me. It takes twice the time of my regular work but I can't charge twice as much, and people often want me doing something I don't want to do, like a gaudy cover for a dignified Bible. And mistakes in custom work are a disaster, whereas in your own work you can simply incorporate errors into the design. Nine times out of ten I screw up on jobs I don't really want to do. On the other hand, I recognize that some of the finest craftspeople take tremendous satisfaction in this kind of challenge, and often do more custom than production work, although this usually keeps them from making much money.

"In the long run I think the craftspeople I've seen who succeed have either been really good businesspeople who get into high production and have lots of sales outlets, or slower-moving, high-quality people who have developed a small but reliable group of buyers. The higher profits are usually in the production category, though not always the artistic satisfaction. There's a kind of pecking order in crafts not related to the amount of money you make, but an order that holds production people, who are making the most money, on the bottom, and those who work more as artists, scrimping by, at the top. A very few of those craftspeople, some of the best, have achieved recognition and do well for themselves, but I'd say that they're the exception.

"Choosing what fairs to attend is important. If I get a letter inviting me to a fair I have to ask what kind of people will be there, what kind of environment will be provided, and who is the advertising geared to? Young marrieds, professional people, little old ladies, and college-educated single people seem to be the people most attracted to a blank book. In choosing fairs or stores, I try to find the ones that attract these kinds of people.

"And when it comes to stores, I advise against leaving your work on consignment because that method often leads to tragedy. As hard as it is, try for outright sales to the store rather than the business of providing the store with its capital and then risking receiving it back unsold and shopworn. If you *have* to settle for consignment at least try for an arrangement where you'll be able to get the money in advance.

"One of the greatest advantages in specializing is not only that you get to know your market quickly and surely, but you can concentrate and become extremely good at what you do. And you build up a regular clientele; as much as anything, specializing cuts down on the frantic search for a market." He tapped yet another design into a notebook blank, and added, "Of course it can be a little boring."

To relieve the boredom, he continues to experiment with new designs on his book covers. Looking through some of his other inlaid journals, I found one embossed with a radio circuit board, another with semiprecious stones scattered in a provocative pattern. "Did you ever notice at the craft fairs that almost all the craftspeople seem to be pretty young?" he asked. "I often wonder what happens to the older craftspeople?

"The future is the biggest puzzle to me. I know now I can make a living doing something that I want to do. But the longer you stay doing any one thing, the harder it is to get out of it. How much longer do I want to do books? It's a nice living but rather precarious, since if I were to be sick and couldn't work with my hands, that would be it. I have to laugh at myself as I see how settled and middle class I'm getting in my ways as the books become more of a business. Instead of figuring out some new hustle for food stamps, I'm now trying to make car payments and to find a good health insurance plan. The more money I make, the more 'needs' I seem to have. It makes me laugh—I'm not as different from everyone else as I once thought." He paused between taps on the leather. "Is that inherent in the human condition, or unique to me?

"Now that times are getting tougher, we all seem to be placing more importance on getting our material trips together. Friends who once were crazies are all busy scrambling to buy property now. It seems that five or ten years ago we had a sense of community that was supportive, and made the security of an income less necessary. I don't know . . . it's funny to see a couple of long-haired craftspeople standing around at a fair, and hear them talking about capitalization and depreciation and tax deductions— but that's what's happening."

I asked for a description of the process of production work, once the leather and the tools have actually been acquired. "Decide what you want to make," he replied, "then devise a pattern for it, cut it out of cardboard or paper, trace it onto a piece of leather, cut it out, and see if it all fits when you put the leather together. It takes a good deal of trial and error before you get a correct, usable pattern for whatever it is you intend to make. Then, once you have a usable pattern, trace it out on a full hide of leather, cut the hide, and once cut, trim to allow for the full hide's wrinkles, then trim the cut shapes to round off edges, mark for grooves and holes. Then comes the design work.

"The techniques you develop for your designs will be as varied as your ideas, and partly determined by the kind of leather you're working with. And, of course, the sequence of events I'm giving you is for my own particular work, and this can vary with the product being made.

"I think dyeing, which comes next, is one of the most difficult aspects of leatherworking. You have to learn a lot of control with the dyes, and that learning takes a long time and serves as a good sign of the overall quality of a piece of leatherwork. Once the leather is dyed, I apply a variety of finishes, depending on what each specific design calls for. Then I saddle-soap and burnish the edges, then put a final finish on the leather. Then I stitch, if any stitching is required, and then I bind my books. All my leatherwork follows this general pattern.

"And that's about all I can think of," he said with a smile. "Well, except, the most important thing of all: Wear gloves and don't breathe the dyes!"

Potters

Tin Top Pottery

"When our 11-year-old son informed his teacher one day that his mother was a potter, she said, 'That's not a nice thing to say about your mother!'

"Our biggest problem is the education of the public," Nita Hafford, of Tin Top Farm Pottery in Weatherford, Texas, wrote me. "This is a problem peculiar to the art business. The general public does not recognize the difference between a hand-thrown pot and one that has been poured in a mold—or worse—made by a machine. Therefore, they will balk at the price at times. We have had to discipline ourselves not to argue or take offense at careless remarks received at art shows. We often take our potter's wheel and demonstrate at such shows. This brings on a new set of uninformed questions. For instance, I was asked at a recent show if I could 'throw a chicken'. I merely informed the dear lady that pots thrown on a wheel must be symmetrical, therefore a chicken must be poured in a mold.

"We are constantly amazed at the general ignorance concerning pottery and the methods employed to make good ware. We must constantly assure our customers that we do not use lead in our glazes and that our dishes are dishwasher-proof. We have printed up a lot of informative papers that we distribute at art shows and galleries, describing various pottery techniques. People are usually interested in learning about the techniques involved in making the piece of pottery they have just purchased."

Nita emphasized the importance of working with good tools, paying a little extra, if necessary, to have the finest available equipment. Because they started potting on a gradual basis, learning as apprentices to an established potter, the Haffords were able to accumulate their equipment over a period of three years. They listed the following as the *minimum* price for good potting equipment.

Kiln	$325
Wheel	200
Miscellaneous tools	50
Scale	40
Chemicals	75
Clay	100
	$790

During their first year of full-time business, the Haffords estimated the following as their actual operating expenses.

Rent (building, furniture, fixtures)	$ 600
Utilities	500
Inventory (equipment, accruals)	160
Travel (art exhibits, other sales)	300
Show fees	480
Legal and professional fees	100
	$2,140

Nita Hafford pointed out that moving from a cramped, expensive, city studio to their 25-acre organic homestead allowed her an artistic freedom she'd rarely known before. "Daily, I discover something new and wonderful out here," she wrote. "I am now experimenting with dyeing the wool fibers I use in my weavings with the plants and weeds that grow on our farm. I also use the feathers from our peafowl and ducks, and pelts from the rabbits we raise for food. Our goats furnish us with milk and cheese, our land with tasty natural foods and clean clear water, and every day is a new experience to share."

Rodney Tidrick

Rodney Tidrick is a potter who lives in Oxford, Iowa, about 20 miles west of Iowa City along Route 6. Rodney is divorced, and has been living with Josh, his five-year-old son, upstairs while building his studio and salesroom downstairs in a building he is buying with a $75-per-month mortgage.

Rodney's equipment includes an electric wheel and a gas-fired kiln. His speciality is stoneware, which is pottery that is fired at cone 10, the hottest "common" firing temperature, although Rodney told me a lot of potters settle for cone 5, "and call it stoneware.

"I hate to think what an operation like this would cost if you didn't do all the work yourself," he told me. "I've built my own kiln and done all the plumbing, I work on a secondhand wheel, and still, with burners and everything, I've got $2,500 tied up. Then I have to meet the mortgage payment, and the propane bills for firing the kiln. I usually fire just once a month, enough stoneware to gross me $1,000, and that requires 75 gallons of propane!

"I've been at this for years, and I'm not yet making it pay," he laughed. "So I'll be driving a lot of nails this spring to make up the deficit. It's mostly a question now of keeping overhead as low as possible while I build up the market. My pots have always sold well, and even though there seems to be a lot of competition around here, the more potters there are, the greater the public's awareness of pots. In other words, competition generates interest. The biggest problem for me in marketing is finding shops willing to retail the pots. Meanwhile, whenever I get in a pinch I can score some work at the union hall in Iowa City. But I don't see that as how I'll do it forever. Eventually I'll be able to make it on pots alone.

"As far as the stores go, they take anywhere from 25 to 50 percent, right off the top, and only a *few* places will buy stuff outright, and that's a very few. Most go on consignment basis, but I'm allowed to set the price, at least. I can always figure a beer mug for $4. Yet I'll throw a planter and think it's great and take it to the plant shop and they'll just shake their head. Other times, a planter I think is trash catches their eye and they say, 'Oh, that's great bring as many as you can!'

Rodney Tidrick

"Crafts fairs are often a good place to sell your stuff. People are always out looking for a bargain, and I sell a lot of seconds at fairs, by offering a lower price. Mencken said, 'No man ever went broke underestimating the taste of Americans.' I sort of have to get a little detatched from my work to price things. If something doesn't turn out the way I planned it—and in the kiln a lot of surprises can happen—I put a lower price on it, and that's just my own taste functioning."

Showing me his kiln, which is in the back room of the three-room downstairs studio, Rodney explained that an indoor kiln separated from the rest of the building is ideal.

"Kilns disintegrate rapidly outdoors from frost action, because of the great porosity of insulation brick. With the kiln indoors, you're also less likely to attract your local hysterical fireman. Just remember that an indoor kiln will make a room uncommonly hot!

"Every kiln is different. With this same pile of bricks, I've made three kilns. Each one had its own personality. Two identical kilns, side by side, will fire differently!"

In the central downstairs room, Rodney keeps his wheels and racks and garbage pails for storing the raw clay that he and other potters in the area purchase together, by the truckload. (Shipping costs as much as the clay, which comes from Missouri.) The front room, which has a large display window, will serve as a salesroom. The idea of making much money from retail pottery sales in Oxford, Iowa, seems a little quixotic, but Rodney believes that once his work and whereabouts become known, he'll be able to earn his entire living as a potter. "We get a lot of traffic coming through here, people from places like Huntsville, Alabama, just off Interstate 80 on their way to see the Amana Colonies.

"Once I set up a display, I think there will be a good market right at my doorstep. Rents out here are one-fifth what they are in places like Iowa City. Take the guy across the street who's building boats for a living. There isn't a body of water big enough for the boats he makes within 20 miles, but the reason he's here is the same as mine: Keeping the overhead down!"

Josh was preparing to visit a friend up the street, and Rodney helped him with his jacket and boots. We agreed to walk with Josh to his friend's, and then to stop in Oxford's tiny poolroom for a quick game. As we were leaving his shop, Rodney showed me

some of his stoneware, explaining his basic attitude toward potting.
"I just try to throw an honest pot, you know. Functional work
sells best, and I try to keep an attitude of staying honest with the
material and not demand that clay do things that are unnatural for
it. Clay has a sort of natural state where it does things well; rather
than try to push it into forms that are imitative of other materials,
like wine goblets and ceramic birdhouses, I try to work with its
natural integrity. I'll admit there may be such a thing as a nice ceramic wine goblet, but I like to recognize that this is clay I'm working with, and treat it that way."

He gave me a small ashtray, saying that small items are very
helpful as kiln-stuffers; the fuller the kiln, the more even the firing
temperatures. In the base of the small ashtray was a knobby pro-
trusion, looking almost like a mistake. "An idea I stole from
General Motors," Rodney smiled. "It's to butt your cigarette out
on."

Spotting a group of large bottle-like containers, I asked what
their main purpose was. "Oh, I don't know," shrugged Rodney.
"They're just a weed vase, really. I've sold a lot of them for 40 to 50
bucks. Maybe some people use them for a very large paperweight.
My ex-wife used to pitch them, so you might say they're useful for
domestic disputes as well!"

Over a couple of games of pool, Rodney talked about the
image of potters, and how a person he knows slipcasts horseheads,
and insists on being known as a "ceramist" and not a "potter."
"Which is fine by me," he said. And for someone who *is* a potter,
with perhaps a different perspective than his, he told me about
Judith Spencer, a woman who bought the old Downey Savings
Bank in a little town like Oxford, on the other side of Iowa City.

Judith Spencer

The following morning I drove out to Downey, Iowa; I started
early because I'd been unable to find Judith Spencer in the phone
book, and I wanted to make an appointment with her before she
started her day. At 8 A.M. I found her beautifully weathered, old
brick bank on a small road off a larger road that connects West
Branch with West Liberty. There was no sign of activity, so I drove
on into West Liberty for a cup of coffee and a look around, and

Judith Spencer

returned to the Downey Savings Bank Pottery at 9 A.M., to find Judith and her potter-in-residence, Wayne Herrick, up to their elbows in clay in the spacious downstairs. Where tellers' booths once were, Judith now has display racks, and the sturdy old bank floor is covered with fine clay dust. When I asked if some time soon would be convenient for an interview, she said, "Now's as good as ever, my time is my own!" and invited me upstairs to her apartment for a cup of coffee.

During the next hour, Judith, who is 32, outlined for me the adventure and difficulties she has faced in establishing a pottery in the rural gut of mid-America. Before moving into the bank she bought in Downey, Judith, who grew up in Vermont, had graduated from Goddard College with a major in psychology, and earned an M.A. in anthropology at Ohio State. She interrupted work toward the Ph.D., and while waiting for a visa to go to the Near East, started potting. The satisfaction of potting illuminates her discussion of the work. "You've got to throw pots just because you love to throw. And you have to be able to love doing what sells, because that's a lot of what you wind up throwing," she added.

"As a woman, you have to bend over backwards to establish credibility. It wasn't quite clear when I first came here that I wasn't a drug addict, that I wasn't purple and didn't have horns. I would expect in any small community an artist per se will have these difficulties moving in. And it just has to do with the provincialism of the area.

"For instance, my purchase of this building was predicated on the idea of uninterruptable gas service. Then it turns out this was not possible: If there was too much natural gas going through the lines they could, in fact, stop service to my kiln. Retaining that kind of power over me was detrimental to me and my kiln, and was clearly not acceptable. I had to go through the company's Washington hierarchy to threaten suit if they wouldn't give me noninterruptable service. It meant phone calls on the hour. I discovered that dealing with the gas company is all subterfuge. They do not like the idea that a woman knows what she is doing. In a kiln, you can see by the color of the flame what it is the meter says you're burning, and I was being charged for pressure I wasn't receiving." She won her battle and a rebate from the company, but only after months of persistent and costly communications with the company.

"Perhaps what was so gross about dealing with the problem is that I had to reach the vice-president of the company before the smaller executives would admit to or rectify a 'mistake' which had cost me some years and took from them only a bit of face. I now have the right amount of gas pressure and my kiln is firing well.

"I think to be a successful craftsperson you have to be at least half businessperson," she said. "And I suppose a part of maturing is learning you're not necessarily paid for what you like to do. I never really thought about what it takes until I met someone who I could tell didn't have it at all. I asked her 'What are your goals?' and *she had none*.

"I do have goals, whose formulation crystalizes over time in direct conjunction with my success. In my first three-year-plan I needed a resident potter, a person who paid me for kiln and studio space. I am phasing that position out now, in favor of the luxury of my own space.

"I think the way the real world does it, like Woolworths or Kresges, is to define the need and to meet it. But for me, I have to decide what my needs are and I just couldn't make it without potting. So I had to find a way I could pot everyday, and I found this building. The first year it was very, very hard, the physical labor of gutting the building and making a living space upstairs. I tied a chain to the outhouse and dragged it away with my truck.

"A few days later a very sweet elderly gentleman came down here and offered to let me use his name because he thought in this community that it was necessary for a woman in business to be in the association of a man."

Judith hates crafts fairs. "I've been on the art fair circuit and I just hate trucking. Lots of motels and you set up in the rain." She paused a moment. "But it *is* how you get known." Because she isn't willing to go on the fair circuit, which would probably pull her away from the wheel longer than she likes anyway, she established her own "Downey Savings Bank Art Fair," an event to which she invited a select group of fellow-artists, three bluegrass bands, and 2,500 or so Iowa neighbors for "a good old down-home day." She sold lemonade and beer, "so people got loose enough to dance and maybe buy, and it really was a good party for everyone."

Judith's approach to marketing is unique. She specializes in Early American "period pottery," which she reproduces "in keeping with the way our forefathers fired when they came to this country, using glazes and materials that pre-date tin, glass, and cast iron." And she sells her work, usually produced in limited editions, to private collectors. She has found that private invitations, specially engraved, mailed to a select group of people, are the best advertisement for the many small showings she offers during the year.

"It's the same with whatever I produce," she told me, "whether it's an edition of pots or a churn, a footwarmer or cheese press or a crock. I photograph it and destroy any seconds. For instance, I produce a limited edition of 10 churns a year; limiting the number helps keep the value up. I sell them, not for $25, but for $100, and let the buyers know they are buying a registered piece. And if I need it for exhibit, I can recall it temporarily. I keep a file with a picture of each piece, containing the name and address of the owner."

"The other part of marketing has to do with knowing how to market yourself. And understanding people when they come into the shop. Sometimes I wonder, 'Why are they so quiet?' for instance. 'Because they want to be alone or should I ask if I can help them?'

"In general, you've simply got to be aggressive: Go out and learn what the laws are and know what the questions are to ask. Experience is the best teacher. I learned by setting up a kick wheel in my kitchen, and going around and learning by watching and talking with other potters. Ask not one but many people, and keep abreast of the legal matters. I have two lawyers: One who figures my taxes, and another for general consulting purposes.

"As it is I'm just getting by, financially, but I'm still alive, and I'm learning and growing. I love the rhythm of throwing a pot, that's my yoga. And I keep the shop open to the public only on weekends, because I am primarily a potter. I think two basic things are necessary for someone like me. First, you have to know your strengths and weaknesses, both of character and body. For instance, I spent three weeks on my back from trying to deal with a piece of Sheetrock. I should have known better. And second, absolutely you have to believe that nothing is impossible. If you persevere. You have to believe in yourself long enough to make it happen."

Judith acknowledges that setting up Downey Savings Bank Pottery has been a painful and difficult experience. But she recognizes the importance in her own life of developing the "nonartistic" capability of dealing with people in a businesslike fashion, and of sticking with the overall pursuit, even when local custom and big business threaten the operation.

"Would I do it all again?" She paused, thoughtfully, and smiled. "I'd have to think about it real hard. I know you have to have a sense of purpose so strong it's all you live for and would die for it. So many other things in my life have nothing to do with my yoga, my art form. So I'm glad I've resisted the forces that would have intimidated me or forced me to become a factory."

Wood 'n' Wheel

Still another approach to making and selling pottery is that of the people at Wood 'n' Wheel, which is a combination studio and salesroom created by John Myers, 34, who rebuilt a barn on his parents' farm in North Liberty, Iowa, only a few miles outside of Iowa City. John is a woodworker, and his wife, Jan, who is 36, is a potter. To keep their large shop full, they rent space to two other potters, Marsha McClelland, 35, and Michael Brannin, who is 22. The rental agreement is kept formal with a simple contract, and the group of potters find that their association is helpful not only for acquiring bulk orders of clay and glazing materials, but also for sales purposes, where the mixture of their different approaches to the craft lends a diversity to their salesroom.

"Because a kiln is not the easiest item in the world to move," said Marsha, who came to Wood 'n' Wheel in 1971, "an arrangement like this has to be a fairly long-term thing." John spoke of his enterprise as the sort of business that often attracts people who are not sure of their commitment to a craft. "It's really too bad there aren't more good opportunities for people to start out and experience the commitment that is necessary, before they actually jump into a given craft. One guy wanted to come here as an apprentice, and I asked him whether he wanted to work in wood or throwing pots. And he answered, 'Kinda both', which is just the kind of answer that tells me he should find his experience somewhere else."

John, Jan, and Jay Myers, Marsha McClelland, and Michael Brannin

Jan Myers told me that bookkeeping for the group is kept simple by using a pool checking account that receives all sales income and from which all business expenses are drawn. "At the end of the month, we simply write ourselves checks for the amount of each person's total sales, less rent and individual expenses, and this provides us with an accurate record."

General chores are shared, including mixing clay, sweeping, and dusting the shop. John said, "We've had lots of shouting matches in the past over what seemed to be ridiculously little things—like who would sweep or who refused to clean the windows, but now, fortunately, those people are gone. Some craftspeople are simply too independent for this sort of a shared venture. As a matter of fact, we're very happy with the situation and people we have here now. We're not looking for anyone else."

It was Valentine's Day when I visited, and the small group was beginning to swell as the Myers' two teenage sons and a customer or two came in to share some pink heart-shaped cookies and herb tea. "We aren't enthusiastic about getting any bigger at all," said John. "I think in this way we're typical of many craftspeople. We like to keep it slow and easy, keeping overhead as low as possible by sharing facilities, driving old cars, and fixing things for ourselves. We keep a garden, and we cut our own firewood. We keep our days full and spend as little money as we can get by spending. We know there's a way to get rich at this, and that's by getting a lot bigger and more aggressive than we are. But we know how much we'd lose if we didn't take time off to go fishing and hunting mushrooms."

"And that," added Marsha, "is how we end up working from six in the morning till midnight!"

A Gallery of Craftspeople

Anna Land, Down Home Comforters

Anna Land, 33 years old, started Down Home Comforters two years ago in West Brattleboro, Vermont. "I had apprenticed to an upholsterer for two plus years and realized that while I was in the right church, as it were, I was in the wrong pew.

"I started making comforters after consulting the *I Ching* and then buying about $250 worth of equipment, including an industrial sewing machine. I learned initially by copying. Gradually I devised my own techniques, policies, and procedures. I do all the work and play . . . myself. This involves nearly all my time one way or another. I do have to be careful so that I don't burn out. Sometimes this just means taking an afternoon off for a sauna or a book or visiting with a friend.

"I figure my prices based on my *actual* expenses. Some businesses try to make a profit on everything. And I charge $5 per hour for my labor. At first I tended to minimize myself and found that I undervalued my abilities and underestimated my needs. My other major mistake so far has been not separating the money that should have gone right back into materials. It's important to keep track of how much money you are putting into a product in material goods and to keep that money flowing constantly back into your product."

Mrs. June MacDonald, Hand-Painted China

"You will feel like a new person!" exclaimed June MacDonald. "People think they 'can't' create anything because they have been indoctrinated to the perfection produced by the machine. I say, 'Any machine can do it perfectly but only you can put in those little squiggles that give it character and charm.'" Mrs. MacDonald, who lives in San Andreas, California, has blended a love of flower and herb gardening with a desire to reproduce bright garden colors for the drab winter months. "I inherited some of my grandmother's hand-painted china, which eventually built up a desire in me for self-expression in this medium. I was fortunate in being able to take lessons and finally getting a kiln and teaching others this fine art. I have never experienced such a thrill as when I found I could do something credible!"

Mrs. MacDonald's interest caught on in her neighborhood, and soon her neighbors were studying the art of hand-painting and glazing fine china. "We were soon creating more than we needed for our families, so we sought a market. The best one for me was the Saturday Market in Eugene, Oregon. This is like a renaissance fair and is held every Saturday during fine weather at the county courthouse parking lot. Everything sold there must be made by the seller.

"Whatever is created and whatever the medium of expression, start simple," she recommended. "Just paint the glory of a single flower, not the entire garden. The main point is to be original, do not be intimidated by the inundation of printed patterns available. You will find that if you like a created piece yourself, others will be enthusiastic also!"

Samantha Mallets, Découpage

Samantha Mallets of "Old Barns 'n' Other Things" stapled her business card to a letter she wrote from Middleburg Heights, Ohio. "I'm a 50-year-old grandmother, and not the complete breadwinner, but what I earn on my home craft helps pay a few bills and puts steak on the table once in a while.

"I tear down old barns, bring the wood home, and use the lumber for plaques and wall hangings. Over a period of two years I have accumulated over 500 themes to découpage on the old wood.

"Some people find it hard to believe that a 125-pounder like me can tear down barns," she said. "I like to say I'm better than thumbtacks! I use a hammer and crowbar, and hire a tractor to complete the job. And my husband and three children help too."

Sam, as she likes to be called, has little patience with gift shops, which she finds "too slow," and concentrates her business on restaurants, lounges, offices, and individuals who want a unique decoration for their basements. "Many of my designs are one of a kind, such as old newspaper ads, front pages, deeds, or other old documents."

She does very little advertising, relying on word of mouth, and as her business has grown from hobby status, she has hired a salesgirl on a commission basis. "I just didn't realize people would like this sort of thing so much. And it just grew and grew!"

Drew Langsner, Woodcrafts

Drew Langsner, 33, from Marshall, North Carolina, supports himself by making hayforks "handcrafted from one piece of oak so they are functional and quite elegant." Langsner wrote me that he makes hayforks only 15 hours a week and his wife, Louise, puts in about five hours. Their product is marketed through mail-order catalogues. "We live on a very small income, considerably below the minimum for filing federal tax. We rent the farm for $20 a month, grow almost all our food and feed for two heifers and two mules. So, our real income is that we need little money to live on. We also trade labor with neighboring farmers for any tractor work we need." The only power tool on the Langsner homestead is a chain saw.

"I make an item that cannot be made by machine, and requires more than ordinary skills. It also has historical appeal (I use an old Mennonite pattern). I can make a hayfork quite fast, fast enough to earn $3–$4 an hour at home, on my own schedule. I have some background in cooperage, and we learned basketmaking. But both of these crafts require too much time to make a good product at a reasonable selling price. We don't believe that craftsmen should cater to, or be dependent on, the wealthy."

One of the big keys to his success, Langsner believes, is that he can obtain the oak from his own woodlot and that his craft is not adaptive to a large operation. "Don't fool with stuff that takes too much time, requiring rich customers or compromises in quality," he said. "I would say finding a unique niche is the best approach."

Billie Tyler

Billie Tyler, Woodcarver

Billie Tyler, 50 years old, was an artist and design engineer with General Motors for 18 years before moving to Otis, Oregon, and starting Kozy Korner Homestead with his wife. Tyler told me that he is able to provide total support for the homestead by designing and building small, wood gift-shop items, including "a peg-legged sea captain, horses and billy goats, spice cabinets, and small shelves."

He sells these wholesale to the many gift shops in the resort area where he lives, and from his own retail shop. "Select a product uncommon to your area," he recommended. "Do a lot of research before going into business. Keep your overhead low, provide only quality items at a fair price. And you must enjoy what you are doing to be a success.

"Anyone who turns out a handcraft product and has put forth the effort to become an expert in his field has many other profitable opportunities in teaching his craft to local people, through adult education programs, or through clubs or other organizations, such as the county extension programs." Tyler teaches a course in woodcarving through the adult education program.

And, addressing the primary difficulty of successfully self-employed people, he wrote, "So far I haven't made any big mistakes. I try to keep my business small so I will have time to work my garden, take care of and enjoy my animals, go fishing, and take vacations. Limiting the amount of work I'll do has been difficult, and keeping the business small requires a certain amount of restraint."

Jeff Moses, Boat Builder

Jeff Moses, 26, is the owner of land-locked Moses' Ark Boat Works, in Oxford, Iowa, which is about 20 miles out of Iowa City. Moses' Ark, a converted supermarket, is across the street from Rodney Tidrick's pottery studio. Moses explained that he doesn't need to be on a body of water to sell boats. "What counts," he said, "is to get one of your boats out on the water with your name and address on it." In the meantime, he recommends low overhead, "which means working in a small, dead town with the heat down and the lights low."

Jeff Moses

When I visited his shop, Moses was completing the first boat in a fleet of five 18-foot catamaran-type sailboats for a man promoting the fleet on Clear Lake. "It's too much work for one person," he said, "but the government would be on my back if I had any help. Their goddamn regulations require more fancy safety equipment than I can afford. It would put me out of business. But it takes me two months to build one of these.

"If I were to start over, I'd probably build canoes, which are cheap and sell very well, and I'd probably run a boat repair service. Most people are set up for selling, not for repairs. But I enjoy this work, and I'm the youngest person I know of who's doing it, so it gives me a good feeling to know if I screw up I've got 15 or 20 years of experience ahead of me. If I'm still screwing up then, why, I'll just quit!"

Sas Colby, Artist in Fabrics

Sas Colby, 36, moved from Connecticut to Berkeley in 1975 when she was divorced from her husband of 15 years. Colby is an artist in fabrics who creates special costumes and embroidered designs often used to illustrate children's books. "I've learned to draw on a sewing machine," she told me. "In earlier years, because I didn't have the burden of making money, I was able to develop my work in a personal way. But now I do have the responsibility of making a living, and I'm still trying to do it by making work that is true to me, and it's very difficult."

When I visited her she was about to leave for a weekend teaching job at an art retreat on the island of Hawaii. "Most artists have to teach to survive, but I'd like to reduce the teaching to a minimum," she said. "It's usually a workshop situation where I'm teaching at an institution where I don't need the formal credentials. I just give it all I've got and sometimes it drains me so there's no energy left for my own work."

Colby said that she initially had difficulty marketing her work. Living in Connecticut, her most obvious market was the art galleries in New York City. "I learned that you should never apologize for your work, or sound anything but positive, at any time. If you don't believe in it, you shouldn't be showing it. Onassis said, 'Never tell anyone your troubles,' or, translated into my work,

Sas Colby

'Don't show bad photographs.' Gallery people can be very intimidating. They know how important they can be to the artist.

"I joined the Connecticut Feminists in the Arts, a supportive group that helped affirm my identity as an artist. You want to come out whole, and not everyone is going to approve and you can't let that destroy you," she added thoughtfully. "The most special thing in the world is to do what you want to do and have people get some meaning from it.

"I find the climate here in the Bay Area very favorable to a woman artist. Out here no one seems to be judging anybody and people seem more free than in New England.

"You can only grow at your own pace anyway. Nothing stays the same, it's always going to change. One day you just wake up and say 'Oh it's okay! I can do this!' "

4.
SERVICES

Selling Labor

Any transaction involves a service. When you buy a table, you pay for the wood and also for the service involved in building and marketing that table. When you buy radishes, you pay for the service someone provided you by growing those radishes. But for the purposes of this section, we'll consider a service to be a venture in which the *doing* of your job is on commission, or where you are paid primarily for labor, not for a product.

Services are known to be fast money-makers because they require a minimum of equipment; if you specialize in one essential function, such as sweeping chimneys, you may need only one tool. Because services are "to order," there's no need to worry about retail and wholesale marketing, and presumably no waiting involved between work and payment. On the other hand, many people I've talked with list "collecting bills" as the number one problem of small, service-oriented businesses. In a retail operation where a product changes hands, at least you have the option of repossessing tangible goods, but if someone welches on you after you've swept his chimney, what are you gonna do, climb up on his roof and dump all the soot back in?

For this reason, the terms of all service agreements should be established in writing, using a simple contract form that states explicitly what the details of the work will be, terms of payment, and cost ceiling. You should be paid half the estimate upon signing the contract, and the balance due upon completion of the work. Such a deposit at least half-protects you from clients who refuse to pay because the results of your efforts "aren't what we wanted."

One of the greatest economies you can offer your customers is a price break on the materials you use. You can probably purchase materials on a wholesale basis if you have ample storage space or friends who will share your stock. Just be sure not to carry an unnecessarily high inventory through a fiscal tax period, where your state tax could be inflated on the basis of inventory.

Do It Before Their Very Eyes

Jock Gill, the photographer, told me "people are reluctant to pay for work they don't actually see you doing." I remembered a piano tuner who came to my house, took the movement out of my piano, returned a week later, reinstalled the movement, and billed me $90. When I paid the bill, three months later, I was sure he had taken me for a ride.

If the nature of your service requires that a good portion of the work be done on your own premises, be sure to explain to the customer exactly what it is he's paying for. In services, as in no other self-employment endeavor, word-of-mouth—satisfied customers—will make the difference between a situation where you can choose your jobs, and one where business is so bad you have to go out on risky assignments where likely as not the client will default at payment time. In service occupations, as in others, it's best to be committed to one location, and known by your neighbors. And a telephone, expensive as it is, is especially helpful.

Your Attitude

In a service, as in no other sort of work, your attitude toward the people you work for will determine whether you and your work are sufficiently appreciated. The tremendous advantage the self-employed person has in this respect is that, as the owner of the business, he is directly rewarded for caring about the customer.

John Casserly, who now lives on a farm in upstate New York, finally gave up his garden, lawn, and general maintenance service in Long Island, because "the pace just got too hectic, too much traffic, and I was on an island with only one way off—the Throgs

Neck Bridge." Now working as a hired hand, John misses being self-employed. "Once you've been independent, it's very hard not to be," he said.

"One important thing I learned is that people want someone they can trust to work around their homes. If you work hard for people they don't mind paying for it. Being cheerful, considerate, and alert relaxes the customer and allows a bond of friendship to happen."

New Hampshire repairman Herb Griffin said: "Never promise what you may not be able to deliver. Once a promise is made, break your neck to keep it. And if you have to break a promise, don't procrastinate on dropping the bombshell."

Billing

The only dentist I ever paid immediately was the one who had a sign, in psychedelic colors, located on the ceiling. When he drilled your teeth all you could see was the drill, your mouth reflected in his glasses, or this sign on the ceiling: "Ten Percent Discount if You Pay before Leaving!"

Over and over, small-business people stress how important prompt payment is in keeping them solvent. Herb Griffin singles out credit as a major barrier to good financial flow. "I avoid credit. I don't extend it, because time and money are wasted in issuing statements and keeping track of payments—and if you don't get paid . . . I don't ask for credit either, except when absolutely necessary. The sitting down to pay bills takes time and money, and there is the postage. Besides, most suppliers offer an extra 2 percent discount for cash.

"You simply have to be hard-nosed when it comes to money. If a bill is slow in coming in, you've lost your gravy."

Maintenance and Repair Services

A Small Repair Shop

Although he admits to "repairing anything that's old and rusty," Griffin's main interest, and hence his "speciality," is Model A Ford restoration. All his work is completed in a shop he built separate from his house, after learning that his homeowners' insurance policy would be canceled and replaced with a fire insurance policy costing six times as much if he had his shop in or attached to the house. Upon the arrival of this news, Griffin promptly cleared a site on his 25 acres, and built with the lumber he sawed from the trees.

"I procrastinated too long seeking legal advice and on checking with my insurance agent," he writes. "The insurance company takes a dim view of business *in* the home, especially a repair shop.

"Just to keep my hand in, against the day there aren't so many Model A buffs, I also repair modern automobiles." Griffin finds too that he uses his sandblaster for a lot more than just automobiles. He's been known to restore boat trailers, cast-iron lawn furniture, "and who knows what else in the way of antiques and machinery that need sandblasting. Being a nasty operation, few people do it; thus I receive a good rate for the time spent.

"Ever since infancy, no car has turned me on like the Model A. And old car restoration fits very well into the schedule of this mini-farm, because cars are normally here for a period of weeks so there isn't the kind of pressure I'd have from, say, working on modern cars, where the owner wants it yesterday. When the sap starts to run, I close the shop and tap trees. If the chickens get lonesome, I go talk to them."

Repair Shop on Wheels

Another "specialist" who will take other work is Paul Silvia, from Assonet, Massachusetts. "I claim to specialize in the model 360 Subaru, because they aren't made anymore and parts are running out. I spend many days just looking for old Subarus for parts, buying as many as possible. So my main line is to buy, sell, or repair 360 Subarus. These cars have a twenty-five horse, two-cylinder engine, and get up to 60 miles to the gallon, so why not keep them going!"

An advantage in "specializing" like this is that word of mouth can bring special-model car owners from far and wide, and if your work is good, your reputation for having the parts and specific know-how can bring a lot of work.

But even though he's considered a specialist, Silvia offers a further service: He will perform both major and minor repairs *on site*, which is an especially convenient arrangement for someone with heavy equipment that is broken down in the fields. "As a matter of fact," he said, "I rebuild any engine that needs it, from lawn mower to diesel."

Quilt Repairs

Sarah Gallagher, 31, lives in New York City, where she established Deep River Quilt Restoration Service, which she claims is "to the best of my knowledge the only concern anywhere formally engaged in the activity of quilt restoration."

Because her service is unique, she has found that there is plenty of business for her. And, to insure that this will remain the case, she keeps a list of references, to assure potential clients that their quilts will receive expert care.

"Deep River was the result of a feverish attempt to add to personal income and, for me, this endeavor has absolutely meant the difference. I feel blessed with the good fortune to make a livelihood from work I love whilst I underwrite my adventures with the Great American Novel.

"I'd had a great deal of experience with all forms of needlework. Although I'd not, prior to the founding of my business, engaged in this work professionally, I believed I could make a go of quilt repair . . . that is, perform the work itself. I chose this particular kind of work because, one, the interest in quilts was on the rise, and two, here in New York, people will pay to have anything done for them . . . and there are enough people of substantial income to support quite a range of nonessential services."

Sharing a Shop

Brian Vaughn is the name I'll use for a machinist who has asked to be anonymous. Brian has rented space and equipment in a friend's machine shop ever since the friend offered him space and several customers he was too busy to handle on his own. "We keep our own records and do our own billing," Vaughn told me. "We don't draw hard lines as to who gets what customers, because most people know and trust both of us, even though we do have different approaches to problems. Between the two of us, we plan to keep the shop occupied from 8:30 to 5.

"When you get right down to it, dependability is a major attraction with such an arrangement. We can both pretty much work the hours we like to, and the customer is always certain the shop is open during hours. When he takes his vacation, I keep the shop open full time, and vice versa. Covering the shop, paying my rent, paying for materials and replacing broken tools are my only obligations. But a situation like this won't work without mutual respect and caring.

"My biggest mistakes are lapses from sound business practices—recording time spent on each job carefully at the end of the day or when I leave off a job to fix someone's emergency, etcetera. We now have a sign that says 'Minimum Charge $7.50'. There are a few good customers for whom a quickie 10- or 15-minute job can be overlooked, but if anyone wanders in with a $10 toaster and thinks it should be repairable for $5, we show them the sign. People with no understanding of mass production and custom work still find us and we spend a bit of time each month lecturing. We can't compete with a manufacturer on price, but on time and availability we're as good as they come."

A Jack-of-All-Trades

Vertis M. Bream, 29, of Aspers, Pennsylvania, started Bream's Lawn Service three years ago. During the winter months, he cuts wood, removes snow, and performs other cold weather chores for his customers. Bream's summer business keeps him busy 50 hours a week for half the year; he estimates "thirty to forty hours per week, depending on whether there's snow," as his winter load.

"Remember, if you spend a lot of time on the road between jobs, it is your time and must come out of expenses somewhere. I personally spend 25 percent of my time on the road between my 50 to 60 customers per week, and another eight hours a week servicing equipment." Bream recommends purchasing only the best equipment, and doing your own repairs. "Get a book if you don't know how, and learn," he wrote me. "And, get your own bulk gas tank and buy your gas in volume. Buy oil in 55-gallon drums, buy hydraulic oil and grease by the case. Work out your schedule so that you don't backtrack or drive more miles than necessary."

Bream said that he has never had to advertise. He bought out another lawn service, acquiring the previous owner's goodwill. "I wouldn't do that again; I didn't realize how much demand for these services there was. I would start part time and build my own clientele.

"A jack-of-all-trades is always in demand, especially by retirees and/or widows. Many people could use a person for one or more days a week to do odd jobs like transplanting shrubbery, painting, removing or placing storm windows, etcetera. Anyone with carpentry skills not looking for union wages could make it on his own.

"By all means carry liability insurance!" Bream said, echoing the sentiments of many people who are aware of the risks involved, and the potential monetary loss, if a client should sue. In a business where machinery is involved, such insurance should be your first priority. "Children and adults alike are fascinated by machines," wrote Bream, "and you should always be protected in case of accident."

Aside from the general benefits of being self-employed, working in a service often involves the opportunity of recycling those items that your client no longer needs. In the case of a trash hauler I met, this concept involves an entire storefront just for the refrigerators he is paid to haul away!

Vertis Bream calls it "the best feature of my work: all of the organic matter that I haul away from my customers (grass clippings, hedge trimmings, leaves, etcetera) is applied as permanent mulch to our one-acre homestead garden, berries, and fruit trees. Also, any mulching material which is leftover from a customer's yard is brought home to dress up our flower beds. My customers give me all kindred of plants and excess flower bulbs—even building materials!

"These types of bonuses mean more than money to me. They help feed and shelter us."

Services by Mail

Al and Jane Wonch, Book Composition

Al Wonch, 43, worked in a management job with a major book manufacturing plant until he was fired, in the late sixties, and went to work with his wife, Jane, composing books at their home in Fort Collins, Colorado. "Book composition requires careful attention to details, so that the job is done right the first time," wrote Wonch. The operation is a perfect service opportunity for someone who wants to work indoors at home, on low overhead.

The Wonches use an IBM electric composing machine, their only piece of special equipment. It is an extremely glorified typewriter, available on monthly lease. They have been working regularly, by mail, composing pages for a publisher in Chicago. Because their actual operating expenses are limited to those of running a small office, at home, and the rental of their fancy typewriter, which produces results comparable to those of many well-equipped printing establishments, the Wonches are able to compete for quality jobs while offering the publisher substantial savings.

Earthbooks Lending Library

Lewis and Sharon Watson, 38, and 35, are "public school teacher dropouts" who started Earthbooks Lending Library, a mail-order lending and retail book service, in Sweet, Idaho. The Watsons started their library with the proceeds of a book they wrote and published at home, *House of Stone*, a step-by-step account of how they built their 1,100-square-foot stone house for $2,000. The Watsons report that their 60-page book has sold $50,000 worth of copies, at $3 apiece, during the last two-and-one-half years. "Fascinated by the mail-order business, we then conceived and developed Earthbooks Lending Library," offering rental for 50¢ a month, discountable if the reader buys, Lewis wrote me. "We specialize in quality, how-to books."

The project was immediately successful, "so much so, in fact, that within the first year we were obviously and inescapably headed for a large, nonhomestead business, complete with big building, elaborate office equipment, bureaucratic inefficiency, employees, etcetera."

To cope with their large volume of business, the Watsons "decentralized" Earthbooks by opening several fully stocked "branch libraries" in other parts of the country. "These are all totally owned and operated by other homesteaders right from their rural homesteads. They are loosely united only by a common catalogue that we edit, plus mutually beneficial cooperation."

The Watsons reported that their book-rental program loses money, but that retail sales easily cover the loss on books that are returned after a month. They have found that "pleasure reading" is almost always returned, whereas good, "how-to" books are kept for permanent reference. "Also," said Lewis, "our rental/purchase plan provides excellent feedback as to the worth of any given title. It provides a wonderful filtering process against publisher garbage!"

Following their own successful path of self-publishing their *House of Stone*, the Watson's own Stonehouse Publications will soon release their latest book, *How to Start a Homestead Mail-Order Business*. For $3, you can buy a concise, readable version of their three years' experience, or rent it for 50¢ a month, if you prefer.

Innkeepers

Anyone who has traveled along the major Interstates, and sought a reasonably priced night's lodging in something other than a chain motel knows that innkeeping is one of the vanishing services. Yet the good places, run by simple, honest people, can be found. No doubt, a useful directory of such establishments, as well as a listing of where simple, natural meals are served, would benefit us all when we are on the road. So far, I know of two where a room costs $12 or less, and where the service, and the atmosphere, are unique. One is in California, the other's in Vermont.

Hector Robert and Pat Britton, The Quincy Hotel

In Enosburg Falls, Vermont, on Depot Street, on the other side of the street from the railroad tracks, two doors down from the historic old Opera House, is The Quincy Hotel, a majestic, if worn, survivor of 100 years. Three stories high, it has 24 rooms, a full kitchen, owners' quarters, dining areas, dance floor, and a bar that has a back entrance.

When I first came upon The Quincy it was 1968, and I frequented the bar in the back room, where a pool table lured my friends and me to stay too long, too often. We would wager a beer on each game, and on a streak it wasn't uncommon to see one of us, with a silly smile, behind a row of six warming draughts.

Hector Robert

The Quincy was always a loose place, and its owner, a wonderful man named Marcel, tended bar with the help of his wife and grown children. Marcel's wife's name was 'Ma'—at least that's what everyone called her—and she cooked an honest meal. Upstairs, clean rooms were available; occasional skiiers would discover the hotel, but mostly the rooms were rented on a more permanent basis.

Marcel and his family were an interesting feature of the hotel. Neither he nor Ma spoke much English, and at times they seemed blissfully unaware of some of the shenanigans that went on in the bar. During many winter afternoons the hotel was as good a place as any to find a game of 10¢ pitch, and almost anyone was willing to place small side bets on the outcome of various pool games. Throughout the proceedings, Marcel served beer and stronger drink, while Ma cooked up a daily "special" as well as all sorts of good sandwiches, and you might even say that The Quincy became something of a hangout for many local tradespeople and pool enthusiasts.

With any situation where people are mixing personalities and alcohol, various outbreaks may be expected, and this is where Marcel demonstrated a surprising virtue. While he seemed to ignore from his side of the bar the activities of his customers, at any sign of disorderly conduct, even before voices were much raised in a way that others in the bar knew what was happening, he would be over the bar (how, I never figured out, he did it so quickly) and would use that momentum to literally bulldoze the offender out of the room.

Anyone who witnessed that surprising failure of Marcel's smile, and the strength of his conviction when he wanted you *out*, handled matters discretely and otherwise behaved. Marcel ran an orderly business, and The Quincy was a place where you could go to relax.

When the last of his children was finishing studies at Enosburg's high school, Marcel made a startling announcement: The hotel was for sale! He was anxious to move back to Quebec, to let someone else take on the challenge of keeping the lucrative but leaky keepsake standing. And I think it's accurate to say that Marcel's patrons were stunned and saddened. But two or three years later, we were still sitting around, a little less worried about the urgency of matters. Marcel had received offers, but refused to budge off his $60,000 asking price—and week after week the local buyers' digest carried the same classified announcement: "Hotel for Sale." I remember that finding that ad in its usual place became a sort of weekly comfort.

Then one day the word came, sort of as a rumor, but it seemed pretty sure that a couple from New York was definitely interested. They had looked it over once and were coming back. And two weeks later Marcel started telling his patrons that the deal had been made. Within six weeks, we would, in effect, be under new rule.

Is it imagination or fact that has me remember the pitch games doubling in intensity, everyone a little more alert at the pool table? The change was in the air, and we sensed that no matter who the new owners were, we would never again have quite the same place for a watering hole.

Hector Robert, 46 years old, and Pat Britton, 42, a friend of Hector's brother, who is also named Pat, turned out to be "the couple from New York." Hector and his brother had grown up on a farm in Enosburg, but Hector had left Vermont in 1950, taking what work he could find, "picking potatoes in Maine, logging for 12 bucks a week. I had a chain saw as long as from here to that post over there," and he motioned, with a grin, to a support that holds up some of the ceiling in his dining room. We were sitting in front of a real fire, crackling in the fireplace, one of the new touches that Hector and Pat brought to the hotel, making it distinctly their own in an amazingly short period.

Hector was on holiday from his truck-driving job in New York, and with Barb, his wife, was visiting at the family farm. Hector's partner, Pat, recalled: "Hector's father said, 'There's this hotel advertised in *Buyers' Digest.*' So we got to talking about it and Barb called and talked to Marcel, and the next time she and I were off to go shopping, we left Hector off at the hotel, and Marcel showed him through. And the next day we came back, all together, because Hector had said, 'You know, it's not all that bad!' So we came back and Marcel told us his price and we tried to talk him down and couldn't. So Hector went back to New York, and I remember we all sat around in the kitchen at the hotel, with Hector's brother and Marcel talking in French and Barb and me wondering what the hell they were talking about. But anyway, we negotiated and finally decided to make the deal. I can't remember whether it was that weekend or the next one."

In negotiating to acquire The Quincy Hotel, Hector and Pat paid Marcel's asking price, which did not include any goodwill or old accounts. Further, Marcel agreed to finance the transaction himself, which is indicative of the good relationship that has developed between the former and the present owners. Perhaps most beneficial of all, Marcel and Ma agreed to stay on at the hotel for a week past the final closing in May, to assure that the transition ran smoothly. "I can still hear her," laughed Pat, "that wonderful 'Une semaine,' because she couldn't speak English, but she wasn't about to stay on any longer!"

Pat quit her job in Burlington, and for the month of April, "not knowing what in heck I was doing, but willing to learn," she worked behind the bar with Marcel. Then, in time for closing, Hector moved up from New York. Barb stayed behind while the children finished their school year. And Hector's sister, "a girl off the farm, who'd never done anything like this either," came in to run the kitchen.

Pat and Hector laugh now at the memory of their first days of owning the hotel, without the benefit of Marcel and Ma. "They left on a Saturday," recalled Pat. "All the kids were here helping them move. And we opened on Monday. I remember I stayed late that night with Hector because he wasn't used to tending bar at all."

"Yeah, and I remember the first two weeks I was here, I think every single thing in the place broke down all at once," laughed Hector. "All the tenants came with their complaints. 'My sink's plugged up.' 'The window won't open.' Stuff like that. And meanwhile something went with the furnace, the refrigerator that made the ice cubes went on the blink, a switch went in the french fryer. If I walked up and down those stairs once it was a million times! First the furnace would go in the basement, then the top-floor basin was leaking and it was dripping all the way down here into the dining room!"

"And of course," said Pat, "the place was crazy busy because everyone was coming in to see the new owners.

"Strictly me, I love the business, not so much the slinging hash and cooking as the bar and the people. I don't have to watch the TV, because I can always be entertained by the people. And the challenge of keeping it all peaceful and everybody happy makes this business, for me, a great deal of fun."

Hector isn't as quick to declare his undying love for the hotel business. His responsibility has been the very demanding one of remaking the hotel into a place that reflected his and Pat's idea of what a restaurant-lounge-hotel should be. Among things he wouldn't tolerate were abusive language (to which Marcel and Ma were seemingly numbed, or noncomprehending), gambling, or any sort of rowdy conduct. Hector didn't mind the clientele, but he wanted them to change a few of their habits.

So it wasn't long before the pool table disappeared, and that was the first tangible evidence that Hector was changing things. Within a few months, the bar had been entirely remodeled, the old bathrooms removed, the walls pushed back, new bathrooms installed, and a supporting post or two, somehow determined unnecessary, removed. Hector repainted and reupholstered and as month after month went by, we were astonished to discover that even though the hotel was sure different, it was still a good place to go.

But it's been a difficult transition, and certainly Hector and Pat have lost a few of Marcel's old patrons, just as new people have been attracted to the remodeled facilities. To help promote their business, Hector and Pat regularly bring in live music. "Never anything too rowdy—the place isn't big enough—but good dancing music, just the same," Hector explained. "We're still feeling our way. After all, it hasn't even been two years yet. I've learned quite a bit, and there's still more to learn. As a trucker, working as a mover, I got to know the interiors of buildings, and I learned how people like things to be arranged. For instance, you don't put a bed in front of a window if the room has a large enough windowless wall.

"And I like to work on buildings, I really enjoy the carpentry work, such as I've been doing here. If we had to call in carpenters or plumbers every time something went wrong in the place we'd probably be broke." Hector left the room to serve someone in the bar, and Pat explained some of the remodeling he has done, including all the new bathrooms, rebuilding the dance floor, cabinets behind the bar, paneling throughout the barroom, leveling the hotel, and restoring such historical niceties as the carriage port, which a less caring owner would have demolished.

The fact is that Hector and Pat have taken on a sizable challenge, and are already beginning to see a return on the improvements they have made. Skiiers are beginning to frequent the hotel with increasing regularity. "You know," said Pat, "people talk about inflation. We saw an old copy of the *Enosburg Standard* with an advertisement for the hotel's rates. Two dollars a day. And right now, we charge our permanent guests $15–$18 a week!" It's a no-nonsense, no charge-card, all-cash business, and this helps keep the prices down. And the food is still terrific!

But I think as responsible as anything for the success of Pat's and Hector's venture is their dedication to preserving a worthy building, while asserting the dignity of their business. Pat has lived in Vermont almost as many years as Hector has, and "there's no doubt these hills are my home." Hector may have been out of state a number of years, and he may even have been a stranger to some of the old-timers who were fond of Marcel. "My brother got his driver's license right in this room, but even though I grew up in Enosburg I never had much to do with this hotel. From the time I left Enosburg in 1950, until the time I bought it, I never really did set foot inside this hotel."

And then, as if remembering for the first time, "except one night, Barb and I stayed in Room 9. We were on our honeymoon and the car ran out of gas down the road, in front of a motel. That was our first night, and we couldn't get anyone up, so we slept in the car. But the second night of our honeymoon, Barb and I slept here.

"I never would have guessed someday I'd be an owner!"

Larry and Betty Farchi, Feil's Motel

Larry and Betty Farchi, both 47, acquired a motel in Nevada City, California, and because the motel's business was so well-established, they kept the former owner's name and sign out front: Feil's Motel. Larry and Betty, with three teenage children, took over in 1973, during the last week in August. "We were lucky to start during a busy season," Larry told me. "We sold our house and cashed in our bank account, and a piece of property I'd bought six

Larry and Betty Farchi

years before. We actually had just $40 left to our name after we'd moved into our 'new' motel."

"But it was the answer to our prayers," said Betty. "And we've just done everything on faith, and it's always turned out okay. We had a full house—all 10 units were occupied—that first night, and then we discovered we needed a new roof which we contracted on faith, and a local plumber who had no idea of our financial situation came and gave us $1,000. And my father, equally unknowing of our finances, gave us another $1,000, and we were able to finance the rest."

Janet and Ben and I came upon Feil's Motel at nightfall. We had completed a full day and resolved to spend the night in the first simple-looking motel we could find off the thruway. A red neon sign proclaimed "Feil's Motel, Vacancy," and we pulled into a beautifully treed parking area. I was immediately impressed by the greeting I received, invited into the owner's living room while we discussed price. Credit cards were not accepted and there was no color TV. But each room was equipped with cooking facilities and the price for a night was $12.

We were shown the room, which was spacious and equipped with a clean, sparsely furnished kitchenette. Fresh flowers were in a simple vase on the table, and as we took our suitcases inside, 12-year-old Peggy gave Ben a selected group of comic books. A simple, original, still-life oil painting hung on the wall. As we marveled at our good fortune in finding such a place, I resolved to talk with the owners in the morning, curious about how they could provide so much for so much less than most motels.

"We have a lot of regular customers, some who stay a week or more, and word of mouth also helps. The price didn't change when we took over, and we want to hold it where it is, if we can. For the most part we found that people respond to our not being the automatons that the world is trying to make of people today," said Larry.

"We enjoy seeing the cold, plastic facades melt into friendship."

"But this business would be awful if you didn't enjoy it, and in the big city it would be a nightmare," Betty added. "If you get into a business like this, you just can't get away. It's seven days a week, all year, unless you have that rare acquaintance . . . "

"Making ends meet is easy," Larry said. "We're the maids. When we were first thinking of this, I had a big English-type mountain inn in mind, serving meals and all, but I couldn't find one at the right price. The asking price of a good motel should be four-and-a-half times its annual gross, and we calculate the value of our motel, for insurance purposes, based on that figure."

I wondered about theft. How did they dare leave original paintings in the rooms, for instance? "That's really not a problem," said Betty. "Except with the Bibles. We've had a lot of Bibles taken, but that's just wonderful!"

Karl Buck, Handyman-Electrician

On a beautiful ridge that overlooks acres of rich farmland spreading toward Lake Champlain, in an immaculate house he built and wired himself, lives Karl Buck, 72 years old, a licensed electrician who quit teaching physics 11 years ago, after 38 years. "Electrician, carpenter, whatever needed doing, I did it. If you wanted a cat buried, it was five dollars." He is a short, sturdy man, with strong hands, a gruff sense of humor, and expressive, active eyes.

"But now," he told me, "I'm a little more particular. I don't need to take jobs unless I want them. While I was teaching high school, my wife and I just couldn't live on my salary. A neighbor, who was a superintendant at A&P, had work for me remodeling stores throughout the state, on weekends.

"And after awhile it occurred to me that we could do just as well if I were to leave teaching, and take up this sort of contracting work full time. It had got to the point where I was working all the time, weekends, holidays, and after school as late as 2 A.M. I'd stagger into school, sleep through the day, get home at 4 P.M., eat, and stagger out again.

"I might as well tell you that quitting was like getting out of prison," he said with a quick laugh. "After 38 years, every day at four o'clock was like stepping out of a jail cell!"

The first year after he left teaching, Karl placed an ad in the Yellow Pages, and "just to prove myself," took just about every job

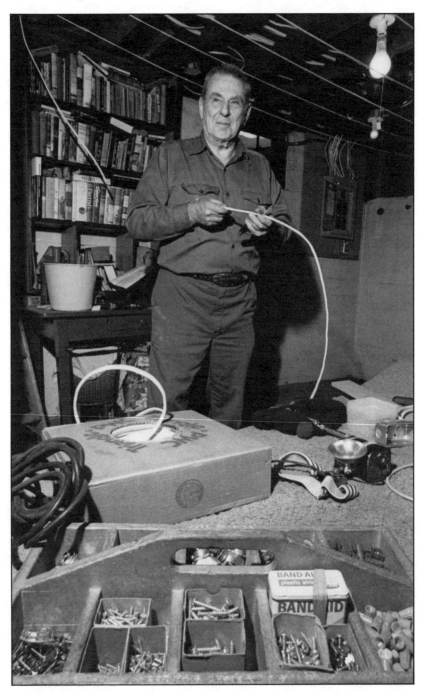

Karl Buck

he could find. "And I discovered that we could live a lot more comfortably. To tell you the truth, I was a little surprised."

During these 11 years of full-time contracting, he has accumulated a lot of savvy about service work in general. His opinions are strong, and thoughtfully expressed. Karl Buck is a very tidy person. Every detail of his house, and a spacious cellar lined with gleaming rows of home-canned foods from his 100-foot-square vegetable garden, attest to his care and thoroughness. He has lived alone since his wife died three years ago, shortly after they moved into their new home. He is obviously a person who enjoys his work, and takes pride in the fruits of his labors. And he is gifted with an objective perspective on his situation. "One time I made the mistake of looking at a job while I was out driving my new Mercedes. I didn't get the job. The people thought my price would be too high. By all means, when you go to look at a job, go in your work clothes. Don't dress up. Take the truck. And though it might be convenient to look at a job at night, when it's raining, you'll never get the job. Go on a nice, bright day when the customer's in a good mood and you can see what you're getting into." He refuses to accept a job until he's had a chance to look it over. "When someone calls, no matter how simple the job sounds, I always tell them I'll stop by to look it over. That's all I say. And then if the person has a nice appearance and the job isn't too dirty, I'll take it. But if my instincts tell me I'm not going to be paid, or the job is too messy, I'll just say I'm sorry.

"For instance, I don't usually work on trailers. They're usually poorly wired, and require a lot more work than the owner wants to pay for. But on one occasion a very pleasant man with a dog that had a friendly tail—of course, it snapped a little on the other end— and a wife who had just come home from the hospital didn't have any heat at all, so I went and made a temporary hookup for them. They had a piece of wire leading into the trailer, a piece of 14/2 with the cap on the end charred to white ash it was so overloaded. And that's usually the kind of situation you run into with trailers."

He has had as many as seven people working for him, but now uses a labor pool exclusively, when he needs extra help. "If I hire somebody, these days, I have to carry liability insurance, unemployment compensation and I just don't want the bother. So I just go to a labor pool, and they take care of everything. I simply pass their bill on to the customer."

His basic fee, he reported, is $9 an hour, "portal to portal." To that, he adds 20¢ a mile for all travel, and what he calls a "Machine Tool Charge," whenever a job requires the use of special equipment. "If I thread a half-inch pipe, the materials I use cost me $500. Sometimes I have to use a hydraulic bender, which cost me $450, so I can't just give the use of these machines away."

Karl Buck will not touch a job unless he has an electrical permit. "It doesn't cost you a thing to get a permit. The customer pays, and you get a certificate upon inspection of the job that exempts you from any liability. There's a business right in Burlington now that's fighting a $600,000 liability suit, which they could have avoided if they'd acquired a permit. So it just makes good sense."

Preparing to leave, I asked Karl Buck if he had any advice to private contractors. "Do the job as quickly as possible, and do it when you said you would. Clean up every day. Make sure that nothing gets broken or damaged. A small item may seem to be of no value, but to the owner it has not only monetary value but sentimental value as well. Do not lay tools on furniture. Put down drop cloths. Clean as you go. Make as little inconvenience as possible. Treat everything as though it were priceless.

"If people trust you, they will not usually ask for an estimate. However, many will ask for an estimate, even after you have started the work. Stress the point that an estimate is an educated judgment based on other, similar jobs, that it is not final, and that they will be billed on the actual cost. It is always good news if the estimate was too high and the actual bill is lower by a substantial sum. Make sure that the customer understands completely all details, in advance. Tell them when payment is due, in advance. Date all payments, at least a month ahead to the tenth of the month. Put it in writing.

"Word of mouth is the best advertising, but I have had several jobs as a result of advertising painted on the truck. Yellow Pages are better than newspaper ads. Making a good impression on a job will often get you another job nearby. Working for contractors in other lines of work is very risky from a financial viewpoint. They are always short of cash, they will not and cannot pay you until they are paid. They want discounts, special prices, and long waits before a 'cash flow'. They want inadequate work done at the cheapest price. Having worked for quite a number, I can say that, in no case, has it been a satisfactory experience.

"Getting 'burned' on the job does occur, but it can be minimized. Experience shows that if you can build up a clientele of satisfied customers over a period of years that it comes to a point where most of your business is repeats with good paying records. Certain types of professions are poor risks, as well as neighborhoods, family size, condition of the house, and many other factors. Young business executives under 30 with families, rising lawyers with sporadic incomes, insurance salesmen who have not built a clientele, highly trained professional people in the sciences are generally poor risks. The best clients are married, over 35, with families about to leave home, take a great deal of pride in the home, live in good neighborhoods. Just good honest people. Just because a client has paid in the past does not warrant the assumption that they will continue to pay in the future. Possible customers who complain, in advance, about mileage charges, labor too high, estimates, are best to avoid. It is better not to always keep busy than to tie up several thousand dollars in a job and have to sue in court with the lawyer getting a third of it after a couple of years."

I asked if he takes on other work now, besides electrical work. Laughing, and characteristically careful, he replied, "Well, let's put it this way. If a job appeals to me, I do it."

Hauling Trash

In Saint Louis, I met a retired 45-year-old professor who for tax and licensing purposes insisted on anonymity. "I guess you could call mine a spoiled academic career," he said. "I was a research psychologist and, when I saw that my career wasn't going any farther, I stumbled into this hauling business. I had an old truck I'd bought a couple of years earlier for a small publishing venture. I ran an ad, 'Hauling', in the local newspaper classified with my phone number and before I knew it, I was getting phone calls at all hours from people who had to move. 'Can you move me, tonight?' A lot of people trying to beat the rent, I guess. This was a little different from hauling and I ran a 'Moving' ad as well as well as the 'Hauling' one and if the job was too big for my little pickup, I'd hire a truck, and maybe someone to help me.

"Salesmanship helps, and can be used with real subtlety. For instance, I know my customers before meeting them. Someone who spots my ad in the classified section is probably trying to save money so when they phone, I ask them to describe what they want hauled or moved. And if the job won't require the hiring of a truck, and most jobs do not, I'll say 'Oh, that's a small enough job, I'll bet we can get by with the pickup truck.' And they're thinking, 'Oh good, he's going to save me money.'

"For a business, this is a perfect weekend deal. Full time it would be a little tighter, although it is verging on becoming full time for me. I started a refrigerator business because for some reason people discard a lot of refrigerators. I'm paid $10 to haul them away. I was hauling three or four a month, so I rented a store and I pay a man to clean and repair refrigerators, and then he puts them out in the front of the store, and we recycle them at a good profit. In a way we're part of a racket initiated by the repairmen who put a ridiculous price on their work so they can make a bundle or sell a new refrigerator. But I find the work very stimulating and interesting, and it sure beats any factory work I could do. My only tools are a two-wheel dolly and a government-surplus pickup."

He granted me the interview on the condition that I accompany him on a visit to one of his clients (where, by the way, he made an interest-free loan of $20), and we were driving along a one-way street in a busy residential section. He took a sharp left. "Here, I'll show you the shop," he said, and pulled to the curb, pointing in through a store window. The man inside, next to a refrigerator, stared out, seeming puzzled. We pulled off quickly before the man in the shop recognized the driver. "Come to think of it, he's never seen this car, and he doesn't know I ever wear a tie. I'd like to keep it this way.

"It's strictly a cash business. I name the price over the phone, depending on whether I need to hire help or a bigger truck. I also run an ad 'We Clean Basements Out,' and people who have just bought a house will take the good stuff that's been left by the previous owner, and we get all the rest. 'All the rest' can sometimes mean something sentimental, which has actual value. Letters. American flags that were draped over caskets. Things people cannot bear to rid themselves of so they leave behind. It can be very sad. But I retail this 'all the rest' at drive-in swap 'n' shop Sunday specials. People will tell you, 'Haul off this trash. It's a lot of junk.' And it's an antique! I also have markets for paper and scrap metal. Any furniture I can't resell, I lease, which is profitable storage!

"I realize you might call this a fly-by-night operation. I carry no insurance, and I avoid declaring this income as deriving from hauling by listing it as part of my little publishing business, which shows a small profit. There's a risk involved in all this and it bothers me very much right now. I'm very inexperienced and just sort of stumbling along trying to stay hidden. Especially from the authorities with their licenses; for instance, what kind of workman's comp would I have to carry, and what kind of equipment would be necessary if I acknowledged that I occasionally hire a helper?

"So I wonder if I were to cut all these risks if I might wind up having to charge the same as Mayflower. But other than that it's a very straightforward, legitimate business. I like the exercise it provides, and the dealing with people. It's a lot of fun, whereas I really get uptight in the teaching situations I sometimes get in with cheating and misrepresented projects.

"Frankly, I'm the wrong age and way overtrained for any position at the beginning level. I probably scare the hell out of people. I was considered for a programer's job paying $18,000, but they wouldn't take me because I was creaming their exams. I could fake it, lie about my background and say, 'I've been hauling trash all my life.' Then I'd probably make it. And maybe someday I'll go back to teaching. But for the interim this is an extremely good business."

Jock Gill, Photographer

Like printing, photography is a craft that can require a large amount of equipment and/or a high degree of specialization. One of the major considerations here is whether to attempt to equip a darkroom, or instead to find a reliable developing-and-printing service. Conceivably, finding no such reliable service, you might decide to go ahead with the darkroom.

"One way to be successful in the photography business is to offer your community a service you know to be missing and for which you have strong evidence there is both a need and a market." Those are the words of Jock Gill, a free-lance photographer living near Boston.

"Or you might conclude that you can offer better service at a more attractive price than is available from existing businesses. If you work hard, and are shrewd, imaginative, resourceful, and just plain lucky as well, your business ought to prosper.

"In which case, you will find yourself faced with a difficult decision. Should you expand beyond a one-person operation and hire a receptionist? An assistant? An accountant? A lab person? The answer to these questions will largely be determined by the lifestyle you are pursuing.

"For myself, I have found it useful to recall some rather brash advice, freely given by some former compatriots: 'Kiss Kiss' or, 'Keep it simple, stupid.'

Jock Gill

"I don't have a darkroom because there's a zillion people taking advantage of the large market for black and white. It is true that I began with black and white, but since going free lance, I've specialized in color. Although the market for color is smaller than that for black and white, there is far less competition in color work, and I avoid the problem of trying to be all things to all people. One should develop some special skills to differentiate himself from the rest of the herd. So I decided, 'No darkroom—save space, money, and time.' It is also important to remember that people are willing to pay considerably more money for the time they can actually *see* you working than for the time you're hidden down in a darkroom out of sight.

"There's a real danger in this business of being seduced by the equipment and becoming a hardware freak. More often than not new equipment isn't really necessary, and you wind up with a foolish capital investment. For instance, I bought an expensive color meter that I've rarely used. Should I take at least a 50 percent loss and sell it, or hold on in case a job comes up where it might be necessary?

"In the end, it is the quality of your thought and imagination, not the hardware, that is truly important."

It was a lazy Saturday in mid-December. Jock's wife, Johanna, an art historian, had flown to Kansas that morning to visit her family for Christmas; Jock was going to finish up a few jobs and fly out the next Saturday. He drove Johanna to Logan Airport at 7 A.M., then returned to the large downstairs apartment they rent and slept until 10. "I work whenever the hours demand," he said. "Today I've only got one job, and that's over at the TV studio at 2—you're welcome to come along." He poured me a cup of steaming coffee. It was 11:30. "Diamonds and Rust" floated from the stereo into the kitchen. *"Where are you calling from? A booth in the Midwest."*

"When you work for yourself, you're a jack-of-all-trades, but for your own sake keep the trades limited!" said Jock. "You can stay purely free lance, or go into a limited partnership as I have done with Dennis Purcell. We have certain projects that are cooperative in nature, for which we split the costs and the profits and assign individual credits or faults. We also sometimes cover for one another, or turn jobs over to the other if we are busy. Beyond that, we keep our clients separate.

"An alternative to total independence or a limited partnership is the studio, but in order to finance that you have to be too busy to process your own film, which means you hire a processor, and then you also need an assistant. This means an accountant to figure taxes, and retirement and insurance programs to cover your employees and their dependents. Figure their salaries as 12 Ks each × 3, that's $36,000, plus fringe benefits, plus an accountant's fee, plus rent on the studio, plus hardware, etcetera, etcetera. Then add your own salary. *Ugh.* Keep overhead low to maximize profits!

"The goal in working for yourself is to earn what you want but not to be a slave to your obligations. The man I apprenticed with, before his heart attack, was earning 80 to 100 Ks a year. Now he's on the Cape with 8 to 10 Ks a year, supporting only his own household. The last time I saw him, he allowed that getting out from under his studio obligations was the best thing to happen to him in a very long time. You might say he lived to tell the tale. With a limited partnership you need to coordinate your acts just enough so that you're not working for other people when you need to work together on a cooperative job."

Jock's speciality is color; he works principally in Polaroid, which requires no darkroom, and in color slides. All exposed slide film is sent directly to the Kodak color processing labs, "because they offer slide processing cheaper than most custom labs I know. More important, Kodak can usually do a better job than other labs. They are big enough to be able to afford more and better quality-control measures than a local lab. Also their chemistry is in such large volumes that a small chemistry error will not have the same impact as it might in the smaller developing tanks at a local lab.

"But local labs do have a very important place in my business. If I need a roll of slides developed in three hours, I go directly to the local experts. If I need color prints, I *never* go to Kodak. Their print quality is targeted for consumer appreciation, not professional standards. As in most things you pay your money and make your choice. I choose to pay my local labs their rightful premium and in return I get color prints of a quality that mass-produced, machine-printed consumer prints can never hope to match.

"As for billing the client, I make no attempt to profit from the sales of my prints. I bill on the basis of time, starting at $25 per hour, and pass on all expenses, including film, processing, prints, and so forth, to the client. I mark these items up 5 percent for handling.

"While this scheme works well for me and my type of business, clearly it would never work for someone in either the wedding, portrait, or commercial studio business. Such businesses bill by the job, not by the hour, and are consequently able to make a great deal more money than I."

A room in the Gills' apartment serves as Jock's office. The room is equipped with a large flat desk covered with notes and photography manuals, a couple of chairs, and a lot of boxes with lighting equipment and cameras. A telephone with an automatic answering device allows Jock to respond to clients, even if he's out on another job when they call.

"You could start in photography with minimum capital, especially if you were willing to learn a certain kind of photography, and equip yourself for just that," he said.

"Simply take a look around and see what *isn't* being done. For instance, one of my specialities is making color slides from flat art, such as books, drawings, prints, etcetera. Among my clients, the slide library at the Boston Museum of Fine Arts has not yet been able to find students willing or able to do the work of copying reproductions of artworks found in books. And this is very easy work—technically like taking candy from a baby—requiring very little equipment. And, both Polaroid and Kodak have little books to show you how to do it. Just write their technical salespeople, or ask at your local camera store.

"But no one wants to do it, mostly, I suppose, because it isn't glamorous enough. For me, work like this provides the bread-and-butter money. And the slide library at the Boston Museum of Fine Arts has been one of my principal, mainstay clients. I make color slides for most of the museum's television shows as well as for just about all their audiovisual productions. I have found several different departments which use my services under the one organizational umbrella of the museum.

"Another of my umbrella accounts is Polaroid. Something like half the cameras sold in America cost $25 or less. Polaroid is very aware of this and addresses itself to that market by working to debunk the idea that one must be an 'art photographer' and buy lots of equipment. My job is to demonstrate, with artistic results, what their cameras can do.

"Umbrella accounts are worth their weight in gold, even if

they cost you a couple of glamor jobs because your time is tied up.
The opposite of this situation is having lots of clients on one-time
jobs. Some guy down in Florida charged Polaroid big bucks for a
job I would have charged $200 for and that's the only job he'll ever
get from them. The ongoing job is far more rewarding because it's a
form of friendship as well.

"At the same time one of the things about being a free lance,
your availability, is a major part of your value. So if a bread-and-
butter job is ruining your availability, you'll wind up losing your
other clients. You have to strike a balance."

Jock's training in photography started in 1963, when he was a
senior in high school. From 1968 to 1971 he worked as a full-time
cameraman and photographer for WGBH-TV in Boston.
"Experience, the school of hard knocks, is one of the best ways to
learn. And by reading books, magazines, and the many, excellent
manuals published by Kodak and Polaroid, to name but two
sources. And there are also the *Peterson's Guides to Creative
Photography*, as well as the very excellent *Life Library of
Photography* series books. Read the publications and do the work
that interests and challenges you. What better way to learn?"

In 1971 Jock decided to break away from the employee relationship when he saw that the creative jobs were being directed
toward outside photographers, while he was expected to stay
within the bounds of his "speciality."

"One night I went to a dinner party and by pure blind chance
sat next to the now-director of a Rhode Island museum who by
chance had gone to the same prep school I'd attended, and by
chance had a photography gig. And all this, coinciding with the fact
that management where I was working couldn't see how important
it is to give creative opportunities to full-time staff members, plus
the fact that I had already been offered another free-lance gig, gave
me the confidence to quit the full-time job.

"I lay in bed all night giggling and poking Johanna. And the
next morning the supervisor couldn't believe I was going to quit. I
had to go back and tell him again. They hadn't understood that if
they'd given the in-house workers some flexibility, I might still be
with them. And it would have been cheaper to hire a free lancer to
cover my job than to bring one in for the job I wanted.

"I've learned that, in free lancing, there really are no rules except to find out what works well for you. I think it's important to always feel that you're a beginner: The joy of constant discovery is what makes it work. As soon as you think you've got the hard and fast rules figured out you might as well pack it up and quit.

"If you're looking for work, take just a few samples of your work. Hide your bleeding heart creativity. If you're looking for copy work, take examples of your copy work. If you're hustling for picture stories, take examples of your picture stories. Show your experience. The first few free-lance hits are the hardest to make because you don't yet have anything published to show. So make up samples of the kind of work you want to do. If you're dying to photograph ketchup ads, set up some sample ketchup stills.

"Remember that the cost of the photographer is just the tip of the iceberg, so the client wants to start with something good. After he's bought your work, he still has to pay for the reproduction, layout, printing, and all related work. Each step of the way involves more and more people, as well as more and more money. You and the art director meet at the tip of this pyramid and he's being hounded by 50 other photographers, all wanting work.

"I'm not qualified to give advice on portrait work, but if I were going to pursue that type of work, I would devise a price schedule that wouldn't scare the client off with high daily or hourly rates. Instead, I'd concentrate on the quality of the image and show the client a good proof, and then make my profits from enlargements. Another way to make money is to go to the fairs and to Santa's appearances and set up a booth. There's lots of income there just waiting for the person who wants to take it on. Just be sure to check with the owner or manager.

"One of the worst things about being in business for yourself is the cash-flow problem." We were driving downtown to Channel 2—where Jock worked until that day in 1971—to photograph Saturday's only job, making a "still" from a videotape. I was surprised when, in preparing to leave, Jock merely slid a collapsible tripod ("one of the most underrated tools in photography") and a four-by-five view camera with a Polaroid back into the trunk of his car. Kiss Kiss.

"As a businessperson, I am now a firm believer in asset management, not debit management. It took me a while to learn this lesson, but a couple of back-to-back zero-dollar-income months in my first year taught me quite a lot. One of the things I learned the hard way was that giving up on that regular paycheck habit made no difference when it came to the rent and other regularly scheduled bills.

"Now, five years later, the bills still come like clockwork, and my income still comes at very irregular intervals, but the marvels of modern banking have solved my problem. Cash flow. My bank put a line of credit on my checking account so that I get a loan, not a penalty charge, if I am forced to overdraw the account to pay my bills. If I pay the bank before they invoice me, I even escape paying interest for the few days I used their money. To avoid overdrawing myself into a bottomless pit, I have a rule of thumb never to borrow more than one-third the amount I have outstanding as receivables."

He stopped the car at a camera store, ran in and came back with two large boxes of Polaroid film. "For some photographers, the advantage of Polaroid is in copying work where the client doesn't want to leave the valuable original with the photographer—so Granny's visage never need stay away overnight. And the photographer and client can see, on the spot, whether a workable image has been produced. For me, Polaroid's greatest attractions are the films the company offers. I love the gray scale of Type 52 (four-by-five, black-and-white) film and I love the color offered both for SX-70 and in four-by-five Polacolor 2. Polaroid films are not the answer to all questions, like anything else. But when they are right, they're fantastic!

"More important than anything else is having satisfied customers. Bad word of mouth will cut you dead. Courtesies really count and you can be dropped like a bad habit simply by failing to extend yourself in a friendly way. Courtesy, promptness, and follow-through. The job isn't finished when you push the button. After you find the job, find out what the client wants, do it, deliver, bill, and follow through with courtesy, every step of the way. If there's any problem that is in any way your fault, even if the lab blows it and ruins your film, do it over on your own time if you can, and never send a bill when the results are not satisfactory. Far better not to take a job than to make an ass of yourself. Don't be afraid to say it isn't my speciality, and to recommend someone you know who will do a first-class job."

Charlie Lee, Farmer and Farrier

Bakersfield, population 600, is a farming community in northwestern Vermont, about 15 miles from the Canadian border. Charlie Lee has lived there since 1971 when he bought the 555-acre Rupert Hyde farm with two partners, Carol Crawford and Paul Haible, who live and work off the farm, but occasionally help with the seasonal chores. Charlie, who is 28, grew up on a dairy farm just 100 miles south, in Bridgewater, "where I learned about half of what I know. The rest I got the hard way."

After a few halfhearted attempts at college and a series of varied jobs, Charlie realized that he was simply postponing his return to the farm, and he set out with his partners to buy a spread.

Six years later, the old Hyde Farm is finally getting to be known as the Charles Lee Farm. And with good reason, for Charlie has changed a number of the old routines, and substituted a brand of farming that really can't be called by any name. The Hydes milked cows up there for 50 years. Charlie had milked a lot of cows in his life, and he prefered the slightly more flexible schedule allowed by raising heifers, which he sold to neighboring farmers as replacement stock. Then, "the horseshoeing business became more than a part-time affair, and I sold off all the heifers to become a full-time blacksmith. Business demand for a blacksmith was that heavy!"

The buildings were in rough shape; the farmhouse, more than

Charlie Lee

100 years old, large and creaky, is being renovated slowly. One of the partners calls it "a regular lightning trap." The house and barns are at the end of a mile-long dirt road, perched on a knoll surrounded by open fields of hay. West of the house, a valley lies below, with undeveloped land as far as you can see. Rising to the north is a beautiful sugar bush and the ancient sugarhouse where, every spring, Charlie and partners produce about 250 gallons of Vermont's finest pure maple syrup.

Charlie thinks of Maple Mountain Farm as a giant garden needing yearlong management. The woodlot is an extremely important part of this plan: Working the woods is a weeding, thinning, and harvesting process. The weeds and thinnings are used for boiling the 10,000 gallons of sap into their 250 gallons of syrup, and to heat the house and shop in winter, when, were it not for "the best wood furnace in the county," the big old house could lose just a bit of its charm. And the harvest: timbers cleared from the woodlot are used for the unending series of building tasks that Charlie seems to face happily. Most recently, he built a new horse barn, and is planning this summer to build a new sugarhouse. "That should let us grow a bit," he said with a smile. Charlie has a dry wit and his eyes sparkle at what seem like a thousand secret jokes. His manner is common to many native Vermonters; the words come slowly while facial expressions do most of the talking.

He loves to work, and it shows. The drive is lined with long rows of maple and beech chunks, split and stacked at least a year in advance, while neatly racked maple and birch planks season under cover. On a summer day, chickens scratch and chase each other in their yard, and Charlie's team of Belgian draft horses, Pat and Charley, if they're not working in the fields, might snort a greeting and amble over to the fence. Charlie has also been raising two Belgian mares that he bought in Canada as three-month fillies. These he plans to breed, to sell young stock. He has been training the mares to work in the woods, skidding logs.

Pat and Charley work all winter, and during the summer visit local parades. During sugaring, when the snow is still two to three feet deep, they negotiate the maple rock slope that's far too steep for any machine. Charlie guides them among the giant maples towing the sled that carries his helpers who empty the buckets and hang them back on the spouts. One spring he loaded them into the truck and drove to the New York State Ploughing Contest, where they won a ribbon.

"These horses really keep me going," Charlie admitted. "There's bad days when you wonder if you've taken on too much and maybe it would be nice to jump in the truck and head down the road saying 'See you later everybody.' But I guess I'll farm and farm until something better comes up."

It wasn't long after he bought the farm and established his own routines that Charlie's love for horses got the best of him, and he applied for farrier's training in a unique three-month course that is offered to only one or two students a semester by Harold Mowers at Cornell University's Veterinary College. He was accepted for January through March, and Carol tended the farm.

Charlie takes a great deal of pride in having worked with Mowers; in the three years since he completed the course, he has driven the 400 miles back to Cornell a number of times to visit his teacher. I made the trip with Charlie that early January, when he first enrolled. We had been offered meals and floor space for our sleeping bags at Kosmos, a wonderful natural foods restaurant and gathering place outside Ithaca, in return for help in the kitchen. Charlie was looking for a place to live, and he had just completed his first day of training. We had washed the dishes for the restaurant, and a live band was setting up. I remember dancing for awhile and suddenly wondering where Charlie was. A little later, outside, I found him sitting behind the wheel of his car, carefully examining a pair of forged tongs—his first project in the training program.

When he returned from his apprenticeship, Charlie was determined to set up his own farrier service, and offer his neighbors something that was badly needed. He had a telephone put in, "reluctantly," he said. And he equipped his truck with anvil and forge and the many tools required in the exacting business of removing worn shoes, trimming a horse's hooves, and constructing new shoes and corrective fittings. Charlie was fairly sure he'd have enough business to justify the expenses.

What he didn't realize was that the shortage of qualified farriers in Vermont reaches all corners of the state, and that within a year he would be using the services of a woman in Bakersfield who takes his calls while he's on the road—visiting and tending as many as 15 horses at three or four stables a day. "It's become a full-time business," he admitted, "and it really does hurt sometimes at the end of the day when I straighten my back."

"It really strikes me as unpleasant work," I admitted.

"It's *hard* work," Charlie corrected. "That's why there aren't too many blacksmiths." I speculated that it must be hardest in the summer, with heat and flies complicating difficulties. "Not really. It's hardest in winter because you can't wear gloves in this work. Horse barns aren't usually very warm, and when the temperature drops below 0°F., your hands can get a bit chilly." And then he smiled and scratched his chin, "But I love it. I love working with metal, I love working with horses, and I enjoy seeing so many different farms."

Charlie told me that he does his own billing. I asked if he ever has trouble collecting. "Yup. Some folks don't pay. Curiously, it's the wealthy people. I'd rather work for the farmers—they're more easy going, and they pay on time. If I had my way, I'd have a shop right here on my farm, and work only on horses that were brought to me. But I don't figure I can do that quite yet. I feel I need more experience before the business will come to me, but ideally, I'd work only on draft horses.

It has been a busy and tiring afternoon. Charlie shod a nag and three very high-class mares for a horsewoman down south of Stowe. The mares had to be just right for a hunt the next day and one of them was for sale. My curiosity overcame me and I asked how much. "Twenty-five hundred dollars. But let me tell you," the lady replied, "she's a helluva good ride. I've ridden many an animal in my time, believe me, and she's the best." Charlie looked up from under the best ride in central Vermont and winked.

"Part of the job is meeting so many different kinds of people," he said as we were driving to Enosburg, where he would shoe Harvey, a racehorse. Figuring up the day's profits: Charlie gets $18 for a regular shoeing job if he provides the shoes; $12 if the owner's shoes are used. This had been a fairly typical day; three clients in his date book with a total of five horses. Charlie had supplied all the shoes today, and the tally came to $90. "Not bad for a sweaty old blacksmith," he chuckled.

The August chill was just beginning to come on as the sun went down and, as he did south of Stowe, Charlie wrestled his anvil off the back of the truck, which wears on each side a handsome, hand-painted sign:

Charles Lee
Blacksmith
Welding   Horseshoeing
Bakersfield, Vermont 827-3741

It was almost dark and he had hammered three shoes into a perfect fit, and was working on Harvey's fourth hoof. The barn took on the smell of hoof parings as Charlie shuffled back and forth from hoof to anvil. I asked if he had to take special care when shoeing a racehorse. "Well, the angles are more critical," he replied, "but you're really supposed to take special care with every horse.

"Sometimes I don't straighten up because my back hurts less if I just keep bent to hoof-height." He bent at the waist and Harvey's right front foreleg pretzeled up and between Charlie's legs. Charlie had shod Harvey twice before and they apparently trusted each other. Harvey's lower lip jumped around a lot and his tail worked hard to keep the flies off balance but otherwise he did seem relaxed.

Behind Harvey, the length of the barn, a dozen sulkies rested against old stanchions and two blue ribbons proclaiming "Enosburg Horse Club Raceway 1974" hung among the tack. I had a lot of questions, but I could tell that Charlie would rather work than engage in conversation. I looked back over my notes and realized I didn't know the correct word to describe what kind of a racehorse pulls a sulky. "Would you call Harvey a sulky horse?" I asked.

"Call him a trotting horse," said Charlie. "He'll trot when I get done." And he bent back to the twentieth hoof of the afternoon.

5.
COUNTRY FREE LANCERS AND URBAN HOMESTEADERS

Independents

Jock Gill, the Boston photographer, introduced me to the term "urban homesteaders." "I equate homesteading with economic independence," he told me. "And though it may be a lot easier to be 'independent' in this way where the cost of living is lower and the materialistic temptations are fewer, the idea that one *must* go up-country to lead a simpler, more basic life is ridiculous. It can be done in the city as well.

"After all, freedom is what homesteading is all about isn't it? You can find freedom anywhere. The limiting notion that freedom is spelled country is unimaginative, dull, and in the end, irrelevant."

For the most part, farmers, craftspeople, and those who perform services for a living have a fairly narrow range of financial expectations. Their operations are based on a regular, annual pattern, where income is proportionate with effort. The people I call "country free lancers and urban homesteaders" are less likely to have any real year-to-year financial pattern.

They are often artists who have dedicated years to the developing of a special interest. Combine talent with special interest and you often get obsession; "unrecognized geniuses" are a lot more common than we think. They are the artists who enrich the lives of their neighbors and of other artists, but whose names never become household words. Generally, they like it this way, though everyone in this category has probably daydreamed the thin possibility of momentary fame and the end of financial burdens.

Hayden Carruth, a poet and free-lance writer, describes the free-lance situation in financial and emotional terms: "A free lance puts his income together from many different sources—for me judging contests, writing reviews, poems, and working as an editorial consultant provide this income—and the really discouraging aspect is that after all the energy's expired, even when you're well paid, *it's finished*. None of the continuity exists in a free lancer's life that prevails in other work situations. Each project is a new start, a clean slate, which suggests a free lance needs a special kind of energy to get himself started each morning."

I include inventors in this section because they, too, work obsessively long hours on any given project, developing ideas and constructing prototypes that may never find a profitable spot in the marketplace. And I also include people whose means of self-employment may offer a regular financial pattern, but whose work relates especially to the city, where commercial recycling projects show substantial profit opportunities.

Recyclers

Mike Keiser and Phil Friedmann, Recycled Paper Products

Five years ago, Mike Keiser and Phil Friedmann, both 32, started Recycled Paper Products, Incorporated, in Chicago with an initial investment of $15,000 and the cooperation of a printer who could supply 100-percent recycled paper, and all their printing needs, and who agreed to defer billing for a year. Keiser and Friedmann came upon their idea as a brainstorm, not even knowing whether 100-percent recycled paper was obtainable. Should it be, they thought, they could perhaps start small with Christmas cards, which would provide free publicity and distribution through customer use.

"Selling Christmas cards is selling art," they wrote me in a letter. "We found our first artists in the Yellow Pages under 'Commercial Artists', and proceeded from there. Once we had a product, all we had to do was see as many stores as possible, and the rest came naturally."

Presently, Recycled Paper Products has gross sales of 1.3 million dollars a year. Because they work in "near-tenement" conditions, Keiser and Friedmann report that the company could withstand a 50 percent drop in sales, "and still make money."

Employing 20 full-time assistants, Recycled Paper Products is the largest business discussed in this book. Keiser and Friedmann attribute their success to recognizing a real market for recycled paper products, and developing a profitable means of advertising their goods. Their most important asset, they told me, is "people who consider working for us to be an opportunity, and not just another job."

Robert Cote,
Unregistered Wastepaper

Robert Cote, who lives in Saint Louis, De Terrebonne, Quebec, started his unregistered wastepaper business three years ago, when he saw an advertisement placed by a giftware distributor who needed clean newspapers for packing. "All it takes," writes Cote, "is the family car and a trailer, or a pickup truck, a few tables in a garage or basement, and a few kids 10 to 14 years old, who receive 15¢ per bundle for making 25-pound oval rolls of the larger size (23-by-29-inch) papers. The smaller, 14-by-23-inch papers are

Mike Keiser and Phil Friedmann

simply unfolded by the middle and wrapped in 50-pound bundles, using string bought from a farmer who salvages it from hay bales."

Cote has made arrangements with about 25 newsstands, libraries, bus stations, and apartment superintendants to collect all unsoiled newspapers on a regular basis, usually twice-weekly, on the same day the municipal garbage collectors arrive "leaving the owner the option to put them with the garbage if I haven't passed by that time." The paper is usually free, but Cote offers to pay up to $20 per ton, for clean newspaper in big lots. Although he negotiates different arrangements with various suppliers, he makes a practice of remembering all his contacts at Christmas with a generous gift. Cote has found that apartment building superintendants are as willing as news vendors to separate clean newspapers from their trash, and "a ten dollar bill makes the deal more interesting than three or four dollars."

Cote's present clients include a lamp factory and a giftware factory. Both pay $30 per ton for the 14-by-23-inch size paper, and $70 per ton for the 23-by-29-inch size, for which he pays $12 per ton to his young helpers for bundling. "After a month or so for setting up, you find yourself averaging three tons of paper a week, and spending about 15 to 20 hours per week of your own time. Assuming that one half of the paper is of the large size, and a half is small, the average gross is $150 a week; after paying my help and figuring gasoline for the truck and heat and light for the garage, I clear between $100 and $125."

Douglas and Jackie Eichhorn, Antiques

Douglas and Jackie Eichhorn are college graduates in their mid-30s. Jackie is a talented graphic artist, and Douglas is a poet of growing national reputation who was, until his contract expired, instructor of creative writing at Earlham College in Richmond, Indiana. Both Douglas and Jackie enjoyed collecting antiques as a hobby; Douglas was growing weary of his teaching chores; both share a commitment, discovered during their Peace Corps duty in Peru, to recycling. So it was natural for them, when Douglas lost his position at the college, to swing their professional energies into a full-time antique business, rather than look for a new teaching job. They bought the house adjoining theirs and started filling it with antiques.

Their business is both wholesale and retail, but their greatest number of sales is to other dealers, which qualifies them as "pickers." Jackie explained that the traditional picker is someone who goes from door to door, asking if there's anything old for sale. "He buys for 10¢ and sells for $100." Douglas added, "That's the *successful* picker." The Eichhorns know a picker who lives in Jacksonville, New York, "when he's not vacationing in the Bahamas." And another who is literally on the road, door to door, 42 consecutive weeks of the year. "He actually goes home just once a year to get his mail. He lives with his mother when he's not out picking."

Centerville is about six miles west of Richmond. Douglas and Jackie live on West Main Street, three blocks from the town traffic light, on Route 40, which is one of those broad two-lane Midwestern highways that stretches across the flat countryside between farm towns. Centerville has one traffic light and eleven antique shops! I asked the Eichhorns about the competition, rather stiff, I'd thought, for such a tiny town. "Not at all. The more shops the better. Centerville's antique shops help each other by attracting buyers to the community." Isn't such a spread just the picker's dream, eleven shops lining West Main, all in a row? "Nope," answered Douglas, "it doesn't work that way. If the picker has something good to sell, he'll unload it at the first shop he comes to. Otherwise he'll leave Centerville with as much junk as he brought with him.

"Never buy something you don't like. That's how we operate. If you don't like something it's hard to convince someone else to buy it. Also, as a buyer, you have to be aware of the subtle differences in things that render them priceless or worthless. We sold a quilt once for $85 that was worth $2,500!" Douglas' voice trailed off as Jackie sighed and explained how they let the treasure slip by. "We only paid $18 for it. We were satisfied with the *profit*, having no idea that if we'd sent a photograph of that quilt to Madison Avenue, we could have sold it for $2,000. I saw it recently on the cover of a prestigious New York catalogue."

"But what are you going to do?" asked Douglas, "let it screw up your life? You can't fret over it. Money means nothing in this

Douglas and Jackie Eichhorn

business. As long as you've got it to buy with, that is. When the merchandise comes up you have to be equipped to buy it. So sometimes we have lots of beautiful stuff all around us and nothing to eat!"

Jackie thinks the best way to start in the antique business is the way they did—collecting as a hobby "so you develop your knowledge and your interest at a leisurely pace. I suppose you could start an antique business without any gradual preparation, but I doubt you could live off it very easily—unless you made two or three big, lucky deals right off. But the business requires very little overhead. It helps to have a wagon or a truck, and it's nice to own a house, but you can always rent. And there are some pickers who live in the front and deal out of the back of their trucks."

This is one business where location is of extreme importance, assuming you are going to maintain a shop, and where competition is an asset. In a sense, all the antique shops in Centerville have transformed the tiny town into an antique district. Real estate prices are generally depressed in this area of Indiana, which made it possible for the Eichhorns to acquire a shop that was just right for their purposes, and ideal because it is adjacent to their living quarters. Both are brick row houses built in the 1830s. Because they live right next door to the shop, the Eichhorns rarely need to use the "Closed" side of their sign. A note is securely taped to the window of the shop door: "If door is locked, please come to our house, adjoining, and we'll gladly open the shop."

Even being only one block off Main Street could cost a lot of business. Further, explained Douglas, theft insurance is almost impossible to carry, because their inventory is so flexible. "We carry fire insurance on our house and its contents, but there's no way we could keep a theft policy on the shop up-to-date. So it really helps to be located in the center of town." Jackie added that their inventory is not of a type likely to attract burglars anyway. In the antique business only the portable items, like jewelry and coins, are really vulnerable to theft.

"Bookkeeping is simple," explained Douglas. "We maintain our inventory on a perpetual monthly cash basis. We have a sales record book, which is divided into months of the year, in which we record our gross sales on a day-to-day basis. We keep wholesale and retail sales separate, as we must send in the sales tax on retail sales at the end of every month."

The Eichhorns recommend specialization. Although many dealers do well buying anything and everything, "that would make it too much just 'business' as opposed to business and a growing-learning experience. After awhile other dealers get to know what you like, and you find buyers whose needs you can anticipate. We've been in business three years and already we know about a hundred dealers pretty well." Douglas told me about a purchase he had made recently. "We saw this advertisement for a 'Barn Sale' so we went, and this guy takes us out through a field of rotting pumpkins to his barn, where there isn't a thing we want to handle. Lots of old heavy cast-iron bells and telephone insulators, the kinds of things you'd buy if you were only looking for profit. Although we definitely specialize in American novelty items, we don't buy unless we can imagine owning whatever's in question, or at least know a dealer with a real weakness for that sort of item.

"Anyway, this guy doesn't have anything in our line. But as we're walking through his toolshed, I spot this weird tin helmet hanging on the wall, and then just outside the door I see this incredible tin ax—it had to be tin because if it were real no one could lift it—just leaning up against the shed surrounded by rotting pumpkins. So I ask if he wants to sell the ax and he laughs because he thinks I think it's *real*. 'Oh, you don't want *that*,' he says, 'that's just a ceremonial ax.'

"But I convince him I'm serious. 'Well, I can't sell it anyway,' he says. 'It was a gift, from a friend.' So I say, 'Well, just assuming it wasn't a gift, how much would you want?' So he gives me this ridiculously high price, thinking that's going to end the matter.

"So I say, 'I can meet that price, and not only that, I've got cash—not checks—to pay with. And I want that helmet you've got on the wall as well.' And he starts talking really fast. 'Now you just wait right here, I've got to go call my friend. I'm sure he won't mind if I sell it.'

"And when he came back, having called his friend, I said, 'Now that we know you can sell, it's time to talk business because your price is ridiculous.' And to give you an idea how crazy this business is, there's probably no other dealer in the country, except maybe one, who would have paid 50 bucks for that ax. But having seen it there among the rotting pumpkins is what drove me not to leave it. And I figure that because it's made out of tin it's worth at least twice as much as a real ax. It's from the Knights of Pythius, about 1875. Well, his ridiculous price was $250. We paid $200 for the ax and helmet and I know there's one dealer who eventually is going to give me $250 for it.

"Half the game is letting other people think you're crazy. We bought an extremely valuable quilt for 50 bucks from a dealer who said 'I'm so glad to be rid of that dusty old blanket!' Then he showed us his Tiffany lamp, saying 'You fools! You haven't even noticed this. It's worth $3,500. I bought it yesterday for $50!' We're just picky about what we buy. The big money in this business is in big fancy ornate stuff we don't even like to look at, so we make a decent living just buying the stuff we really like. If we were willing to deal with things like heavy furniture and brass beds we could clean up. Four or five years ago you could buy all the brass beds in Syracuse for 10 bucks apiece, and sell them today for up to $1,000.

"But I would never buy that ax again. We felt we had to rescue it from all those pumpkins."

The Eichhorns' enthusiasm for their work is typical of people whose business combines personal aesthetics with a sense of ecological responsibility. Douglas explained. "We try not to see it exclusively as a business. I like the personal investment and the emotional involvement with money not being the thing of value. The sense of preserving things." This philosophy spills over into other areas of the Eichhorns' life. "We buy our clothes at yard sales, our appliances at auctions, and we drive secondhand cars," said Jackie. "We view the money we spend on an item as *rent*. The concept of 'owning' often leads to terrible destructiveness. I know this beautiful old 150-year-old house someone bought and ruined through remodeling. He kept saying, 'Well, I *own* this house.' When we lived in Peru *nothing* was thrown away. Old tires were cut up into sneakers or sandals, every object went through a second life after its first life was exhausted. And in America you can get perfectly good sweaters for 50¢, wool ones."

"Everything that's *used* is dirt cheap in this society," added Douglas. "Which in some ways is a good thing because it helps poor people who are intelligent enough to see that the used items have already withstood the test of time. Our refrigerator, for instance, cost us five bucks, and it's just as good as the new ones costing 50 times as much! But if all that firsthand money weren't spent, this economy would collapse.

"Once we saw that we preferred old things, and that we didn't need to operate within the firsthand society, we began to perceive that we could earn our living doing what we *pleased*. But if everyone were suddenly to stop lusting after new items that exist a few days beyond their warranties, this country would fold. So the government doesn't exactly encourage people to pursue their hobbies and dress warmly in the clothes of their predecessors!" He let out a sigh. "So I don't see much hope for it.

"The people who buy our antiques aren't usually rich. They are making sacrifices, which is nice, because we see they have the same quirky appreciation for the antique that we have."

"And," said Jackie, "it's the only business I can think of where you *bargain* with people. While we were in Peru, you could buy anything that way. If you didn't like the price you could make an offer—buying was a way of striking up human contact. In the antique business it's still true. There is no ultimate value you can place on anything in this business. You go on feeling: *There is no way to prove the value of anything*. What I loved about the Peruvian economy was they felt that way about anything they were selling."

"This money-is-the-thing-of-value attitude has pervaded America," said Douglas, "to the extent that not only can't you bargain with the owner of what's for sale, but you pay the printed price to cashiers who, in Richmond for instance, go out of their way to make the food-stamp victims feel like rats. They act like Jack Webb on TV questioning a suspect."

The Eichhorns have done their share of door-to-door picking, but without much luck. So now they buy almost entirely at auctions and from other dealers. Because they have such a favorable location, they can sell both from their store, and out of their 1969 Rebel station wagon, and they sell both retail and wholesale. Each retail tag bears special code which tells the dealer his discount. Because state property taxes are calculated as of March 1, the Eichhorns try to pare their inventory during February. Yet they rarely sell a piece for less than they paid. "The biggest loss we've taken was $200, which is a lot, but it was on a $1,000 table," said Douglas. "More often you hold something for a year, and sell it at 20 to 30 percent profit. Where else can you tie up your money with such good return? And meanwhile you have the pleasure of a fine object."

"It's best to let the seller name his price," said Jackie. "If he asks you to make an offer, you might offer too low and insult him."

"Or worse," added Douglas, "offer too high.

"You should take a look at something and calculate quickly what you think you can sell it for, then cut that figure in half and hope the asking price is in that area. It can be a very emotional thing, but you should try to be calm and not try too hard to buy or to sell. Of course if something is really great in its category there's no price you can put on it—it is worth whatever someone will pay.

"Remember that there's a difference between merchandise, which you buy and sell for a profit, and something you're really excited about having around your home. Whenever you see something like that, it's a good idea to inquire whether it's for sale. I don't mean in the homes of good friends, unless they happen to be dealers, but driving in the countryside. If we see something really great rusting away on the lawn, we don't hesitate to stop and knock on the door. And, should the answer be 'no', we can always ask if there's anything else that is for sale. People usually just love to show you their things."

"Never buy an antique just because it's cheap," warned Jackie. "A lot of the things we've bought cheap we can't get rid of. But you do have to be a gambler in this game."

Douglas laughed. "One reason I don't think I want to go back to teaching again is I don't know if I could stand the security."

"We both thrive on the unknown," added Jackie. "I'm sure if we ever get to the point where we can't stand it we'll find something else to do. But we love it. We've even tried to buy things back from people just to be able to sell them again. We've known antiques that have traveled two or three times between the East Coast—which is pretty much picked out—and here."

Douglas starts circling spirals with his hands to describe "this great walking stick with a snake curling up the body of a beautifully carved, naked woman about to bite her on the ass and the woman who owned the shop was really embarrassed to have such a cane in her store, and had it way in the back. 'I can only take $5 off the price,' she said. So I paid $45 for it. This was in Maryland. We took it to another dealer who offered me $85 immediately, and I decided that wasn't enough, so we brought it back here.

"Well this same dealer from Maryland was passing through Richmond on his way to a large antique show in Indianapolis, and he came through Centerville and stopped at our store and saw the cane, and he'd forgotten it from when we were in his shop the year before. 'How much you want for this?' he asked, and I told him I didn't really want to sell it. But he was a friend and so I finally named a price—$110—and he bought it. I was sick to have sold it. Of course he sold it in Indianapolis for $195.

"Then it went to the man behind him for two and a half, and the last we heard it's for sale in Rochester, New York, for $850. The same walking stick I paid $45 for and couldn't sell for a year!" His eyes filled with reverence. "That cane was unbelievable. When you grabbed it, your hand just encircled that girl."

And Jackie added, "When you've bought something and then you sell it you still feel as if you've always owned it."

Hugh Starr, Real Estate

"Any dodo can make a million bucks in real estate if he has the desire for it and enjoys the experience." Those are the words of Hugh Starr, a 32-year-old Hawaiian, homesteading on the island of Maui. I have known Hugh since we lived in the same freshman dormitory at college. Hugh's wife, Erin, is also a good friend of mine from college days. We have stayed in touch, over the years, exchanging letters, and photographs of children. Forest is five, Brook is three, and Amber is one and a half. Hugh and Erin have built a simple one-room cabin, with loft, toolshed, large garden, and a guest cabin on three acres of beautiful craterside land near Makawao, which is the location of Hugh's real estate business.

Like so many other people in this book, Hugh became involved in the business because he was first interested by the field itself. "I had my degree in agricultural sciences, and I came to work at Ulupalakua Ranch. But we saw friends with their own places, and that appealed more than my working for someone else. So we took our savings, about $6,500, and put it into a piece of land, which in those days (1969) was possible. At first we considered pooling our resources with some friends, but the legal ramifications of that kind of deal encouraged us to look on our own. Everyday we'd get into our van and drive around looking for the perfect piece of land. And one day my brother-in-law said, 'Look at this potato from Olinda,' and I said, 'That's what we want a piece of land for! We don't need a spectacular view!' And so we bought this piece where the soil is good, and we're away from the main road. I

put our $6,500 down and owed another $9,000 for these three bare
acres. I'd quit the job at the ranch, and I decided that since I had
acquired so much knowledge about land, I should take a real estate
course and get a license to pay my debt.

"My first year I went to work for a real estate company, five
days a week, selling in Wailuku on a commission basis, and though
I didn't sell but one or two properties that year, I got to learn by
watching and by studying ordinances. And unlike some of the
other real estate people who were already making lots of money, I
was slowly becoming an expert on ordinances. And I liked raw
country land; just studying it, the trees and the view from the
slopes and gullies. Successful salesmen have a system whereby
they persuade people to buy, and I'm just not like that so, during
my first year, Erin supported us teaching."

The Starrs have electricity within 100 feet of their cabin, "but
just haven't got around to stringing it up yet," Erin explains.
"Actually, we've just been too busy to notice."

They light their cabin with kerosene lamps and candles; a 12-
volt automobile battery is rigged to provide power for occasional
stereo or television. Their water comes efficiently and free through
a gravity system, and during a heavy rainstorm the afternoon I arrived, Brook bathed outdoors in a large washtub, singing lustily as
he soaped and splashed throughout the downpour. Later that
afternoon, when the rain was melting off the greenery as steam,
Forest proudly walked me out to the chicken house that is just
above two well-endowed banana trees, to show me how he
performs one of his major chores—feeding scraps to chickens and
turkeys alike.

"We can grow just about all the food we need," said Erin.
"And, living like this, which we enjoy, keeps our overhead low so
that Hugh can turn most of his earnings back into the business. The
only trouble is, as perfect as it looks—a good business and a wonderful home—he works more than full time. Seven days a week,
and he starts at the office before daybreak, so he can have a few
hours to himself before the phone starts ringing. He's usually not
home until supper, or even later. I think he's a workaholic."

"It never occurs to her that I might enjoy it," added Hugh.

I was only able to visit with the Starrs for 24 hours, but I felt
from my brief stay that I received a fairly complete picture of small-

island life. Erin greeted me, barefoot, at the airport. The sun moved in and out of the heavy clouds that later dumped shower water for Brook. While I held Forest's birthday cake, or what was left of it after the morning's school party and a subsequent invasion of ants, she drove us into Wailuku, where we found Hugh and the two boys in a little store where a fan circled uselessly overhead. "Hugh often takes the children with him to work," Erin explained. "It's all very easygoing here, and the outdoors is always an option they can choose if Hugh has indoor dealings to make."

Hugh had suggested that he keep the children for the afternoon, but Erin decided to have them come with us, so he went off to inspect some construction projects while Erin, Forest, and Brook showed me their home, about three miles from the sleepy town where Hugh's office is located. Hugh occupies a strange position in the community. He grew up on Oahu, a neighboring island. Although he knows the customs and the language, his features are distinctly "haole." He has acquired leases to buildings in a substantial portion of the downtown area, and is known to rent on a completely fair basis—even to hippies. Hugh's personal style is very low key, which probably further confounds those who see him as a local celebrity who happens also to look like a movie star. One can see how such a person would engender a certain amount of controversy.

"It's really not cool these days to be a businessman, and a lot of people would never consider doing what I do," Hugh told me when he came home for dinner. "They're at a point of going through an experience I had years ago, and it's interesting to see them go through the evolution. Being known as a businessman is therefore a drag, though I really enjoy the actual work. It involves a lot of variety, because I do as much of the maintenance on my buildings as I can, all the plumbing. And I derive a lot more pleasure from this sort of work, using my hands, than from sitting around a conference table with a bunch of businessmen. But you have to be willing to absorb a lot of negative energy: I know some people think I'm a slumlord, even though I'm working to improve their mosquito-ridden lots."

Hugh worked the state-required two years as an apprentice to an established real estate company, after completing the prerequisite eight-week, intensive, real estate training course. During his apprenticeship he concentrated on country property. "And all this time I studied any topographic maps, soil studies, water studies, or aerial photographs I could find. I was acquiring these sources of information that are most helpful in understanding the land. And I spent two years selling country property for this company then took the broker's test and passed it, and stayed on with the company because it's run by an ethical broker, and I like to be with him. I just wanted to clear my debt and then live off the land.

"But one day a friend said, 'Hey, you've got to get some form of real income for yourself. You've got to get into making money!' And I did a subdivision with him, and he introduced me to a new kind of client: businessmen with money who have an interest in making money on it. They're sitting over in Honolulu, hoping to invest some money over here. This was a big change in my approach, and I was now getting heavily into subdivision, contracting the labor when I needed to. I learned to lay water lines and we managed to reduce a $90,000 water line job to $35,000 by doing it ourselves. We divided the land and improved it ourselves. I took a 6 percent commission on whatever lots I sold, and received a 4 percent fee for the developing services involved in improving the piece.

"I found this kind of work a lot more appealing than just straight selling, because I was participating in actual work with the land. I really didn't like being associated with the concept of persuasion that seems so important in salesmanship. 'Anything that walks in the door, sell it something!' is the attitude of lots of slick realtors. So I moved into other subdivision agreements with these same people, and I got into another deal where I took 33 percent of the profit investing my expertise as a developer instead of cash. I was made an actual partner.

"Then one day I heard about a group of attorneys who had bought a piece of land with four small houses they wanted removed. So I went and saw they were good houses, and the demolition man was only too glad to give them to me, since that saved him the trouble of demolishing them. I took out a loan to have them moved to a piece of land I'm leasing. By making similar agreements, I have acquired a total of eight houses that I rent out for an average $225 a month, apiece. I pay $200 a month for the land, and about $200 a month on the loan that paid to move and fix up the houses. So, theoretically, for 30 years, which is the length of my lease on the land, I have a guaranteed monthly income of $1,500 from these houses alone. Old houses are a good deal, if you can find them. They cost less than 20 percent what a new house would cost, and they're often more appealing to the types of people I rent to than the sterile boxes made by house factories today. The income we don't use to support the family is reinvested."

The phone rang. A friend was calling to confirm Hugh's promise to come at 10 P.M. for a meeting about a land deal he had under consideration. "That's another part of it," Hugh explained, "staying open to the friendly aspects, and helping people avoid unnecessary mistakes." He invited me to come, meet his friend, a near neighbor, and to enjoy a hot soaking in his friend's furo bath outdoors, overlooking Wailuku's lights, and the oceanside beyond. I soaked as they talked into the night, and about midnight I walked back to the cabin and visited more with Erin. She explained Hugh's idea to reach a financial goal by the age of 35, and to retire from business then. Within the last six months, they have seen their debts diminish, and the savings toward their goal take a dramatic leap. Hugh says they are "ahead of schedule, at this point."

Hugh came home about 1 A.M., and sat up with me, completing our scheduled interview at about 2 A.M. He excused himself shortly after I closed my notebook, explaining he had an early day ahead of him, he'd have to be at the office by 4:30 if he was to get any work done before flying over to Honolulu on the 7 A.M. shuttle. Before retiring, he gave me a complete rundown on his real estate dealings, and I could see that diversification and a willingness to do most of the work himself have blended well with his own deep appreciation of the land, and an ability to deal evenly with back-to-the-land and conservative interests alike. None of his success has been realized without heavy cost, however. Like many other self-employed people, he works about twice the hours of "conventional business," and operating within a small community as a conspicuous "outside force," he has been the recipient of a certain amount of community and police harrassment.

"In a small town, I'd advise staying as anonymous as possible," he told me as we were wrapping it up. "If possible, do business in the name of your company, or partnership, or something obscure. If I drove around in a fancy car and wore silk suits it might be dif-

ferent. But there are a few people in this community who don't
think I'm a legitimate businessman. They say I live with a bunch of
hippies, and our house is too small. They ask my friends, 'Where
does Starr get all his money?' So the notoriety is no good; I can
understand from what little I've had how Elizabeth Taylor and
Jackie Kennedy must feel!

"You see, I have four separate deals going in town. Two are
leases on commercial property, then my housing project, and a
subdivision I'm doing with an old schoolmate. All told, it makes up
for about half the real estate business there is to do in town. And
it's a small town, and my every move is watched."

Hugh said it is possible to get a start in real estate with little or
no money, "especially if you're a really good talker. The most important aspect is experience. With that, it isn't too hard to find
people with the money, and for putting a deal together you receive
a share of the profits. It's important not to overextend your credit;
some guys leverage themselves to the hilt so that if one deal
collapses they've had it." Hugh's big break came when, with two
partners who put up the money, their Makawao Properties acquired a 35-year lease on a grocery. Hugh and Erin took over the
management of the store, built up its inventory and clientele, so
that within two years the monthly gross business had risen from
$9,000 to $40,000 and was still rising. At that point, the company located a successful grocer who wanted to move to the islands. He leases the store, technically a sublease, from Hugh and
his partners. In this way, explained Hugh, his company has the
use of 56,000 square feet ("improved so the property is worth about
$250,000") for $200 a month. They are paid $1,000 a month or a
percentage of the store's gross sales, whichever is greater.

"You have to have an attorney," said Hugh. "I simply give all
my business to one lawyer, and he's helpful with any potential
problems. I'm really a businessman and that's all. I just like to
drive secondhand cars, and I choose to go around in slippers
instead of being a big shot. I simply want to take my knowledge
and use it to provide a steady income projected into the future.
Even though I've gotten out of the raw land aspect of the business,
my commitment to this place remains strong. By investing in in-
come-producing real estate, I should be able to live very comfortably without too much hassling. But it takes a lot of effort to set

it all up. There's a lot of deals I could be making that I'm turning down now, because somewhere along the line I have to learn to decide how much energy I want to expend, and how much money I want to make. Every deal takes energy.

"One day or another you always pay for it, and I don't want to be consumed by the business, so the big trick is knowing when to kick up and get out. My goal was just to set up my scene. I'm amazed by how little people who are our age and younger know about business. I think it's because we grew up in an environment where everyone was denigrating the system, saying, 'This is bad because it's capitalistic,' and now I'm on the other side of the fence. I go to a lot of public hearings and find myself surrounded by two, distinct attitudes: That of the hippie who doesn't want any more change, and that of the real estate man with an interest in developing.

"Really, I'm more a developer now than a real estate broker, but the term developer has so much unfavorable connotation. I try to do it with sensitivity, relying on instinct, and it requires a thick skin about what others think you're doing. In Maui there is a particularly high percentage of educated dropouts, and they have a very critical attitude, and at the same time they're really naive. But I like the variety involved: Eating at a fancy restaurant with prominent businessmen in Honolulu at lunch, and back here in shorts planning a subdivision the same afternoon. The experience day to day is all you're ever going to get so you'd better enjoy it. I'm striving for no personal goal other than to be more patient with my children.

"It's the money trip basically, and I'm just doing it the most efficient way I know without sacrificing my life for it. I want to do it fast so as not to spend the rest of my days scratching, but if I went out and leveraged myself to the hilt and got sued and lost the business, that would be alright because I'd have learned from it. I could go and scavenge a shack and survive. We have learned to live anywhere—for a year we lived out of a VW van—and that gives us a lot of freedom. The balance between the personal, emotional needs and the external, material needs is a hard one to keep."

"Well maybe I should let you go to bed," I said to Hugh, who just laughed. In two hours he'd have to be up and off to the office. Just before he blew out the kerosene lamp and climbed up into the loft to join Erin, who'd drifted off long ago, he said, "I often wonder what I would do if I lost all the money. And I decide every time that I could trade my experience for a scene that would keep us going. We would survive. I wouldn't jump out of a building."

My next memory of the visit is fuzzy. Before daylight I heard a door close gently, followed by the sound of light footsteps padding across the wooden floor. "Bye-bye, Daddy," called one of the boys through the screen door. A few hours later I woke to full daylight, and a warm cup of cocoa and homemade cornbread with Erin.

Rosalie Sorrels, Musician

Six years ago, working under the direction of the English department of Boise State University, I was browsing in the
university bookstore and noticed that one of the English teachers,
poet Thomas Trusky, listed a record album for one of his poetry
courses. The album's title was *Travelin' Lady*, and when I met
Trusky briefly, I asked him about it. He replied that music is very
properly a part of our poetic literature, and that the writer in question, Rosalie Sorrels, is native to Idaho, so that her songs are
doubly appropriate for a literature course in a western college.
Before I had a chance to pursue the conversation, Trusky was
whisked away mysteriously. Not so mysteriously, about three
weeks after I returned to Vermont, the album in question arrived
in the mail, and I got my real introduction to Rosalie Sorrels.
When I learned last year that she was living in Burlington, I
phoned and introduced myself, and was graciously invited to spend
the afternoon in conversation. The next morning she took me to
the recording studio at Philo Records for a preview of her album-
in-production, *Moments of Happiness*.

Rosalie is unique because, at 43 she has raised five children
and has, since 1966, when she and her husband separated, pursued
music as a full-time career. None of this has been easy, and
Rosalie's not apt to hide the joys or the pain in her music, which is
what makes it so good. How was I to think she'd be holding back
when I came to her with my notebook in hand?

Rosalie Sorrels   *Photo by Bob Griffith*

"Well for one thing," she started, after greeting me at the door of her rented four-room Burlington apartment, cluttered with books in cartons, records and a portable stereo, lots of guitars in hard-shell cases, "having a manager is worse than being married." She paused, thoughtfully. "Unless, that is, you can find one who will work for you, rather than have you work for him.

"The big record companies are really weird. I've worked for them and I don't think any amount of money could make me do it again. They're usually not dishonest—just stupid. They acquire your publishing and your personal services. Then they wait around to see whether you turn into a commodity. In my case I'm a 'female Jack Eliot' or a 'lady Kristofferson,'" which serves as a kind of hook for publicity. Then they wait for me to establish a reputation and begin to sell, and only then will they commit any funds to promotion.

"One time a company that had an interest in me split with its subsidiary, and since then neither company has been able to tell me what's going on. I go to them with money in hand trying to lease the masters, so I can re-record and re-release *Travelin' Lady*, and do it right. But the contract says I've got to wait five years for the copyright to belong to me. Well, they can just sit on it and spin as far as I'm concerned. Those big companies are not always literally dishonest, but they are often stupid and corrupt.

"The contract I have with my present recording company, which is Philo, stipulates that if the company no longer keeps the record in print, the master automatically belongs to me. But with the big companies, they'll hold everything they can waiting for the day you turn out a hit." Rosalie told me about something called a "BSR rating," which is a process whereby companies attach wires to the skins of hundreds of teenage "consumers," then play the songs they're tempted to promote as singles. The wires are monitored by a computer that measures "basal skin response." The more the merrier, and those songs that according to the meter really get the skin churning are given a special BSR rating.

Given such rampant commercialization, Rosalie chooses to remain managerless and to record her music with a poorly promoted but technically sophisticated label. "I sing a lot of benefits. I'll sing anywhere someone will listen, I don't care if it's a boiler room with just a couple of friends. I am not a big-concert person, and I will *never* sing, for instance, at Madison Square Garden."

Rosalie has had to pay for this lost "efficiency," and has had to learn to do her own promotion, booking, and getting herself from place to place with little more than the gigantic car from the sixties she was trying to sell to anyone who would tow it out from under Burlington traffic tickets on the day I visited. She has probably spent more time on the road than most musicians do, which is plenty, and her children radiate a kind of hip intelligence that is rare in young people and always in danger of souring into cynicism. Rosalie's independence does not seem chosen, nor does theirs; they are strong enough to deal with the bad hours and the times when she is on the road.

Though she has recorded 10 albums, many of them featuring her own songs, Rosalie has at times had to rely on friends to help her financially. "I personally consider myself to be successful. I have the respect of those whose respect I crave and I do what I want to do: I conceive projects and find a way to get them done. There's no way a major record company would allow you to begin an album with a seven-minute monologue from *Archy and Mehitabel* by Don Marquis, as I do on *Always a Lady*, let alone a whole side with no up tunes on it. A company like Philo helps me put up with gray Burlington skies. They give the artist complete control of the album. They say 'we have nothing to do with this! It is all her idea.'

"I started by collecting and singing Mormon and Idaho folk songs, and sang in Salt Lake ski resorts for years before going to New York. In total I've spent 20 years getting where I am, which is nowhere according to lots of folks, because I still don't have any money. But the worst thing I ever did was to try to get myself put on the market in New York City with a manager who pretended he knew what I wanted and proceeded to treat me as if I had no mind of my own. This kind of treatment is accepted by those people who want to be big stars, a commodity—'flesh' is what you're called when you go on the block. 'Very interesting, but not a marketable item,' they say." She let out a long sigh.

"And that would do some damage to the dumbest, most naive human being alive. But we let our poets die, so what the hell. I also think they encourage that self-destructive streak in you, because it's good press to have you flame out in some memorable way. It's enough to keep you alive wondering what some fool will do to memorialize you once you're gone.

"The New York scene is a market, and going up for sale is a drag. I sleep on people's couches instead, because the human contract is worth far more than being rich and famous, even though at times I have an incredible yearning to be alone. But I'm a city addict at heart, I think cities are fascinating, falling apart as they are, so interdependent. And I know how fortunate I am to know how to do what I do in an independent way. I know I'm not washed up because I don't buy that idea that I have to make more money each time I perform or else it means I'm through. I didn't start until I was 33; in terms of show biz, 25 is old. I was already 'too old', and that mentality leads you to believing that the older you get the more washed up you are.

"The most incredibly difficult aspect of being a musician is trying to maintain any kind of family, trying to keep any personal relationships together. So many people want your undivided attention at all times and giving it away leaves you with the feeling you've been torn apart, rent asunder, little pieces taken away. I don't think it's glamorous at all, and the problem of being misinterpreted is always there, particularly when you're as personal as I am.

"In order to do it you have to know what you think and believe it's worth conveying and then be incredibly stubborn. The only way I could ever recommend taking a manager is if you find someone who will work for *you* and not vice versa, and only then with a contract that leaves a *mutual* option, so either of you can get out, and only then with a music lawyer overlooking the deal, and a good mother too. Watch your publishing rights like a hawk. Read *This Business of Music*, by William Krasilovsky, who is a music lawyer with fabulous integrity. And avoid like the death any romantic attachments with the people you work with."

As we talked, Rosalie was interrupted occasionally by the telephone; one caller was interested in the car, another was reminding her (she hadn't forgotten) that tomorrow's benefit dinner would start at 5:30 P.M. A door closed and her 18-year-old son David, who was leaving by bus for Salt Lake, came in. He had hoped to catch the afternoon bus, but now he'd have to wait till morning. Rosalie was glad; they'd have more time together and he could advise her on the car. The phone rang again, and after that conversation ended she simply pulled the plug. Holly, Rosalie's daughter, came in, worrying about the effect of a braid on only one side of her head. "Do I look funny there?" she said, turning her head and pointing. "You look fine," said Rosalie after a thoughtful pause.

"I've been very lucky to have parents as understanding as mine. For instance, I don't know of any other parents who, when their 33-year-old daughter came home and said, 'I've left my husband,' would be encouraging and supportive, yet firmly prevent her from soaking back into a childlike relationship with them.

"Housewifery doesn't prepare one for too many fields of endeavor, and the decision to be a folk singer came with the realization that I had to do something, and singing was all I could do aside from sling hash or waitress.

"So I went to New York, and made a series of mistakes that have encumbered my music and forced me to seek legal counsel. A manager gave me $1,000 and a contract which I *did not know how to read*. You do not need a manager, you need a music lawyer, do not sign anything until your lawyer has seen it, their lawyer has seen it, and probably another lawyer who's not even involved has seen it. Above all, I'd recommend anyone considering a career in music read Krasilovsky's book, and find a real music lawyer, someone who knows that business and practices nothing else, not a friend who happens to be a lawyer.

"My trip with the manager was a disaster, and I simply broke my contract on the advice of a lawyer who also told me: 'Don't make any money for six years or he can sue for it.'" Rosalie uses free-lance agents, and says she would never sign with an agency unless they offered a guaranteed income of $15,000 minimum. "And at that, I would *never* sign for longer than a year! But the free-lance agent doesn't feel he owns you. I book a date in an area, then write the free-lance agent who's closest to that place saying 'I have this date and will pay 10 percent for every contract you can get me around it.' I make it very clear that this is a one-time agreement, and I will not pay a commission for gigs at places where I've previously appeared. In other words, I pay agents only for helping me break new ground.

"Some agencies ignore your work, and I've been booked into

places where a barking dog would be more appropriate. One time it was a beer cellar where the students had all come to drink. They didn't want to hear my songs. I played a couple of numbers and then said, 'If you're not here to listen, I don't want to interrupt your conversation. It's been a long time since I needed money that bad, so good night!' Then I went over to the guy who'd set the show up and said, 'You don't have to pay me.' Then this couple came up to us saying, 'We drove all the way from New York to hear you!' So I said to the guy, 'You give me a room and I'll sing all night for these people, and you can pay me or not as you please.' He couldn't find an unlocked room except, finally, a smelly, but large, photo lab with nothing to sit on but large metal stools. It was the funkiest room I ever saw, but people started trickling in, until there were 30 or 40, and the man did pay me. But the point is that this particular agency got into the business because the people in it love artists and want to help, but they don't know how to go about it. If I could find someone who knew how to promote me, rather than writing my own letters—'Listen, I'm really good, you should hire me'—I would be delighted.

"But since I haven't found that person, I promote myself by having good copies printed up of reviews of my appearances and albums, and passing them around and mailing them to the free-lance agents. And I ask artists whose work is similar to mine, 'Where do you work?' and I send my promo materials to those places.

"A lot of people are competing in this business, but I'm not. I am the only me there is, and the only way to discover that me is to start doing it. It costs because you can't really live anywhere. You have to go to all these places and sing for church suppers and all sorts of people and be positive and find those people to whom your songs are useful, because more than anything I want to feel that what I do is *useful* to other human beings.

"This realization has helped me know where and when I belong, and I do not take gigs—after 20 years of learning—where I might face an unresponsive audience. I do not sing well for big audiences, and I don't always perform well outside. I don't have that kind of energy, and I want to see who I sing to. I've seen Pete Seeger work with audiences of 15,000, and he can get them all on their feet singing because if Pete Seeger tells you to sing *Guantanamero*, you do, because he believes—he *knows*—you will. I tried something like that at the Peoples' Bicentennial and someone pitched a tomato, one of these big, beautiful, fully ripe, bright red tomatoes, the kind you only find on stage, and it hit me just below the breast, and all I could think to say was, 'That's a perfectly good tomato.' When the real Bicentennial Celebration began just a few hours later, I just cried and cried because all they could think to do was set off hundreds of guns and cannons. My God, what is wrong with us?"

The next morning Rosalie and I drove to Philo Records in Ferrisburg, where Bill Schubart has converted an old dairy barn into an amazing musical retreat, with a fully equipped studio. Philo has quickly obtained a number of fine artists because of Schubart's reputation for trusting his musicians. He shows them how to mix, and hands complete artistic control over to them, if that's what they want. At the same time, he is extremely discriminating, and the sort of people who record with Philo are, like Rosalie, people a little too folksy to have their music taped to basal skin machines. Schubart, a native Vermonter, runs an honest recording studio. Philo isn't likely to become the label of the stars because Philo isn't concerned with creating or promoting stars.

Schubart offered us coffee and showed us downstairs to the mixing room so we could hear early takes of Rosalie's *Moments of Happiness*. The title song was first, with Rosalie's voice counterpointed with piano, and if I'd been wired for response, my goose bumps would have stuck clear through the tapes and gummed up the meters of those basal readers. Rosalie smiled in satisfaction as the song climaxed and faded. Her voice carries long notes into an almost breathless, plaintive cry. When you think she's going to stop for breath, from some mysterious place she finds another shot of air and the voice rises from its cry back to music, sweet and pure.

Later, back at her apartment, we talked more, and Rosalie would sometimes sing, full voice, a cappella, to demonstrate a point. "The thing we need the most," she told me, "is to learn to respond to people in a human way and that's what I think I'm up to. And to remember to tell the truth and realize that what was true yesterday is not always true today. And to own up to that."

Rod Ruth, Free-Lance Artist

Rod Ruth lives just outside Chicago. He is 64, and has been illustrating books on a free-lance basis since 1971, when he quit regular, studio work in downtown Chicago. Rod has been drawing for as long as he can remember. "My mother started saving my drawings when I was four. In school I found this was the one area where I could excel. I remember in second grade, the teacher gave me a special blackboard between two windows. But from then on I did poorly in art class because they'd make you cut out paper or draw a potted plant, and I was always adding a bug or something behind the plant and would be marked down, especially if I refused to erase it."

Janet and I had taken the train up from her family's farm in southern Iowa to visit Rod and Mary, who have been close friends of Janet's since she was at college with their son Rick. Rick, who was visiting his parents when we arrived, met us at the train station, explaining that Rod was—as usual—up to his neck in work, and a good three weeks behind a fast-approaching deadline. "It's really good that you've come," he said, as we pulled into the driveway, "he's been at it so hard, and your visit will give him an excuse to take a break."

Rod's studio is located upstairs, in a bright room that is insulated from the carpeted hallway by the master bedroom. After greeting us at the door, Mary called up to Rod, who came bounding down the stairs with his characteristic, enthusiastic welcome. I

Rod Ruth

suspect at these times (we usually manage to visit the Ruths once a year) that Rod and Mary share with many other self-employed people the conflict of feelings that accompanies the arrival of company. Everyone likes to take a break, but when the flow of work is interrupted, it can take as much as twice the duration of a visit to get back into a productive routine.

Rod has been a free-lance artist, on and off, all his life, and during the early years of his marriage, from 1941 to 1957, supported his family by illustrating *The Toodles*, a syndicated comic strip that ran in "Sixty or seventy small-circulation papers, but since I was paid by the unit of circulation, there wasn't that much money in it. I got up to about $9,000," Rod said.

"It only took me three days a week to do the six dailies and the 12-panel Sunday strip, so it would have been a good job if there had been enough money in it, and *much more importantly*, if I'd had my heart in the work. As it was, to augment my income, I got so I was spending the other three or four days a week doing other kinds of artwork on the side, which seemed increasingly more interesting than the comic strip itself. So at age 45 I finally got it through my thick head that it simply wasn't what I wanted to do, and I quit the strip.

"One of the bad prices I paid for staying with it for 16 years is that my work in comics became such a cliché, and I feel it still affects my work."

During the years from 1957 to 1971, Rod commuted to downtown Chicago, working at advertising studios, and realizing a peak income of $26,000 a year. He compares that life with the one he now lives. Even though he presently earns less than $20,000 a year, Rod said that "we just got wise to what we really want. During the years I was working downtown, we bought a new car every four years, and took two big trips to Europe. I needed more clothes then than I do now that I can dress as I wish. And now, I work in the garden when the weather is right, not just on weekends. I can shovel the snow when it falls, and anything else that has to be done, as soon as it needs doing. I *like* being at home, and the price isn't as steep as it was to be downtown." He paused for a moment. "You know, there's really only two things I miss from the studio: association with my peers and all that fantastic equipment, free paper, free enlargements, and photostats." Rod reported that the only item a studio does not provide its artists is brushes, which now cost as much as $70 apiece!

Rod's persistent interest in the outdoors has created "a hunger to do animals. While I was working for the advertising studios, I would be just dying to do animals and I'd be including cats in refrigerator ads, and the note would come back, 'Delete cat,' but eventually the tail got to wagging the dog and they started asking for my animals. I've really lucked out because I've built up a reputation for fanciful illustrations and wild animals and prehistoric animals. It's very hard to get photographs of wildlife, and impossible to obtain them for fanciful animals, so my speciality is in great demand."

Now, instead of vacation trips to Europe, Rod and Mary enjoy inexpensive camping trips to American wilderness areas, where Rod studies the animals carefully. "One of the biggest dangers of being an artist is developing a facility and being able to crank 'em out: stereotypes, clichés. You've just got to back away from stereotypes," he said. "I spent 12 weeks taking life drawing and working to stamp out the cliché impulse, forcing myself not to draw standard ears, but to look at this particular ear and do it the way it really is. It was an exasperating experience, very hard. When you draw something, you should draw it as if you've landed on another planet and they ask you to draw some earth phenomenon. Draw as intensely every time as you would in these circumstances.

"And that's all well and good, but when you come home and face a deadline, and bills are coming in, and it has to be done by Tuesday, you can be sorely tempted to fudge it rather than to study and render exactly what you see." Outside at the window, we were distracted by a fat squirrel on the bird feeder.

"Of all the arts, it's easiest to make a living in graphics. There's such a wide spectrum in what you can paint, from a 'For Sale' sign to the ceiling of the Sistine Chapel. The society is visual, and needs visual representation. There are thousands of reasonably paid middle-ground artists earning good livings that you'll never hear about. Maybe it's the same in writing, but if you're going to be an actor or a musician you have to be among the best. One reason is probably that television has reduced actual public demand for live entertainment."

Rod has just completed the illustrations for a children's book titled *Album of Prehistoric Man*, and he took Janet and me up to his studio for a look at some drawings. He carefully removed layer upon layer of tissue paper from a large square box, showing us the overlays on which he calculated the initial composition, and on which he later created the details. "Almost half the work in a job like this is research. I have a friend at the museum, an anthropologist, who was extremely helpful with this book. He'd challenge me about the details of a weapon, for instance. 'How did I know it was really held with just one hand?' And in some cases I had to re-do a week's worth of work to get it right!"

Rod stresses that being willing to go over and over a drawing to make it right, and not a stereotype, requires a certain kind of temperment. As for learning, he has little good to say about art schools. "I don't think you can teach a person to become an illustrator, any more than you can teach someone to become a clown. You can create a climate in which a talent can grow and as far as illustration is concerned—as opposed to 'fine art' painting—I think starting from scratch in a big, varied art studio would be better than going to art school. The catch is that you usually can't get a job in a studio unless you show evidence of art school training. And art school training, I'm afraid, some of it you'll have to *unlearn* if you get the job. If you do go to an art school, for heaven's sake, don't think you'll get all your art training there! Get *varied* learning.

"If you want to do it badly enough, the question isn't 'Should I be an artist?' but 'Can I live *without* being an artist?' When younger artists ask my advice, if they're not really good, I say, 'How nice you have this avocation you can pursue in your spare time!' But if they've really got good work, I start throwing roadblocks in their way, and if they can climb over them, they'll be alright. But anyone starting out in a field like this has just got to love concentrating for long periods of time on work that most folks might call monotonous!"

Writers and Editors

Hayden Carruth

Concerning Necessity

It's quite true we live
in a kind of rural twilight
most of the time giving
our love to the hard dirt
the water and the weeds
and the difficult woods

ho we say drive the wedge
heave the axe run the hand shovel
dig the potato patch
dig ashes dig gravel
tickle the dyspeptic chain saw
make him snarl once more

while the henhouse needs cleaning
the fruitless corn to be cut
and the house is falling to pieces
and the car coming apart
the boy sitting and complaining
about something everything anything

this was the world foreknown
though I had thought somehow
probably in the delusion
of that idiot thoreau
that necessity could be saved
by the facts we actually have

like our extreme white birch
clasped in the hemlock's arms
or our baybreasted nuthatch
or our mountain and our stars
and really these things do serve
a little though not enough

what saves the undoubted collapse
of the driven day and the year
is my coming all at once
when she is done in or footsore
or down asleep in the field
or telling a song to a child

coming and seeing her move
in some particular way
that makes me to fall in love
all over with human beauty
the beauty I can't believe
right here where I live.

Hayden Carruth, 56, lives with his wife, Rose Marie, and their son, David, in a small farmhouse sandwiched between a dirt road and a year-round trout stream just outside tiny Johnson, Vermont. Carruth has worked as a writer, in one capacity or another, all his life. He made his retreat to Vermont 16 years ago after half a lifetime in the South, the war, Chicago, New York, etcetera, ending with eight years' confinement at a place he refers to as "the hatch."

Writing has been in his family since his grandfather founded the first newspaper in the Territory of Dakota, in 1885. Hayden's father was also a writer, and one of his brothers works in New York with a major publishing company. But Hayden's career in writing has been unique in his family because he has not only managed to live by the pen, but he does so in the country, away from the martini-and-olive luncheons, without an agent. I will add here, just quickly, that this "career in writing," is founded—paradoxically— on the least-paying verbal genre of all, the poem. Hayden Carruth is a poet, well-recognized, widely admired, and often imitated by other poets, and this mini-notoriety, based on five or six very good books of poetry, has established his credibility in the eyes of editors and publishers who might otherwise be too busy to read his writing carefully enough to appreciate his abilities.

"I have always come to writing—other than poetry—out of necessity, not choice," he told me. "What I do for a living is basically editorial and journalistic, even though much of it may be concerned with literature. My *writing*, as such, is my poetry. In other words I definitely consider myself an artist who is supporting himself, like most others, by doing what he can. The fact that in my case this money-making work is also in a way literary and does entail some kinds of writing confuses the matter somewhat, but in my own mind there's a clear distinction. This has been the one way I've been able to support my family and still work at home, even though my yearly income has always been extremely modest. If my personality were a little different, and I could get a job and make a decent living, I probably would. But writing and editing at home are among the few things I can do. Of course I benefit from the few years I spent working in publishing and as an editor, before I became ill. A free-lance writer needs to have a good notion of how a publishing company operates.

"Experience is the best way to get this. And that usually means working in a publishing firm for a few years, as a copy editor, advertising writer, secretary, or whatever work is available. Today, some colleges offer courses in book publishing; perhaps these are an alternative to a year or two of actual experience."

Carruth lists two potential clients for a free-lance writer: the publishing company and the author. He has worked for both, in many capacities. "With a publishing company you get assignments to ghostwrite, rewrite, read manuscripts, copy-edit, make indexes, type, any kind of fixing-up work needed before the manuscript goes to the printer. The work is paid for on a fee basis, and is basically the kind of work you get by knowing somebody in the publishing business. I started with the help of some friends in publishing and my brother, who at that time was an editor with Thomas Y. Crowell.

"The other employer is the author, who may be anyone from the rankest amateur with a hopeless manuscript to a corporation executive too busy to write his own book, or a scientist who needs help with stylistic problems, and your work can consist of almost anything from typing up handwritten notes to making the prose of a science book readable. And there's ghostwriting too, which is a little trickier, because sometimes you find yourself involved with somebody who hasn't a chance of producing a salable book."

I asked Carruth if his move to the country had upset his career. "Of course, being near the city helps a good deal," he answered, "especially in keeping up contacts with publishers and editors.

"But we have a big garden, and even during the years when my total income was less than $3,000, we've been able to get by without welfare or food stamps. It's good to remember, also, that 90 percent of publishing in this country is not by the big, commercial New York houses, not the books you see reviewed in the big periodicals, but annual reports and ghostwritten speeches, technical manuals, even labels. Clear directions on how to assemble a toy can be a big boon not only to a manufacturer but to the customer. Some of the most profitable magazines in the country are trade magazines and university magazines, specialized publications hardly anyone knows about. But they all hire editors and copy editors, writers and rewriters.

"And I've had some pretty lousy jobs, such as manuscript typing for $100 a manuscript, and sometimes the manuscript would be seven or eight hundred pages long. Once I started to rewrite a book for a Cuban refugee and then quit when I learned he was promoting the assassination of Castro.

"But there have been good jobs too. I spent two years completing the *Encyclopedia of American Literature*, from the typed manuscript copy and handwritten notes when its editor died. When I finished that, I rewrote a dictionary of American slang, which was interesting, especially because the original definitions were very sloppy and I had to make them concise and lucid, which was quite a challenge. These were both big jobs, paying only $1.25 an hour—but they were steady, long jobs, and they paid the doctors' bills, and gave us room and board.

"In recent years I've tended to stay away from this sort of work because book reviewing is more lucrative—provided you can get assignments from the five or six large newspapers in the country. They pay $100 to $150 for an average-length review. And I still read manuscripts, mostly for the university presses, on scholarly manuscripts or collections of poetry. I still occasionally do copy-editing. If you have a special area of knowledge, of course, that helps you find these sorts of jobs: science, education, ecology, etcetera; the publishers prefer someone who approaches problems not only as verbal, but as problems of substance. A lot of writers specialize, setting themselves up in technical editing, indexing, translating, and many other areas."

Carruth is the first to admit that free-lance writing, like most other free-lance work, is time consuming and emotionally draining. "You're trying to sell the product of your own brain, which is bound to be somewhat irregular, and unless you're well-known or highly specialized, the uncertainty and irregularity of income are tremendous pressures. Even with money in the bank you're worried all the time because you don't see enough jobs or sales coming along. There's no financial security at all unless you're very well-known. There's no such thing as a pension, insurance, or sick pay, and you have to pay both shares of the Social Security tax, which is often higher than the income tax.

"But for me, the really discouraging aspect is after all the energy's expired, even when you're well-paid, it's finished. There's none of the continuity in a writer's life that prevails in an office worker's. Each project is a new start, a clean slate, which suggests that a writer needs a special kind of energy to get himself started each morning."

Carruth led me out to his studio, a converted milking room, about nine feet square, separate from the house, known as the cowshed. Inside, a small chair, a stove, and large desk were encased by walls of books and stacks of paper. Three or four framed photographs hung from otherwise unused wall space. "And there," he said, pointing to a sizable stack of book-sized and personal envelopes, "is the day's mail. Most of it," he added with a shrug, "one way or the other has to be answered. And that's the kind of free-lance writing no one pays for but you and your family."

Vicky Thompson

Vicky Thompson is not the real name of a 31-year-old friend of mine who has traveled extensively, mostly with a pack on her back, mostly by hitching rides. She taught five years with the English department at the University of Hawaii, and now is in San Francisco, teaching Saturdays in a Graduate Record Examination score-boosting preparation course, a job that provides her steady income that guarantees she can always pay rent.

"The best source of income I know," said Vicky, "is free-lance copy editing. With the belt-tightening of the seventies, commercial and university presses had to drop a lot of their full-time copy editors, and assign the jobs to free lancers.

"The first assignment is the hardest to get. Thereafter, your experience will get you the jobs, because that's all the editors ask about over the phone. College degrees don't carry nearly as much weight as experience does. The first thing they ask is, 'What copy-editing have you done?'

"When I get to a town where I know a commercial or university press is located, I simply call and with a confident voice announce, 'Hello, this is Vicky Thompson. I'm visiting in town for eight weeks or so, and was wondering if you had any copy-editing for me to do.'

"The main point is to sound confident, not apologetic. If you know grammar, and can spell, you've got it made. Just work slowly, carefully, and make legible notes. Almost all manuscripts are riddled with grammatical problems; a good copy editor can make all the difference between a mediocre book and a good one.

"As in all free-lance work, it doesn't hurt, once the job is done, to ask for a reference from your senior editor."

Fresh Seafood

I was driving south out of Burlington, on Route 7, past all the franchise stores and gas stations and discount hamburger joints that line the roads to our cities. As I slowed for a red light, I saw a green truck across the street at the edge of a parking lot with a sign painted on its side: *Fresh Maine Seafood*.

The owner of that truck, who was friendly and anxious to describe his business, repeated, "I don't want no books written about me," and made me promise not to use his real name. "I've got friends all along my route," he told me. "My customers know me and my schedule. They always know that on Fridays, say, between 10 and 5, I can be found right here. Last night, some friends threw a party for me in Essex Junction."

He owns, not only the truck that is equipped with a small, well-insulated van, but a good-sized fish locker at his home in coastal Rockford, Maine. "I devein shrimp all winter and sell 'em when summer comes. This trucking is only for six months a year; I drive May to November. Wednesdays I load the truck. Thursday I drive to Essex Junction [Vermont], and sell there from 4 P.M. until supper. Fridays I drive to Burlington, and sell all day. Saturdays I drive down to Barre [Vermont], sell there all day, and on Sundays drive home for two days off. It's a good living, I've got lots of friends, and I stay in the same motels each time. Last night's party was a good-bye party, because this is my last trip over to Vermont until next spring.

"I have to have truck-peddler licenses for three states: Maine, New Hampshire, and Vermont. I don't usually sell in New Hampshire unless someone sees my sign and buys from me at a red light or the counter where I stop for lunch. My only real advice is keep your overhead low, don't try to sell without a license, pay the store a commission for letting you have a piece of their parking lot, sell as cheap as you can, and if it's food you're selling, take it where they need it.

"Lobster, $2.40 a pound. Sounds like a good deal to you, especially because just three days ago it was walking the ocean floor. But that's because you live inland. Down East I'm lucky to get $1.25 a pound."

Inventors

Surely inventors are artists of sorts, dreamers who practice the discipline of developing their fantasies. The difference between the dreamer and the artist is that the artist takes the time and effort to sketch it out. The inventor goes a step further: After sketching it out, he attempts to reproduce it according to his plans. No one is willing to say for sure what sparks the inventive idea to begin with; laziness often gets credit, as does necessity, or brilliant parentage.

Inventors seem to have a sense of play that doesn't dissipate when the need for precision comes into the picture. Eric Darnell's window shade is a masterpiece of studied precision, yet for one reason or another the only way he is able to convince it to retract is by hammering the windowsill in such a way and at a point that only he knows. Richard Fatigati's enthusiasm for chess led him to wonder how a truly portable game could be designed, so the pieces would stay in position even as the players carried the chessboard from city to city.

The niceties of patent law often require that you hire a patent lawyer to search patent files to be sure your invention doesn't infringe on established rights. My brother invented a sand-spray system which the automobile automatically triggers in emergency skidding situations. He did a lot of the legal legwork for himself, and saved money that way. But by the time his patent was registered, he'd spent close to $1,000 in legal fees. His current problem is to convince automobile makers that a sand-spray emergency braking system is a wise addition to their growing battery of safety devices.

The world needs better ideas, and an inventor spends a lot of his time analyzing the realities of dreams. Anyone short of ideas can start with problems that haven't been solved, like a punctureproof, low-cost container for maple syrup, which must be pressure packaged at a temperature just below boiling. Or mouseproof insulation, which surely doesn't *seem* that hard to figure out. Or women's stockings that don't self-destruct at the first snag. My father used to say the run-proof nylon stocking is cheap to manufacture, and locked up in patents so the disposable society can continue its gallop.

The history of inventive ideas that endure, however, has nothing to do with planned obsolescence, and a whole career could be made of sniffing out just those oversights, intentional or not, that big industry builds into otherwise worthy inventions. Ferreting out such examples of unclear thinking and redesigning with an eye toward long-term efficiency seems to be a major priority of serious inventors.

Although I cannot define the components that make some people "creative" and others not, I am probably not the only person who has met many brilliant "inventors"—people with good ideas who, for one reason or another, never pursue their instinctive nature. I have two good friends in Boise, both college English teachers, who have a wonderful gadget idea for fly fishermen. Although they could construct a prototype for less than $200, they are content to joke about the grandiose money-making potential of their idea without making the practical effort to see it happen. I have the same sort of reluctance with ideas of my own, and you probably do, too. But I heard a remark on a radio show one night that made a real impression. The inventor of "Pet Rocks" was quoted as having said, "When you've had one too many and you get a crazy idea, write it down before you have another," or words to that effect. From that point, a true inventor is optimistic enough, or foolhardy enough, to give up lots of time and energy and money in the effort to see his brainstorm become reality.

Additionally, an inventor needs a certain amount of persistence, in case the legal aspects of obtaining a patent become too discouraging. Paul Kiepe, who has just sold the license to produce his patented "Back Country Booster," a device to improve daylight radio reception, wrote me that he could never have seen his idea to completion without "persistence in fighting with the patent office to get a patent on something 'so damned simple'." The word 'patented', once you have it, helps sell the device to the point of the customer's being willing to try it."

Eric Darnell

Just outside tiny Sharon, Vermont, in a reconditioned chicken coop, lives Eric Darnell, 32, whom I met just after dark last fall in a heavy November downpour. I had been driving on an unfamiliar mud road over hilly countryside when the rain started splatting down in a continuous curtain of water. My windshield wipers took that opportunity to stop working, and I edged into the general store parking lot in the next village I came to, which happened to be Sharon. The rain showed no signs of letting up. I was prepared to spend the night.

"How do you like your new car?" I turned and saw a young man leaning against an old VW, oblivious to the rain. "Not much right now," I answered. "The damn wipers just quit." "Do you have an 11-millimeter wrench?" he asked, and I got the car's tool kit, still fresh and unwrapped, out from under the passenger seat. When he effortlessly tightened two obvious bolts, I felt a little silly, but was glad to be roadworthy again.

Before I could rush off, he invited me to his home for a steak dinner; he was celebrating the birth of an idea. During the meal, which we enjoyed by kerosene light, Darnell explained the concept of his "Darnell Free-flow, Wood-fired, Space Heater," and a number of other ideas he has been developing.

"Books related to the environmental problems facing this planet made me realize the need for a change in personal philosophy toward one of taking less from the earth than I put back." Darnell, who worked as a full-time diesel mechanic for eight years, moved from California to Vermont, "and learned carpentry, plumbing, and electrical skills by doing whatever odd jobs I could find. People seem to keep calling with work at a rate faster than I can get it done, so I must be doing something right."

Eric Darnell

Living as simply as he does, Eric is able to reserve as much time as he needs for sketching out and building the prototypes for his inventions. "I truly hope to warp the world," he said, with a laugh. "Of course, it's a good idea to remember the original meaning of 'warp', which, as a carpenter can tell you, does not necessarily mean unfavorable change." He had recently returned from a trip to Lebanon, New Hampshire, where an organization named "Creare," provides a think tank of engineers. "And do you know what the majority of them were working on?" he asked. "Atomic power protection devices. I try to talk to them, to ask them why they devote their time to systems that are hazards to the planet.

Darnell's Free-flow, Wood-fired Space Heater, which is constructed primarily of interlocking curved sections of auto exhaust pipe, circulates the heat that normally goes up the stovepipe without using any external power source. Another of Darnell's ingenious contraptions is a pair of foot-operated faucets on a kitchen sink. Other Darnell inventions include a small dental-flossing machine which allows the user to crank the floss, as on a tiny fishing reel, between two prongs that form a U-shape at the end of a three-inch "rod." Darnell developed this machine so he could floss while on the job, without soiling the floss with his hands. Other ideas on which he has been working include an automatic 10-speed bicycle transmission, and a hang glider that will use the potential energy of a coiled spring in conjunction with human power to flap its wings in case the glider needs emergency power.

Darnell's meticulous approach to the development of his ideas is evident when one looks at his prototype flossers, that are carved of wood and carefully fitted with the necessary hardware. His attention to every detail of his environment in the chicken coop is manifested by the simple elegance of good carpentry and the careful planning of space and function. Such care is not often associated with playfulness, a quality that is significant in allowing the mind to roam to places where it may never have realized earlier, it is very much needed.

On the bed was a plastic toy airplane shaped like a bird with a small handle projecting from its tail. "I bought that from a boy who was flying them over rush-hour traffic in Boston," he said. "Wind it up." I did, and then released it. The wings flapped and the little plane fluttered, then crashed into the bed. "That's how I got my idea for a potential-energy hang glider," he told me.

"If I can just develop a light, but heavy-duty gearing system, I think hang-gliding can be made a lot safer."

Darnell's interest in flight is also manifested in boomerangs, which he has made and flown since he was 12. "Boomerangs allow you to envision three-dimensional spacial orientations, and give you tremendous feedback on subtle climatic conditions and on your own physical and mental orientation."

Darnell supports himself completely with his odd jobs, and claims to be disinterested in profiteering from his inventions. "I simply want to help make things a little better, and to spread this attitude among people who use my inventions. When I see garden stores marketing solar panels at three times what they're worth I realize the 'how can I save the world and get rich at the same time?' mentality is dangerous and really contradictory.

"I call my enterprise 'Turning Point', because it encompasses all I do, and also the philosophy I am trying to instill in people."

Richard and Evelyn Fatigati

"At first we thought, 'This is great, we're going to make a million dollars overnight,' says Evelyn Fatigati, a writer in her late 20s whose husband, Richard, also a writer, is an avid chess player, with a collection of manuals and chess magazines that takes up a whole wall of the library in their house in Mason City, Iowa. Richard had seen a photograph of Bobby Fischer in an old issue of *Life*. The chess ace was pictured in an airplane practicing on a board that seemed totally portable. It was lap-sized and had tab pieces that stuck in place.

"I was working for a newspaper in Coconut Grove [Florida] at the time," Richard said. "I was commuting by bus, an hour each way, and really wanted a set I could use during this time. So I told Evelyn, and she designed a leather wallet-sized chessboard, and I designed chessmen that could be printed on flat, plastic tabs, and inserted in pockets that Evelyn stitched into the prototype playing board. And I used the set every day and really liked it, so I contacted Evelyn's father, who is a leather manufacturer."

At first, Evelyn's father resisted the idea of portable chess, and the Fatigatis stayed in Florida, where Richard continued with

Richard and Evelyn Fatigati

the paper and wrote a book on a detective. Then they moved back to Mason City, and began to pursue their idea full time. They learned that Evelyn's father's main objection to the chess game was that the board required at least two pieces of leather, and a great deal of stitching. At this point the idea was refined to make production possible with a single piece of leather, which would be printed with chessboard squares.

"But he was very reluctant, still," Richard remembered. "We had to talk to him—over and over, convincing him a pocket set was a salable idea."

"That reluctance was good for us," said Evelyn. "It kept us from rushing into a lot of mistakes. I remember how he got started, in half a garage when I was a child. Now he has three buildings and employs 83 people. We used his factory to produce the whole thing, and once we did, we spent every working hour in the factory, learning all the various manufacturing techniques and materials, and overseeing the development of the idea."

Finally, with the cooperation of Evelyn's father, the Fatigatis incorporated their fledgling game business under the name Era, Incorporated. "We were expecting a greater response to our chess game than we received, and when the sales lagged beyond all expectation, we decided to try the same idea with backgammon, which was all the rage then. A distributor in Florida saw our chess sets and said, 'Boy, you ought to do this in backgammon!' and when we did, and sent him a sample, he never even ordered!

"We went through the same process with backgammon as we had with chess, except we'd solved the problems of how to make a game board; all we had to do was change the dyes to accommodate the new game. And we went to an advertising company in Minneapolis that took $1,000 for what turned out to be unusable promotion. So Evelyn and I worked over their copy, trying to create an accurate picture of what we were offering, and placed ads in a select group of high-circulation magazines, *Esquire, Army–Navy Times,* and *Saturday Review.* In *Esquire,* a half-page ad cost us about $800. We figured that all we needed was one-hundredth-of-one-percent return to the message we estimated would reach a readership of three million. But the actual results," and here Richard shook his head, laughing, "kind of crushed us. Less than one-thousandth of one percent!"

In spite of the fact that Evelyn and Richard describe their projects with Era, Incorporated, so far as "disastrous," they retain what Richard calls "the essential dream." Presently, they are at work designing a Scrabble game, hoping that the company which holds the rights will eventually be interested in the idea and the manufacturing techniques they have developed and applied successfully twice, even though marketing has not yet caught on sufficiently to suggest demand.

Later, Richard invited me downstairs for a game of chess in a room with a fireplace, which he has converted especially for chess matches. "I know it seems unrealistic to follow an idea so hard," he said, as we were finishing our fourth game in half an hour. "We've depleted our savings accounts twice, just paying the manufacturing and promotional bills. But you have to find that star to hang onto, and if people start buying the sets we make because they see that there is a certain artfulness and precision involved, if we can develop an advertising campaign that successfully shows this aspect, I think we'll be able to smile at the hard times we've had putting it all together and chalk the early losses off to necessary experience.

"And by the way," he said, looking at the board, "you just moved into check."

Paul Kiepe

Paul Kiepe, 68, is the founder of Loud & Clear Products Company in Payette, Idaho. I learned of Paul's work as an inventor while I was participating in a "Writer-in-the-Schools" program in Boise, and saw, in one elementary school a curious electronic board upon which the students could place sheets of music. By pressing the notes that are printed on special sheet music, the students played what Kiepe calls "Touch Music." This ingenious device allows young children to learn the relationships among the notes on a musical staff with a minimum of abstract concepts.

Kiepe's other invention is a little device he calls the "Back Country Booster," which provides daylight radio reception in backcountry areas of the Rocky Mountains. So far, he has done little better than to break even producing the 4,000 boosters he has sold so far. Last year, he licensed a manufacturer to produce and

Paul Kiepe

sell the boosters, and he is hopeful that his invention will become a commercial success. He is less optimistic in his projections for Touch Music, and has not taken it beyond the prototype stage. "I consider one of my biggest mistakes to have been not anticipating that we would, as a nation, get into an energy crisis, where electronic inventions, like Touch Music, are counterproductive for the economy," he wrote.

"We're at the end, at the *reducto ad absurdum*, of a once-useful idea—the substitution of fuel power for manpower. Young enterprisers should forget any ideas that come to them about joining this end-game. Instead, start thinking first of humans, *people*: what work means to them, what it means to you. Mass production is not for little guys. Besides, it is generally energy intensive and job eliminating. And what in hell's the use of that?

"Remember, always, 49 percent of the populace has less than 100 IQ: they are entitled to do useful work also, not have wise guys displace what work normally falls to the less-acute by computerology, division of labor (into degrading bits), systems analysis, and all the rest of it. Particularly, stay away from chemistry. The 400 new chemical combinations introduced into the environment every year (or is it 4,000?) no regulatory board can keep up with. The problem of synergism is beyond solving. Proceed on the present course, and the world becomes uninhabitable.

"My own greatest unmet need is to find a group of *economists* willing to deal head-on with pressing social and environmental issues of our time." Along these lines, Kiepe has designed a program he calls, "The Corn Plan," that is "prepared especially for the 50 percent of U.S. citizens who, in a canvass conducted by *Environmental Quality* (The First Annual Report of the Council on Environmental Quality), said they'd like to live in a rural district, 'if they could make a go of it.' The plan suggests offering four-acre leaseholds *only* to applicants willing to agree to limit their family size. Each new farm family would grow two acres of feed corn, and be eligible to receive a federal subsidy over the market price during years the market price proves insufficient for family maintenance." Kiepe cites E. F. Schumacher's *Small Is Beautiful*, as a philosophical equivalent to his plan, which would emphasize energy saving through use of organic methods ("which have now proved in a nine-year test the equal in production of energy-inten-

sive chemical-mechanical imputs"). Water saving would be practiced by application, where suitable, of drip irrigation.
Technological support would be limited to the walking-type
rototiller of a few horsepower.

"Something like this 'Corn Plan' must be started in the United
States. It must be shown to be viable under a certain set of conditions, then these conditions presented to legislative bodies for action.

"Our nation ought not to go on fumbling with major problems,
which grow apace. Rebuilding rural morale with small-business opportunities would make things livable, once again, both for the ar-
tisan and the enterpriser."

Bibliography

This bibliography, by no means exhaustive, lists those books whose titles were most often mentioned by the people whose stories are told in *Working for Yourself*. The bibliography is divided into three sections, General, Arts and Crafts, and Agricultural.

General

"An Information Aid for Inventors." Available from the Department of Commerce, 14th Street, Washington, DC 20231.

CODA, Poets and Writers, Incorporated, 201 West 54th Street, New York, NY 10019.

"Fear of Filing (A Guide to Paying the IRS for Self-Employed People)." From Volunteer Lawyers for the Arts, 36 West 44th Street, New York, NY 10036.

"General Information Concerning Patents." Available from the Department of Commerce, 14th Street, Washington, DC 20231.

"General Information Concerning Trademarks." Available from the Department of Commerce, 14th Street, Washington, DC 20231.

"General Information on Copyrights." Library of Congress, First Street, Washington, DC 20540.

"Grants and Awards Available to American Writers." P.E.N. American Center, 156 Fifth Avenue, NY 10010.

Jones, Stacy V. *The Inventor's Patent Handbook*. NY: Dial, 1966.

Krasilofsky, William. *This Business of Music*. NY: Watson-Guptill, 1971.

Noback, Joseph C. *Life Insurance Accounting*. Homewood, IL: Irwin, 1969.

Steinhoff, Dan. *Small Business Management Fundamentals*. NY: McGraw Hill, 1974.

"Tax Guide for Small Business." U.S. Government Printing Office, North Cap Street, Washington, DC 20401.

The Grants Register. St. Martin's Press, 175 Fifth Avenue, New York, NY 10010.

Thomas's Register. Check local library for this multi-volume listing of suppliers of everything and its manufacturers.

"U.S. Postal Service Mailers Guide." See your Postmaster.

"Your Federal Income Tax." U.S. Government Printing Office, North Cap Street, Washington, DC 20401.

Arts and Crafts

How to Publish, Promote, and Sell Your Book. rev. ed., Chicago, IL: Adams, 1971.

American Artist. 1 Color Court, Marion, OH 43302.

Art and the Law. (Summer 1975). From Volunteer Lawyers for the Arts, 36 West 44th Street, New York, NY 10036.

Art News. 750 Third Avenue, New York, NY 10017.

Artweek. West Coast art news. 1305 Franklin Street, Oakland, CA 94612.

Burke, Clifford. *Printing It*. NY: Ballantine, 1972.

Ceramics Monthly. 1609 Northwest Boulevard, PO Box 12448, Columbus, OH 43212.

Chernoff, G. and Sarnin, H. *Photography and the Law*. Order from AMPHOTO, 750 Zeckendorf Boulevard, Garden City, NY 11530. (Write for their list.)

Clark, Leta. *How to Make Money with Your Crafts*. NY: Morrow, 1974.

Connaugton, Howard W. (C.P.A.) *Craftsmen in Business: A Guide to Financial Management and Taxes*. American Crafts Council, 44 West 53rd Street, New York, NY 10019.

"*COSMEP Newsletter*." Richard Morris, ed., Box 703, San Francisco, CA 94101.

Crafts Horizons. The American Crafts Council, 44 West 53rd Street, New York, NY 10019.

Gassan, Arnold. *Handbook for Contemporary Photography*. Distributed by Light Impressions, Box 2012, Rochester, NY 14514.

Handweaver and Craftsman. 220 Fifth Avenue, New York, NY 10001.

Henderson, Bill, ed. *Publish It Yourself Handbook.* Pushcart Press, Box 845, Yonkers, NY 10701.

Kodak's many booklets on technique.

Lee, Marshall. *Bookmaking: The Illustrated Guide to Design and Production.* NY: Bowker, 1965.

Literary Market Place (LMP). NY: Bowker. Published annually.

Mueller, L. W. *How to Publish Your Own Book.* Detroit: Harlo Press, 1976.

Nelson, Glenn C. *Ceramics: A Potter's Handbook.* NY: Holt, Rinehart, and Winston, 1966.

Nemser, Cindy. *Art Talk: Conversations with Twelve Woman Artists.* NY: Scribners, 1975.

Picker, Fred. *Zone 6 Workshop.* Order from AMPHOTO, 750 Zeckendorf Boulevard, Garden City, NY 11530.

Rhodes, Daniel. *Clay and Glazes for the Potter.* NY: Chilton, 1957.

————. *Kilns: Design Construction and Operation.* 1968.

————. *Stoneware and Porcelain: The Art of High-Fired Pottery.* 1959.

Shepherd Magazine. A.A./Lund Associates, Incorporated, Sheffield, MA 01257.

Smith, Brendan. *Brendan's Leather Book.* Cotati, CA: Outer Straubville Press, 1972.

Stroebel, L. *View Camera Technique.* NY: Hastings House Publishers, 1976.

Studio Potter, Daniel Clark Foundation, Box 65, Goffstown, NH 03045. Published semi-annually.

Sunshine Artists ("lists and rates fairs") Sun County Enterprises, Incorporated, Drawer 836, Fern Park, FL 32730.

The Feminist Art Journal, 41 Montgomery Place, Brooklyn, NY 11225.

Todd, H. N. and Zakia, R. D. *Photographic Sensitometry.* NY: Wiley, 1976.

Westart. West coast's art news scene. Box 1396, Auburn, CA 95603.

Wettlaufer, George and Nancy. *Craftsman Survival Manual: Making a Part-Time Living from Your Crafts.* Holliswood, NY: Spectrum, 1974.

Wilcox, Donald. *Modern Leather Design.* NY: Watson Guptill, 1969.

Williams, Chris. *Craftsmen of Necessity*. NY: Random, 1974.

Wilson. *Jewelry Art*. Hub Material Company, 387 Washington Street, Boston, MA 02124.

Woodcrafts Supply (tool catalogue), 313 Montvale Avenue, Woburn, MA 01801.

Agricultural

Attmore, T. Seven pamphlets on herbs, $1 each, from the author. Turquoise Trail Herb Farm, Bernalillo, NM 87004.

Berry, Wendell. *Farming: A Handbook*. NY: Harcourt, Brace, and Jovanavich, 1971.

Bromfield, Louis. *From My Experience*. NY: Harper, 1955.

Budbill, David. *Christmas Tree Farm*. NY: Macmillan, 1974.

Clairborne, Craig. *Cooking with Herbs and Spices*. NY: Harper and Row, 1970.

Clarke, W. W. "Pennsylvania Beekeeping." Pennsylvania State Agricultural Extension Service, University Park, PA 16802.

Corley, Hugh. *Organic Farmer*. London: Faber and Faber, 1957.

"Dairy Goats: Breeding/Feeding/Management." (leaflet no. 439). American Dairy Goat Association, Box 186, Spindale, NC 28160.

Dempsey, Paul. *How to Repair Small Gasoline Engines*. Blue Ridge Summit, PA: Tab Books, 1972.

Easey, Ben. *Practical Organic Gardening*. London: Faber and Faber, 1955.

Encyclopedia of Organic Gardening. Emmaus, PA: Rodale Press, 1975.

"Environment Action Bulletin." Rodale Press, 33 East Minor Street, Emmaus, PA 18049.

Fatigati, Evelyn. *Bzzz: A Beekeeper's Primer*. Emmaus, PA: Rodale, 1976.

Faulkner, Edward H. *Plowman's Folly*. Norman, OK: University of Oklahoma Press, 1945.

Foster, Gertrude. *Herbs for Every Garden*. NY: Dutton, 1973.

Grieve, Mrs. M. *A Modern Herbal*. NY: Dover, 1971.

Grout, Roy A., ed. *The Hive and the Honey Bee*. Hamilton, IL: Dadant and Sons, 1963.

Hainsworth, P. H. *Agriculture: A New Approach*. London: Faber and Faber, 1954.

Henderson, George. *Farmer's Progress*. London: Faber and Faber, 1950.

———. *The Farming Ladder*. 1944.

———. *The Farming Manual*. 1960.

Hills, Lawrence. *Down to Earth Fruit and Vegetable Growing*. London: Faber and Faber, 1960.

Hunter, Beatrice T. *Gardening without Poisons*. NY: Houghton Mifflin, 1964.

How to Grow Herbs. Menlo Park, CA: Sunset Books, 1972.

Jagendorf, Moritz. *Folk Wines, Cordials, and Brandies: How to Make Them, along with the Pleasures of Their Lore*. NY: Vanguard, 1963.

Kanes, M. G. *Five Acres and Independence*. NY: Dover, 1973.

King F. H. *Farmers of Forty Centuries*. Emmaus, PA: Rodale Press, 1911.

Leach, Coral. *Aids to Goatkeeping*. Dairy Goat Journal, Box 1908, Scottsdale, AZ 85252.

Lowenfeld, Clara. *Herbs, Health, and Cookery*. Hauppauge, NY: Universal Publishers and Distributors, 1970.

Mackenzie, David. *Goat Husbandry*. London: Faber and Faber, 1957.

Morgan, Charlie. *Earthworm Selling and Shipping Guide*. 1972. Available from Shields Publications, Box 472, Elgin, IL 60120. $2.

———. *Profitable Earthworm Farming*. 1975.

———. *Raising the African Nightcrawler*. (rev. ed.), 1970.

———. *The Worm Farm*. 1962.

Myers, Ruth. *A-Worming We Did Go*. 1968. Shields Publications.

Nichols, B. P. "Profitable Herb Growing," Nichols Garden Nursery, 1190 North Pacific Highway, Albany, OR 97321.

Rayner, M. C. *Problems in Tree Nutrition*. London: Faber and Faber, 1946.

Root, A. I. *ABC & XYZ of Bee Culture*. Medina, OH: A. J. Root, 1974.

Shields, Earl B. *Raising Earthworms for Profit*. (16th ed.), 1977. Shields Publications.

Stephenson, W. A. *Seaweed in Agriculture and Horticulture*. London: Faber and Faber, 1968.

Sykes, Friend. *Humus and the Farmer*. London: Faber and Faber, 1946.

Wagner, Philip. *A Wine Grower's Guide*. NY: Knopf, 1965.

Walsh, Helen. *Starting Right with Milk Goats*. Charlotte, VT: Garden Way Publishing, 1972.

Whittock, Gustave. *The Pruning Book*. Emmaus, PA: Rodale, 1948.

Winkler, A. J. *General Viticulture*. Berkeley, CA: University of California Press, 1975.

Index